IMAGES
of America

HOPKINS COUNTY

On the Cover: Robert Hartline and his family stand in a tobacco patch eating watermelon in Barnsley. The photograph is believed to have been taken on Whit Smith's farm around 1920. From left to right are Robert Hartline, Mae Hartline, Martha Helen Hartline, Monroe Hartline, and Geneva Hartline. Hartline also worked in the coal mines, often getting up early to walk 3 miles to the mine to work. (Gail Warren.)

IMAGES
of America

HOPKINS COUNTY

Lisa D. Piper and
J. Harold Utley

ARCADIA
PUBLISHING

ISBN 978-0-7385-6639-9

Published by Arcadia Publishing
Charleston, South Carolina

Printed in the United States of America

Library of Congress Control Number: 2009928273

For all general information contact Arcadia Publishing at:
Telephone 843-853-2070
Fax 843-853-0044
E-mail sales@arcadiapublishing.com
For customer service and orders:
Toll-Free 1-888-313-2665

Visit us on the Internet at www.arcadiapublishing.com

To Maj. Maurice Kirby Gordon and Harold George Ledbetter for their untiring dedication to the preservation of the history of Hopkins County. Together they are responsible for 70–80 percent of what we know about Hopkins County history.

Contents

Acknowledgments		6
Introduction		7
1.	Treasures of Hopkins County	9
2.	Business Ventures	25
3.	Early Entertainment	47
4.	Notable People and Places	55
5.	Tribute to Military and Public Service	63
6.	Black Coal and Rail	79
7.	Character of a People	97
8.	Faith and Education	115

ACKNOWLEDGMENTS

Special thanks go to the Historical Society of Hopkins County (HSHC) and all of those who keep our heritage alive. We would like to thank our spouses, Dennis and Louise, for patiently supporting us with this project. Thank you, Luke Cunningham and Amy Perryman at Arcadia, for giving encouraging words and direction during the course of the planning and writing process. Fragments of the county's history seem to be strewn all over the county in photo albums and in the memories of its citizens. We would like to thank those who have shared their portion of Hopkins County's history with us so that others can learn of our past: White Plains Museum (WPM), Hanson Museum, Nortonville Museum, Jane Rogers, Roger Shelton, Gail Warren, Ronnie Lewis, Mary Hall Porter, Chelsea Babb, Mildred Stanley, Piccola Hunt, Don Ezel, Brenda Jones, Carlos Lamb, Anita Pate Cartwright, Bob Beeny, James Hicks, F. W. Livingston, Helen Brown, Roy Day, John Rash Philips, Allison Goodman, Ann K. Morgan, Gigi Kesterson Smith, Ruby Concrete, and Debbie Hobgood.

INTRODUCTION

Hopkins County was created in 1806 from the southern part of Henderson County. It was named for Gen. Samuel Hopkins, who lived east of Henderson at Zion. He represented the area in the state legislature at the time. General Hopkins was a Revolutionary War veteran and surveyor. He worked for the Transylvania Land Company, managing their holdings of 10,000 acres south of the Green River. Daniel Ashby, also a representative in the legislature, suggested the name in honor of his colleague General Hopkins.

The act creating Hopkins County was signed on December 9, 1806. The first meeting of the court for the purpose of organizing the county was held on May 25, 1807, at the home of Robert McGary. At this meeting, Daniel McGary and Solomon Silkwood produced a writing pledging 20 acres each of their land for the purpose of establishing the county seat. The McGary farm was located where the Big Spring Inn now stands. At the October 26, 1807, term of court at the home of Daniel McGary, the plan by McGary and Silkwood that a town be established was accepted, and it was to be called Madisonville.

Out of Hopkins County, communities were born, and the following cities make up the county: Madisonville, Earlington, Nortonville, Mortons Gap, Dawson Springs, White Plains, Nebo, Hanson, Ashbyburg, Anton, St. Charles, Charleston, Dalton, and Manitou.

Farming was the mainstay of Hopkins County for most of the 1800s. Tobacco was the leading crop, followed by corn. It is not known exactly when coal mining began in Hopkins County. It is thought that early residents may have mined outcrops on their land for their own use or traded coal for hay or grain. It is known that in 1850, John Woolfolk mined a small amount in the Hunting Branch hollow, took it to his blacksmith shop at Hall's Post Office (Earlington), and burned it in his forge. The first mining on a small commercial scale was in Hunting Branch hollow by Madisonville Coal Company (later Victoria Coal Company) and others. The first large-scale commercial mining was by the St. Bernard Coal Company in Earlington when the railroad was built into Earlington in 1871. Mining coal then became the county's major industry and offered employment to Hopkins Countians other than farming jobs. The coal company paid in cash. It also provided a company store where the miners could purchase goods. In 1899, Hopkins County became the first Kentucky county to produce over 1 million tons of coal per year. Hopkins County mines produced 1,265,707 tons of coal that year. Coal mining remained the major employment for Hopkins County until the mid-20th century.

Hopkins County was divided by the Civil War. Union supporters joined a regiment recruited by James Shackleford. Al Fowler recruited troops for the Confederacy. The first shots of the Civil War in Kentucky were fired at Burnt Mill Church in Webster County (actually in Hopkins County before the creation of Webster County in 1860). The courthouse at Madisonville was burned by Gen. Hyland B. Lyon on December 17, 1864, during his courthouse-burning raids through Western Kentucky. O. W. Rash wrote the following record of the account to his children: "When about twelve years of age, being too small to carry a gun, I was sent out on one Saturday night to warn the neighbors that soldiers were coming, and pressing into service every available man and every horse for service, and I could hear the soldiers talking and the rattle of swords and guns only a few hundred yards away, and on the following day, (Sunday), I was sent afoot to Madisonville to gather information and movements of the soldiers. When I reached Madisonville, the Court House was burning, having been fired by the soldiers, stores were broken open, and goods of all kinds, that were of no value to the soldiers, were carried off. In fact, we were in the midst of 'Blue Coats' on one side and 'Gray Coats' on the other side during the entire war. I attended the burial of a Hopkins County Confederate Colonel killed in battle only a short distance from where we lived, and at the burial, they were looking for the 'Blue Coats' to come at any moment."

The Evansville, Henderson, and Nashville (Louisville and Nashville, or L&N) Railroad was completed through the county in 1871, and the Elizabethtown, Paducah, and St. Louis (Illinois Central) Railroad was completed in 1873. The county then had transportation north-south and east-west by rail. The railroads provided transportation for the coal to be shipped nationwide.

Many communities grew quickly as whistle-stops on the railroads, including Hanson, Mortons Gap, Nortonville, and White Plains. Dawson Springs, in the southwestern part of the county, began to thrive in the 1880s as a popular health resort, but its popularity had faded by the time of the Great Depression.

In 1970, Hopkins County was the third largest coal producer in the commonwealth, following Muhlenberg and Pike Counties. In 1971, the county also ranked fifth in oil production in Kentucky. Development of resources was aided by the construction of the north-south Pennyrile Parkway (now Edward Breathitt Parkway) and the east-west Western Kentucky Parkway (now Wendell H. Ford Parkway) through the county in the 1970s.

In 1987, farms occupied 41 percent of the land area, with 72 percent of farmland under cultivation. The county has an area of 552 square miles, or 353,280 acres.

Civic leaders realized that mining and farming would not sustain employment for the growing population. The Hopkins County Development Foundation was created to attract the manufacturing industry to Hopkins County. The S. J. Campbell Parachute Factory located in Madisonville in 1942. Versnick Manufacturing Company located here in 1955. In the years 1966–1974, Goodyear Tire and Rubber Company, General Electric Corporation, American Laundry Company (now Gemtron), Knowlton Brothers (now Allstrom), National Can Corporation, and Borg-Warner Corporation—York Division all located in Madisonville.

The population of the county in 1810 was 2,964, and in 1990, it was 46,126.

Great men and women have been born or lived in Hopkins County. Perhaps the most popular citizen was Gov. Ruby Laffoon (1869–1941). The log cabin birthplace of Gov. Ruby Laffoon was originally located 1 mile northwest of the Liberty Baptist Church on the farm now owned by the Perry family. John B. Laffoon Jr. built the cabin upon his return from service in the army of the Confederate States of America. His son, Ruby Laffoon, was born in the cabin in 1869. Ruby Laffoon was the 43rd governor of Kentucky, serving one term from 1931 to 1935. He was governor during the Great Depression.

In 1986, the remains of the cabin were dismantled and placed at 107 South Union Street next to the Historical Society of Hopkins County. The cabin was restored by the society and opened to the public in 1988.

One

Treasures of Hopkins County

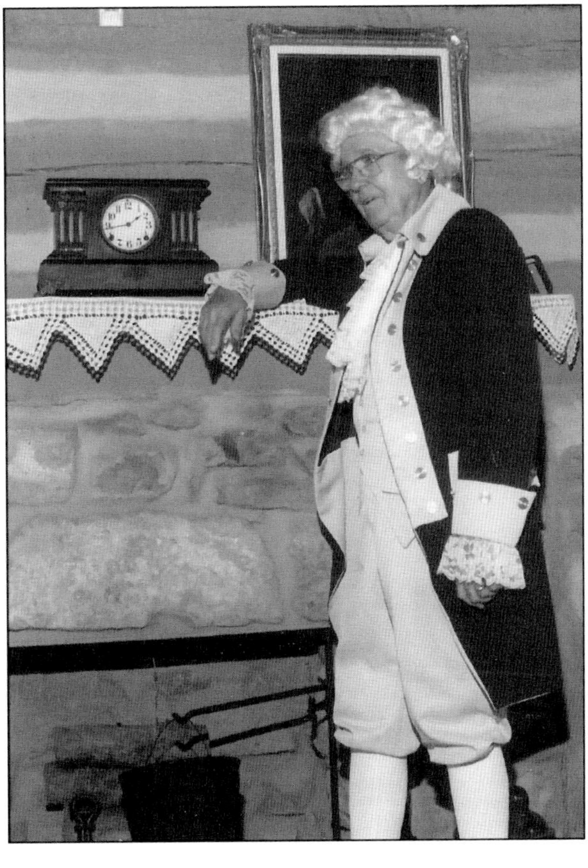

James Madison Days, a festival to celebrate the naming of Madisonville for James Madison, was begun in 1986. Pictured is Harold G. Ledbetter, in costume as James Madison, at the fireplace in the parlor of the log cabin birthplace of Gov. Ruby Laffoon during the festival. (HSHC.)

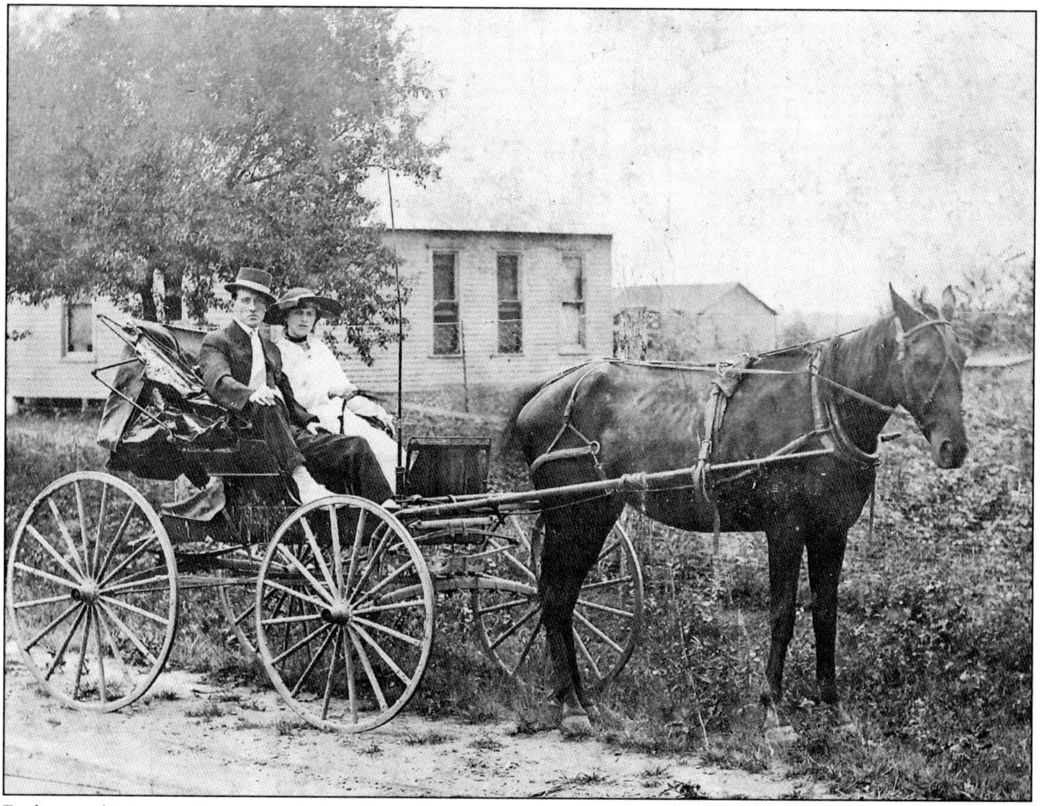

Ruby and Vester Farmer ride in their buggy on their wedding day, June 16, 1916. The typical church building for the era, shown in the background, has four windows on each side and double doors on the front. Vester owned and operated a little restaurant in Nortonville for several years. Ruby ran a pool hall in Nortonville. (Gail Warren.)

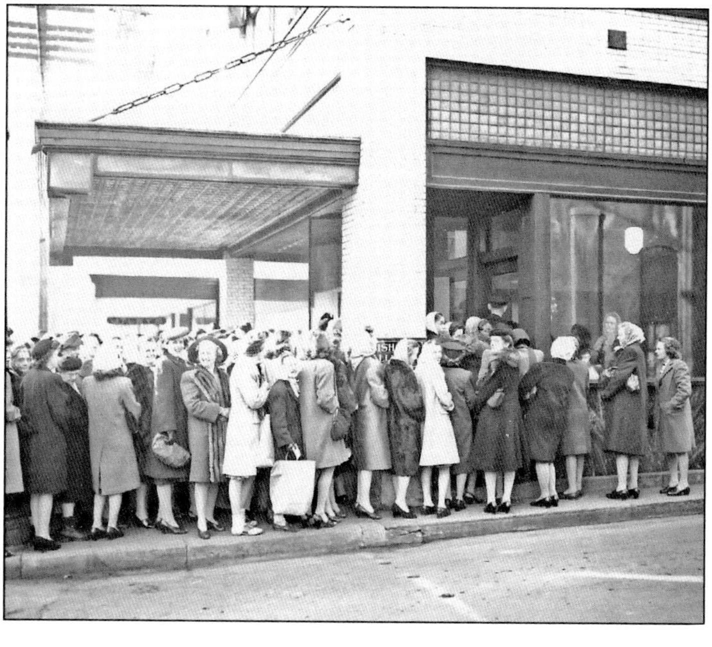

In World War II, there was an acute shortage of nylon hosiery. Bishop's Millinery had just received a new supply of nylon hosiery. This photograph was taken of the women standing in line to purchase stockings at the store. Police chief Pat Collins is standing by the door with his back toward the camera. The chief was present to maintain order in the hose-wearing crowd. (HSHC, photograph by J. B. Moore.)

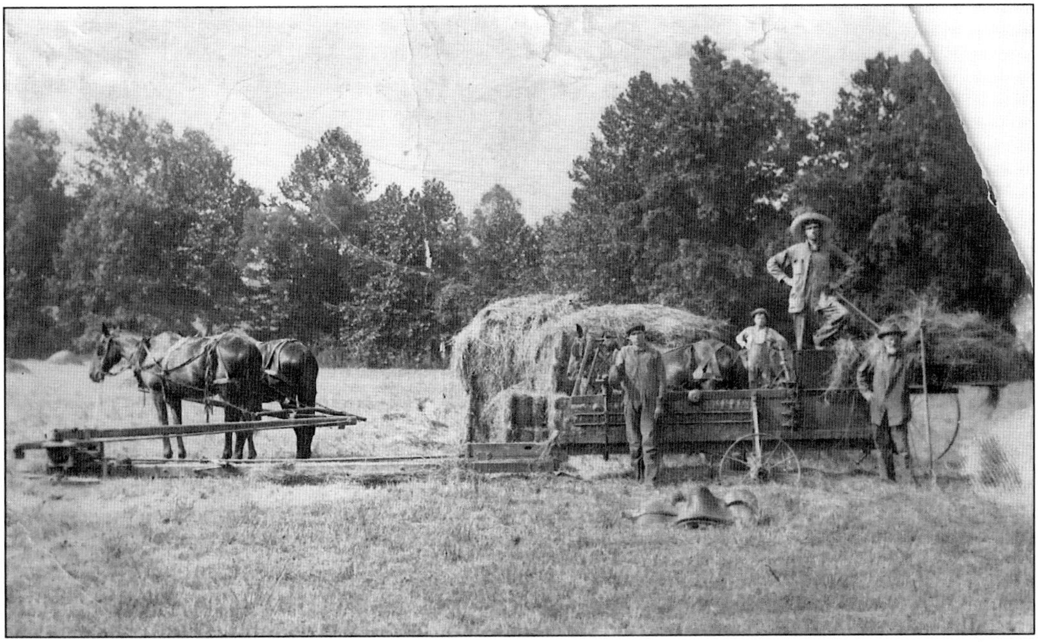

A horse-powered hay baler shows the ingenuity of the early 1900s. Loose hay was baled into rectangular blocks weighing over 100 pounds. The mule or horse walked in a circle to create power after being hitched to a sweep arm. As the compressed hay emerged, workers placed long wires by hand around the bale to hold it together. (Gail Warren.)

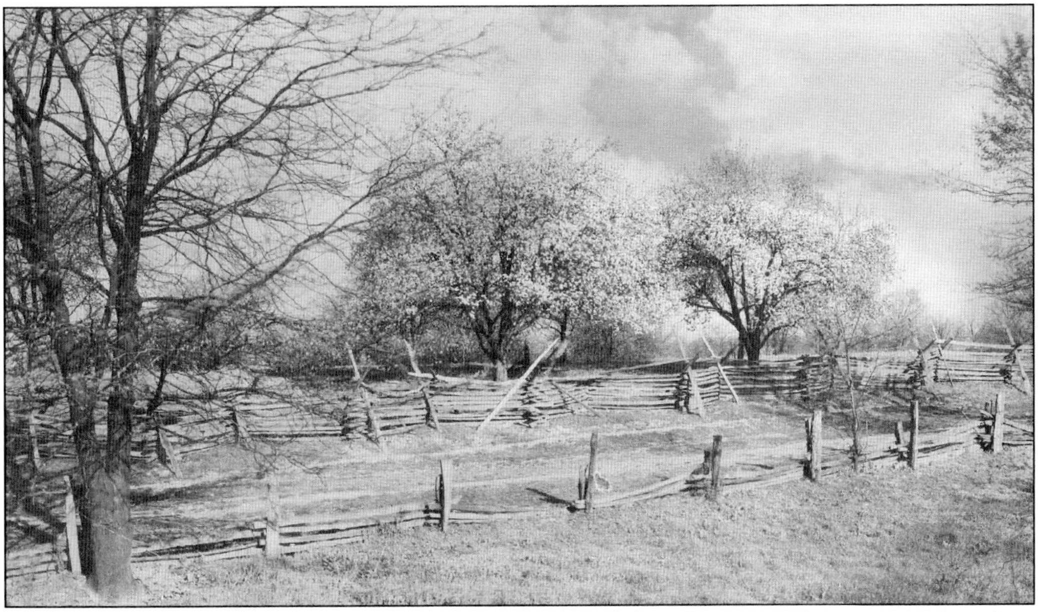

In its early days, around 1815, Hopkins County farmers did not have wire fences to enclose their ground. They made fences out of rails and used them to keep in their cattle and protect their crops. The photograph shows a typical farm lane with a split-rail fence of the Abraham Lincoln era. (HSHC.)

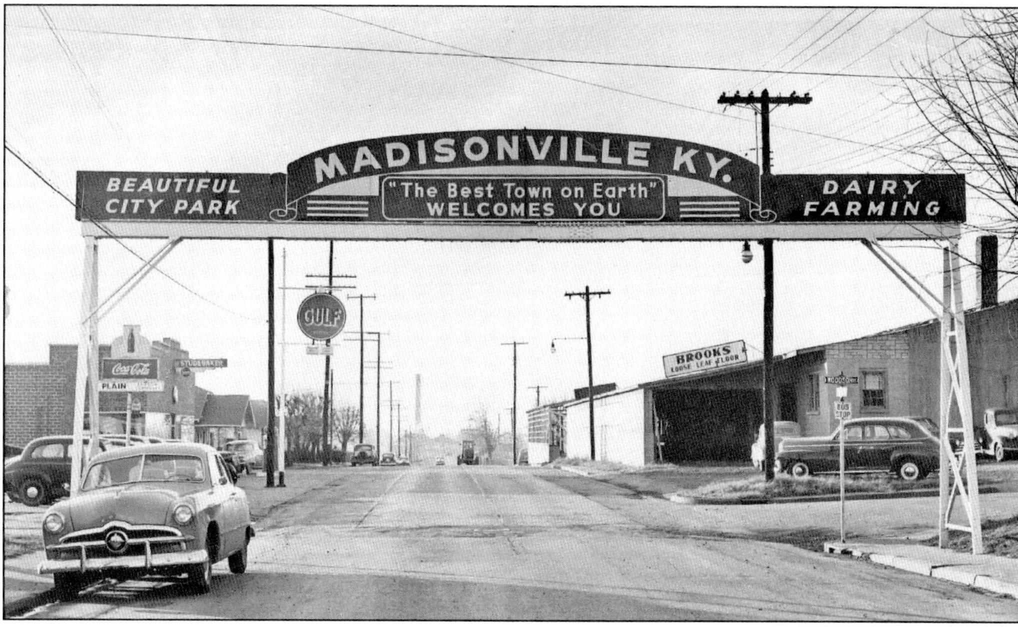

The original Madisonville welcome sign was erected in 1927. It was replaced in 1949. The sign is located on West Noel Avenue. The Brooks Loose Leaf Floor is on the northwest corner of West Noel Avenue and Woodson Street. The Studebaker garage, whose sign is shown on the left, was operated by Dallas Cavanaugh, who later sold it to L. B. Plain. (HSHC.)

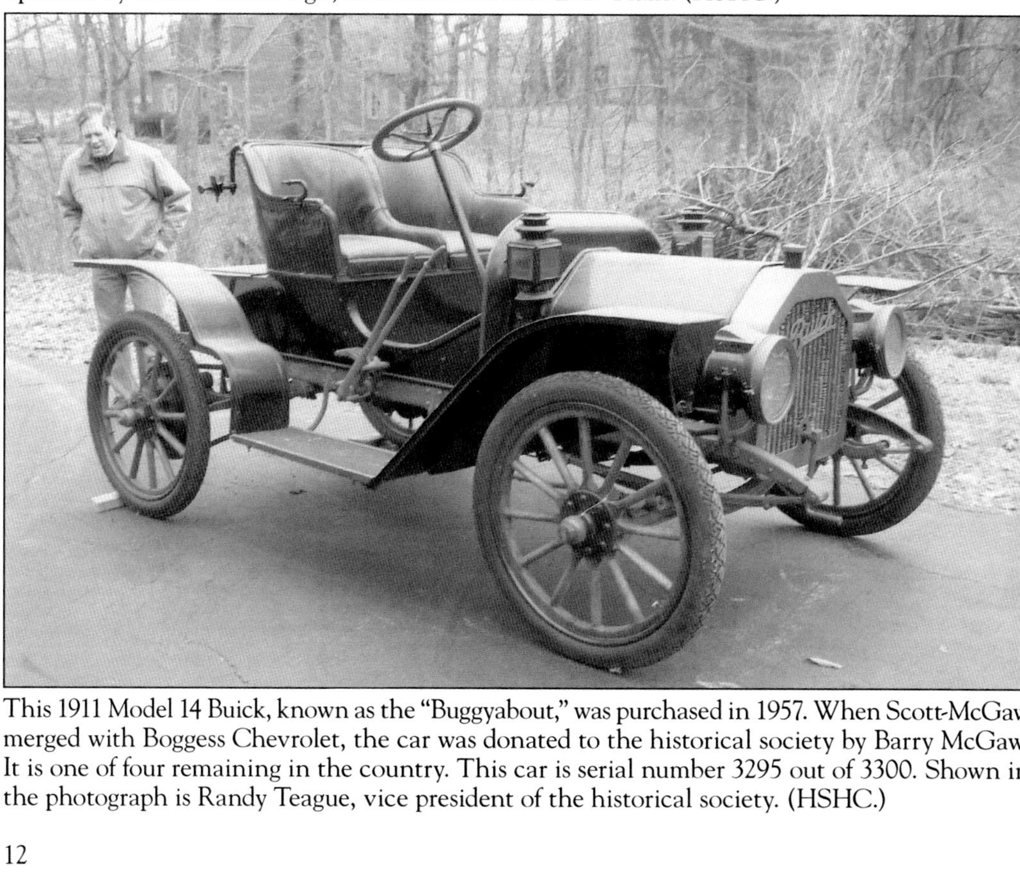

This 1911 Model 14 Buick, known as the "Buggyabout," was purchased in 1957. When Scott-McGaw merged with Boggess Chevrolet, the car was donated to the historical society by Barry McGaw. It is one of four remaining in the country. This car is serial number 3295 out of 3300. Shown in the photograph is Randy Teague, vice president of the historical society. (HSHC.)

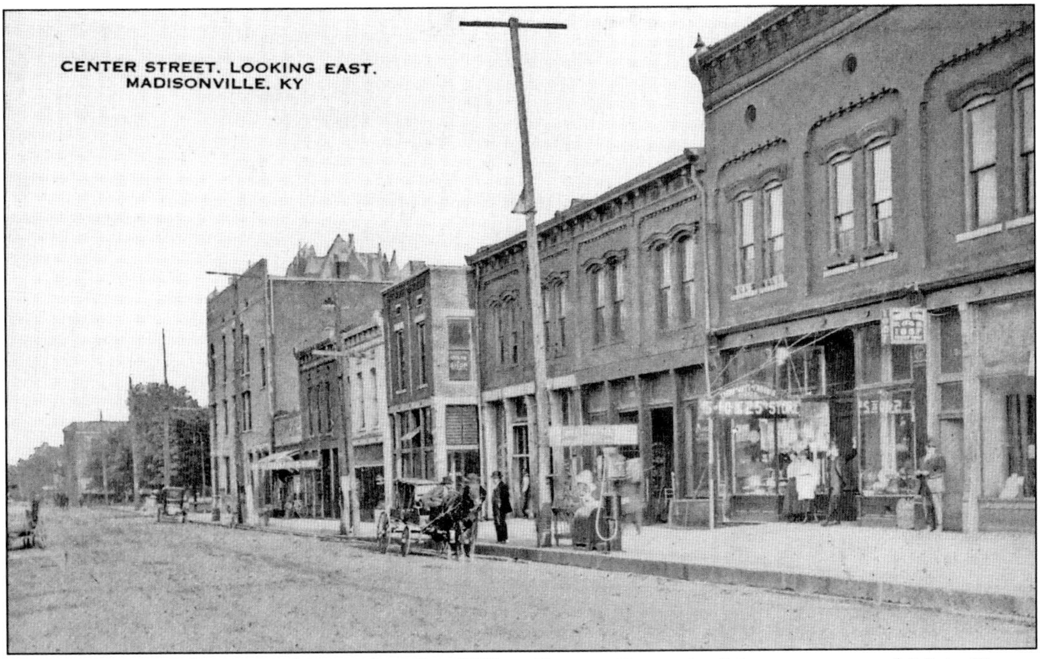

This old postcard depicts the south side of West Center Street looking east toward Main Street around 1910. Note the gas pump on the side of the street and the electric poles. Inkerman Bailey had the first electric generating plant and provided electricity to Madisonville. Today the street is home to the U.S. Bank, Ron Johnson Consulting Engineering, Brasher Mattress Outlet, and Ratliff Shoe Repair. (HSHC.)

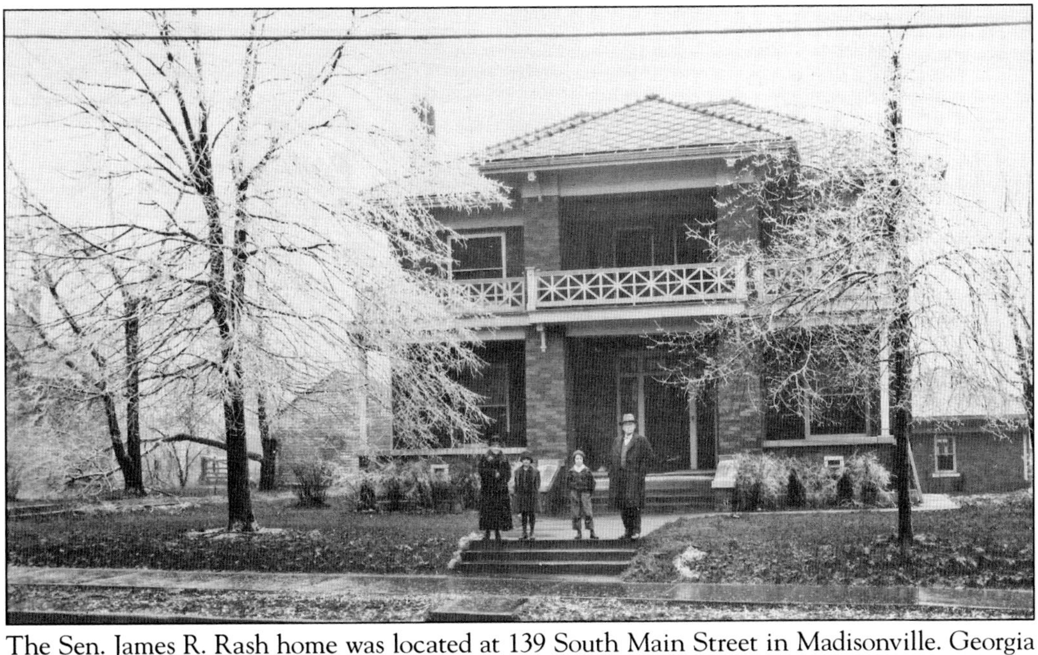

The Sen. James R. Rash home was located at 139 South Main Street in Madisonville. Georgia Rash is pictured on the left in 1925. The two boys with Senator Rash are unidentified. The home was razed in May 1976 so the People's Bank and Trust could expand. The bank purchased the property after Mrs. Rash died in 1970. (HSHC.)

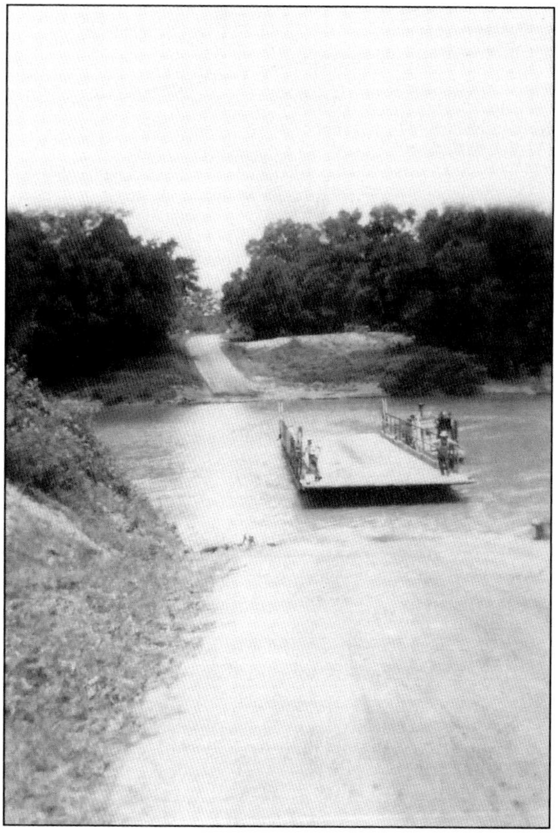

In 1925, a ferry across Pond River was pulled by hand to transport people across at Jewel City. It was at this site that a team of mules accidentally drowned. The driver had intended to water the mules. He drove them too far on the slippery bottom of the ferry. The driver, a Mr. Clarke, was the owner of the tile factory in Jewel City. (Robert and Audrey McCain Collection, HSHC.)

In 1869, the founders of Ruby Concrete Company opened what would become the oldest continuing business in the county. John Ruby learned that the railroad was coming through Madisonville, and he secured a contract to make all of the ties to lay the track. With the money he made from that job, he opened up a general store, which eventually became Ruby Lumber Company and later Ruby Concrete. This undated photograph shows men doing a weight test with three-core block. Today the company block has two holes instead of three. (Ruby Concrete.)

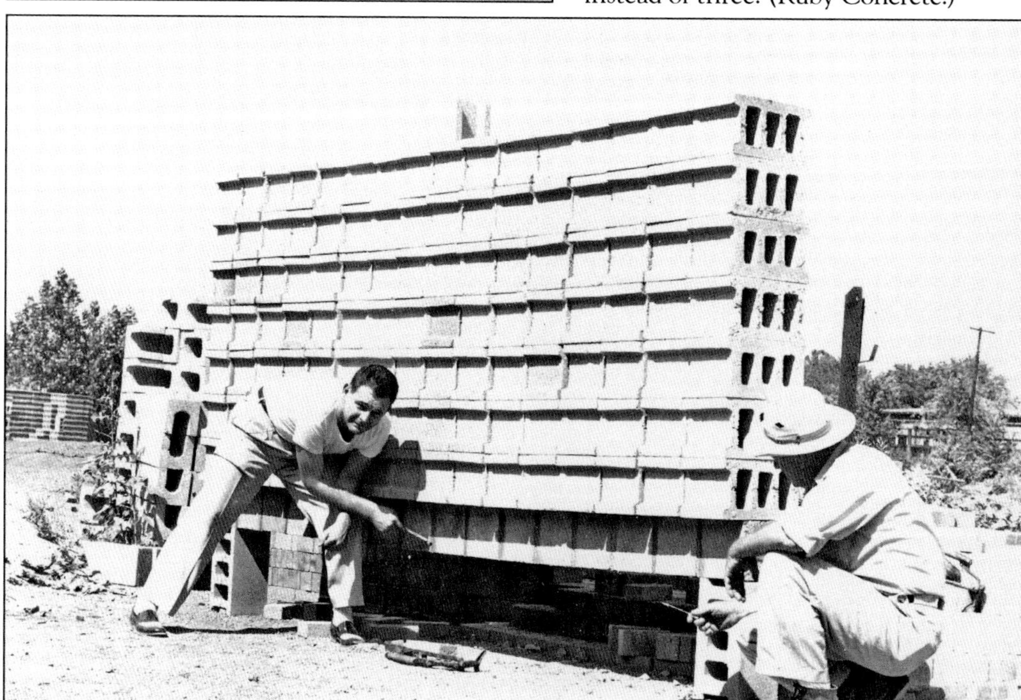

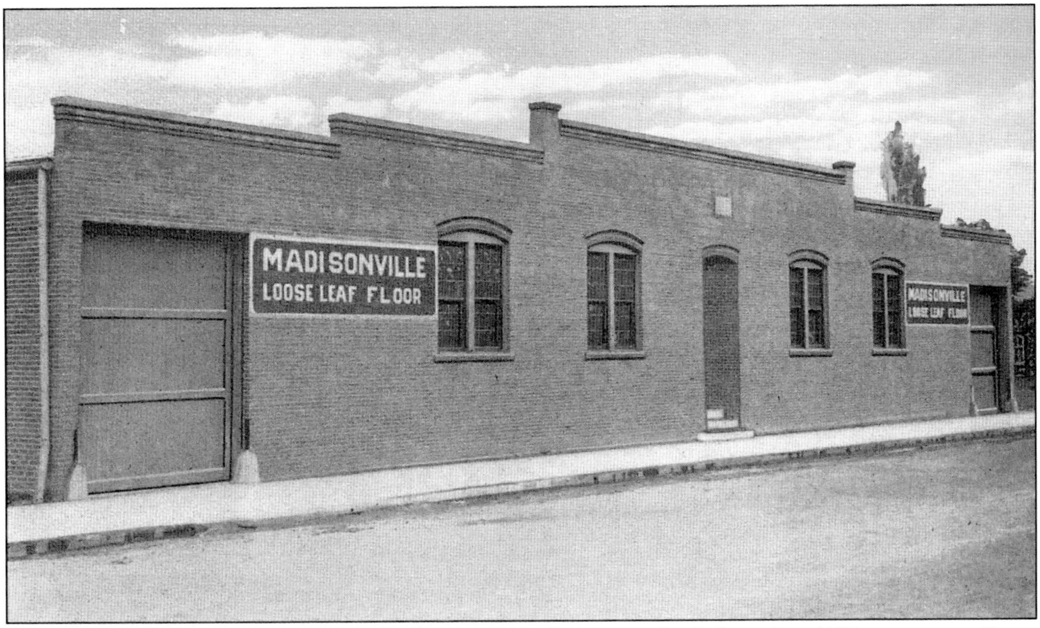

The 30,000-square-foot Loose Leaf Tobacco Warehouse was built by a Civil War veteran, Capt. James Burchfield. The building later became the S. J. Campbell Parachute Factory and, later, the Enro Shirt Factory, which made men's shirts. (HSHC.)

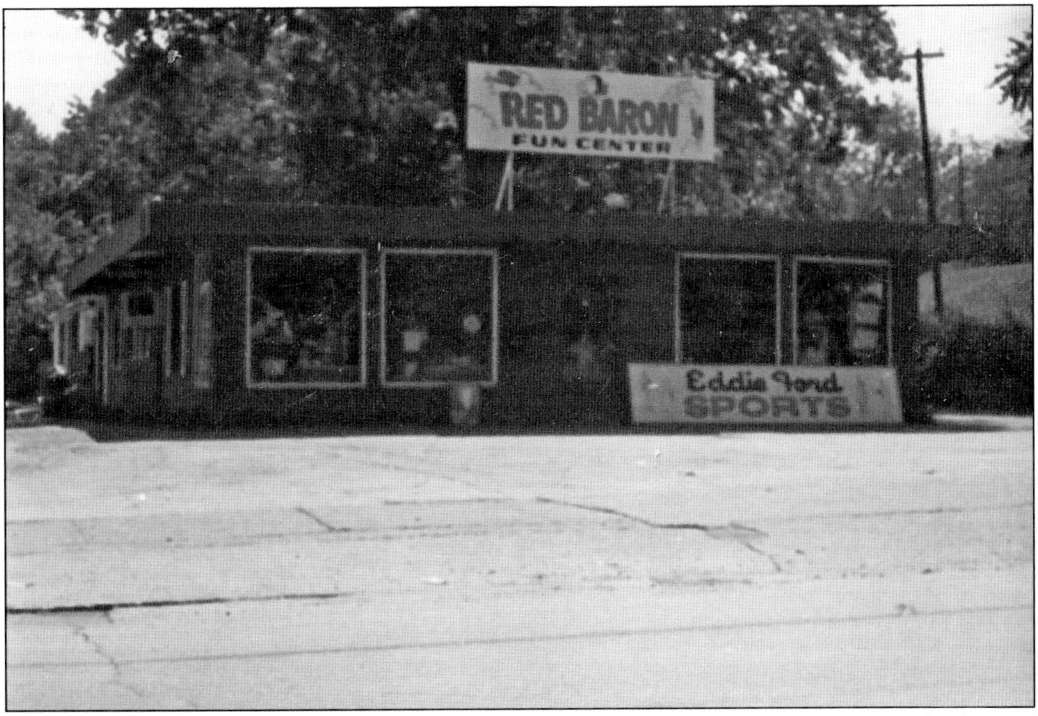

This building was originally the home of the Spanish Inn. In this undated photograph, the Red Baron Video Arcade is in operation on the north side of the building. On the south side of the building is Eddie Ford Sports. Eddie Ford was an outstanding basketball player and the father of Travis Ford of the Charlotte Hornets. (HSHC.)

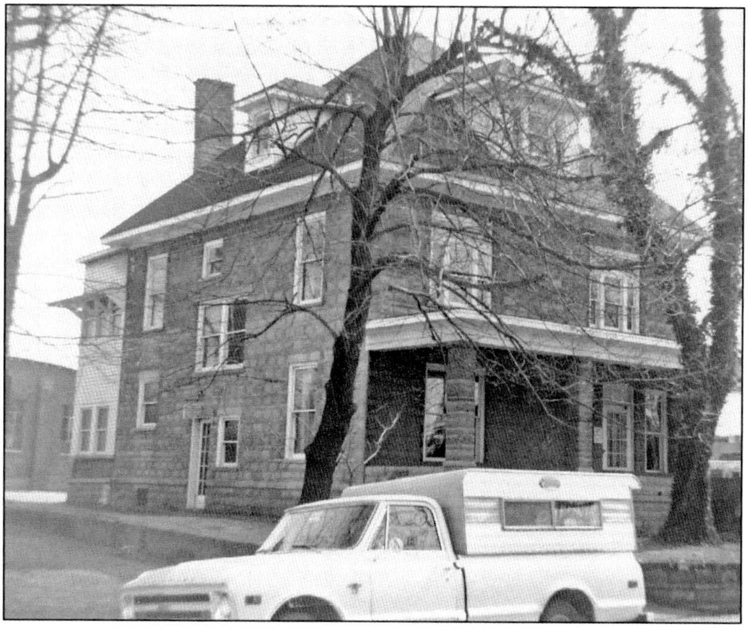

Gov. Ruby Laffoon lived in this home at 38 North Seminary Street in Madisonville when he was elected to the position. When he left office in 1935, he returned and lived at this location until his death on March 1, 1941. After his death, the building became an office of the Kentucky Department of Highways. The building is still standing. (HSHC.)

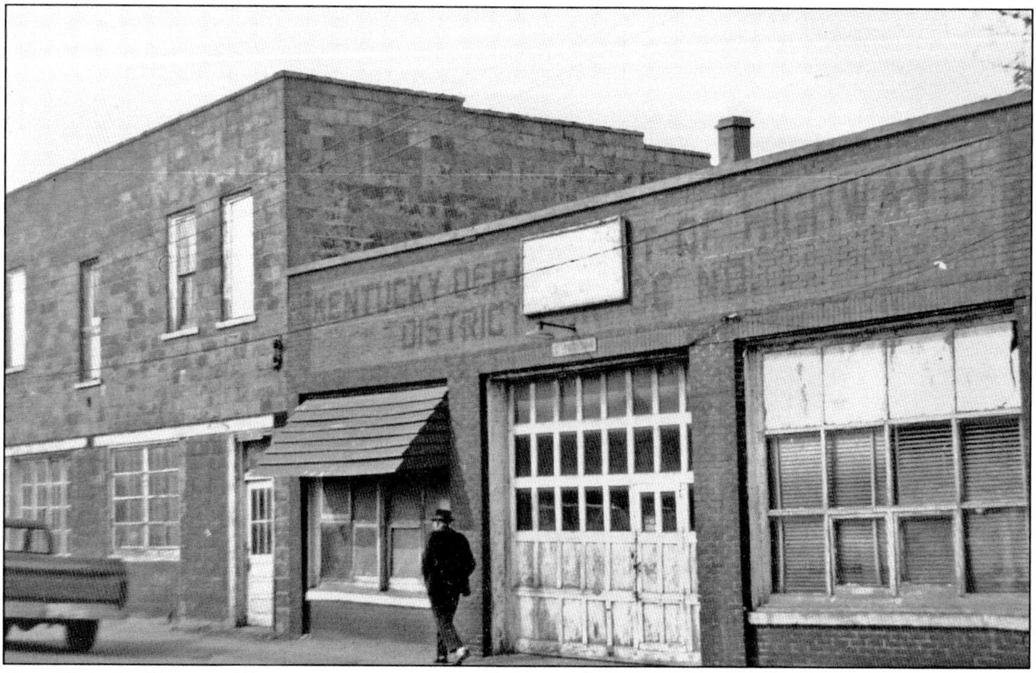

Gov. Ruby Laffoon sold his concrete garage and business house to the State of Kentucky on October 27, 1932, for $15,000. Madisonville was close to the center of the second district of the Kentucky Department of Highways, and the purchase saved the state money. This photograph is how the building looked in 1982. Note the ghostly writing of the former name on the building. (HSHC.)

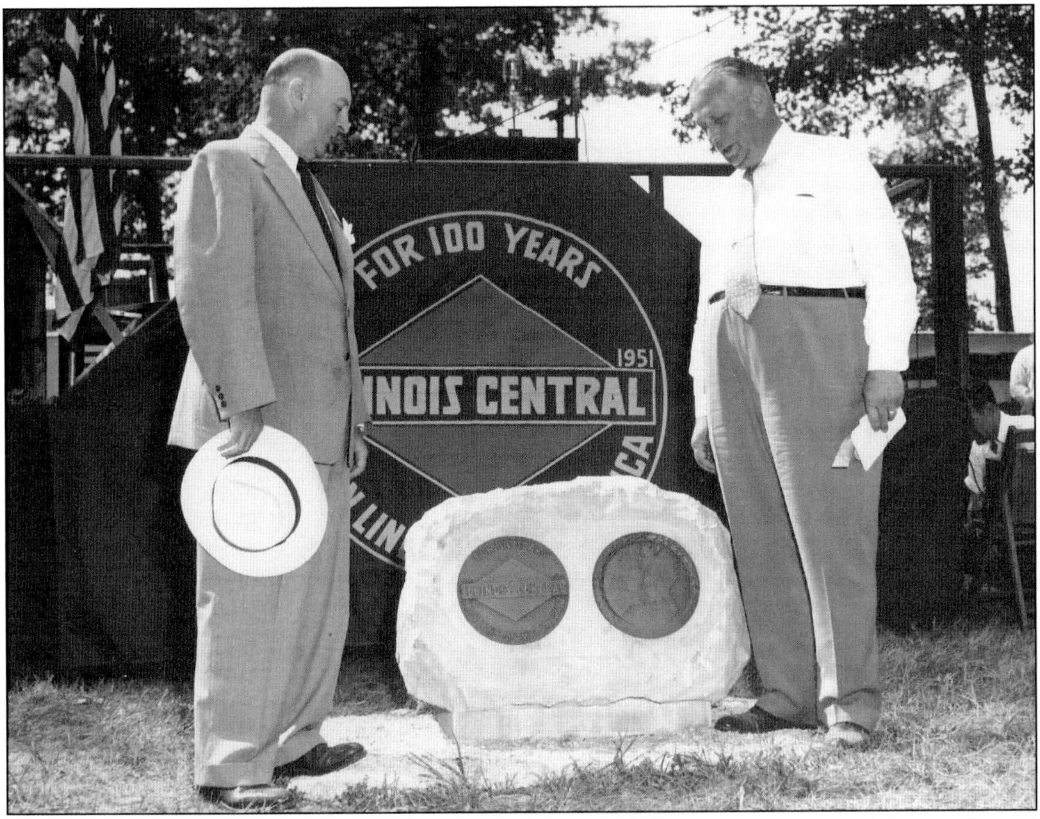

In 1951, the Illinois Central Railroad Company presented this monument to Madisonville and Hopkins County on the occasion of the company's centennial celebration. The monument was presented to Mayor David Parish, shown on the left, by Illinois Central president Wayne Johnston. The monument can still be seen on the northwest lawn of the Hopkins County Courthouse. (HSHC.)

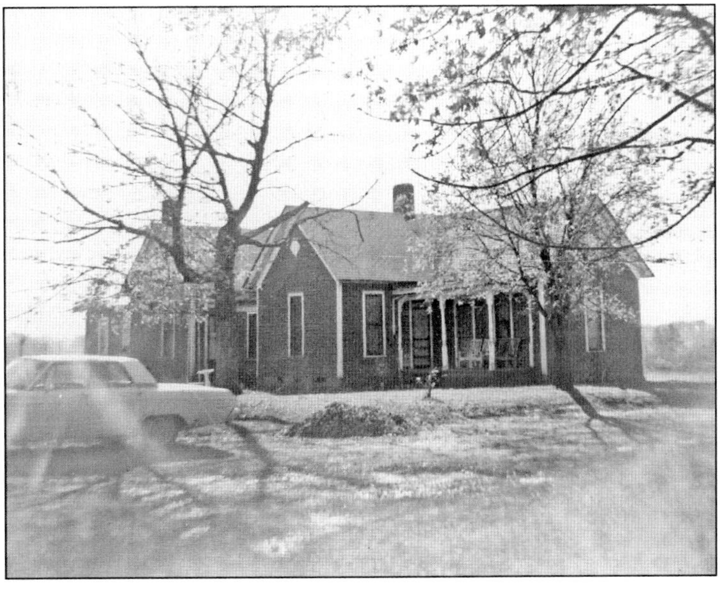

In the late 1900s, the poor without any income were sent to the alms house. The first house rotted down, and on January 20, 1900, Hopkins County bought enough land to build a new house and tear down the old one. The county erected the building shown here, located 6 miles north of Madisonville. (HSHC.)

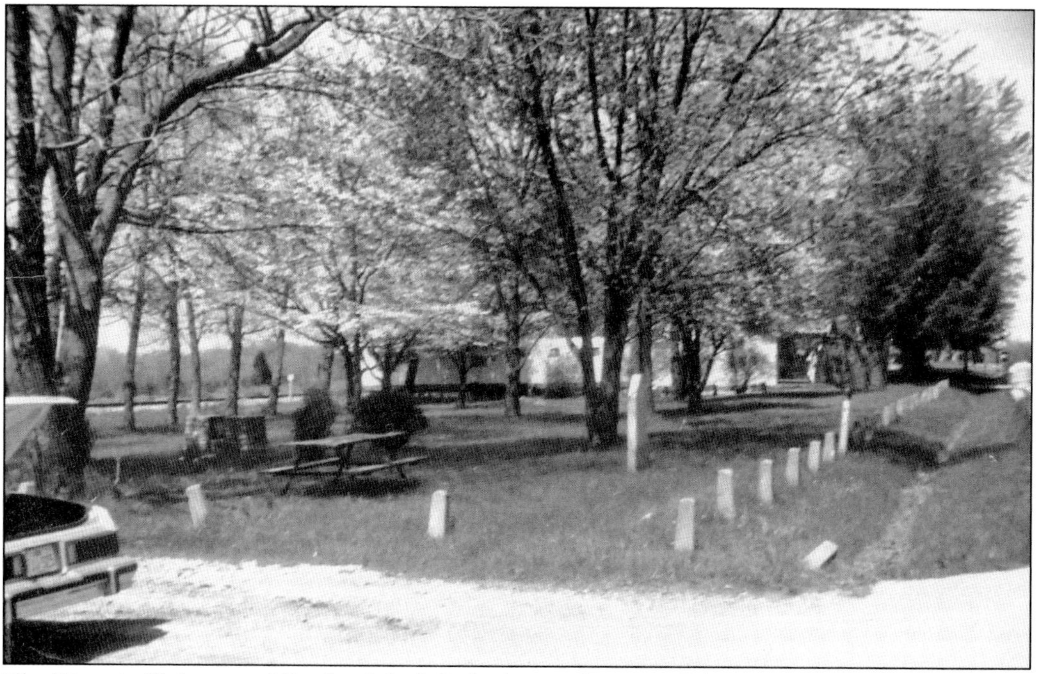

The Kiwanis Club erected Steuben's Lick Park, shown above, on February 1955. It is located on the east side of Manitou on U.S. 41A. A plaque notes that Steuben's Lick was named for the Prussian soldier Frederick Baron Von Steuben (1730–1794) who, according to tradition, visited the site in 1787 to inspect land for military grants. In a skirmish with Native Americans, Steuben was said to have been slightly wounded. Below, U.S. Highway 41-A on the east side of Manitou is shown in an undated photograph. Through the years, Manitou has been called Steuben's Lick, Tywhoppity, and was finally named Manitou for Manitou Springs, Colorado. (Both, HSHC.)

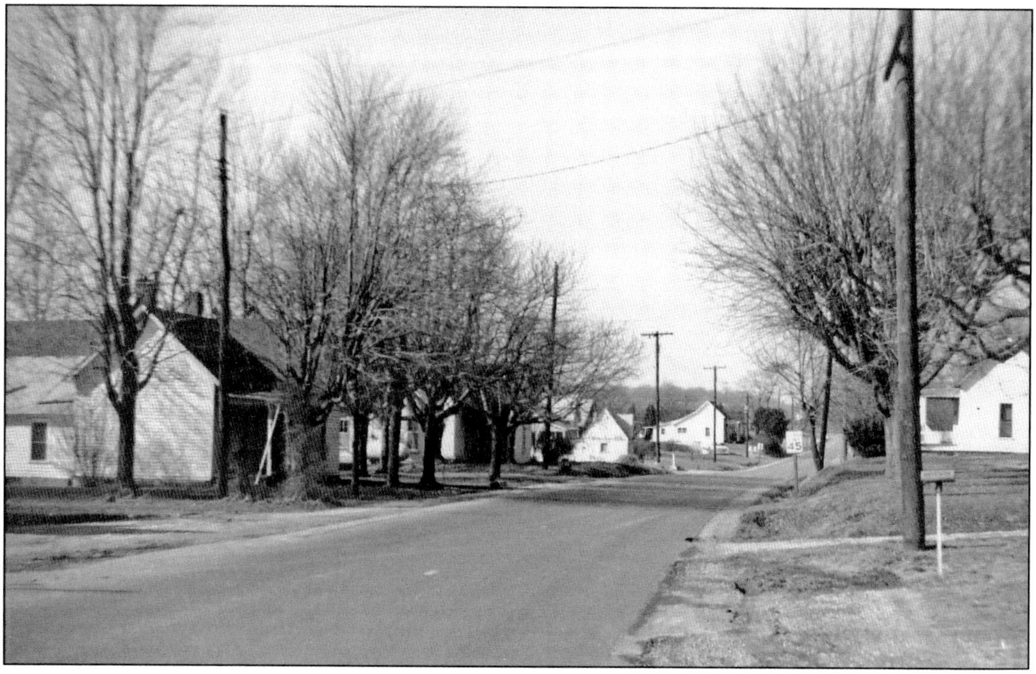

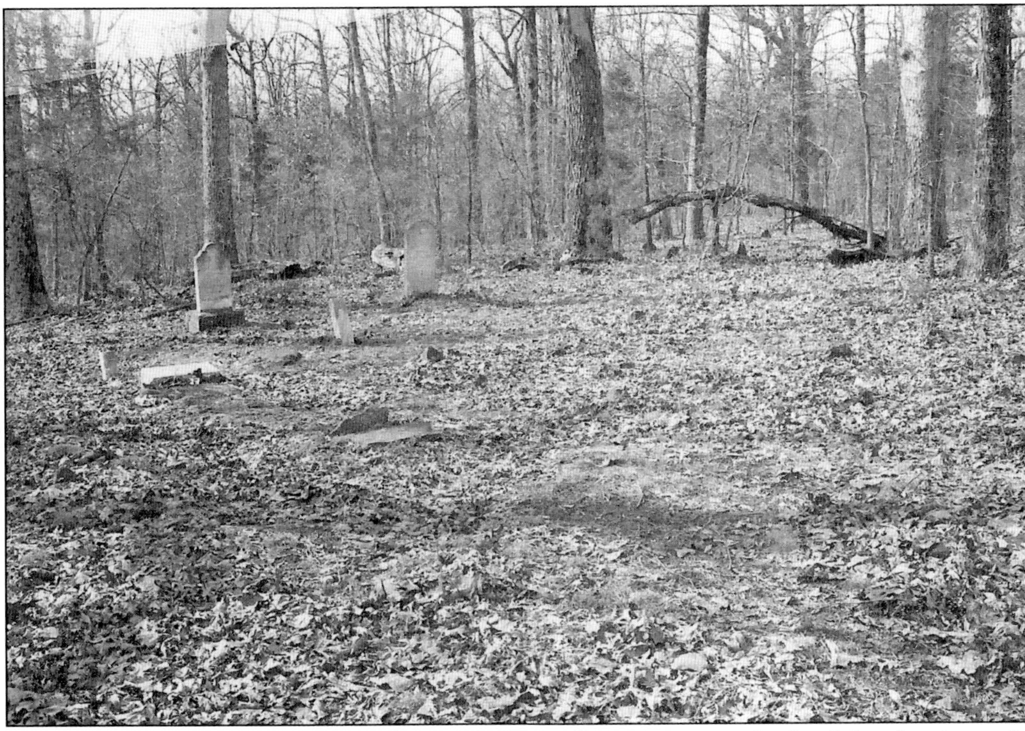

The tombstone of M. R. Brown and Mary J. Wyatt Brown rests on the land that has been the subject of many scary tales. "Wyatt's Cemetery–Hell's Half-Acre" (also known as Lynn Cemetery or Brown's Cemetery) is located on the west side of Highway 109, about a quarter mile from the junction of Highways 109 and 1034. (HSHC.)

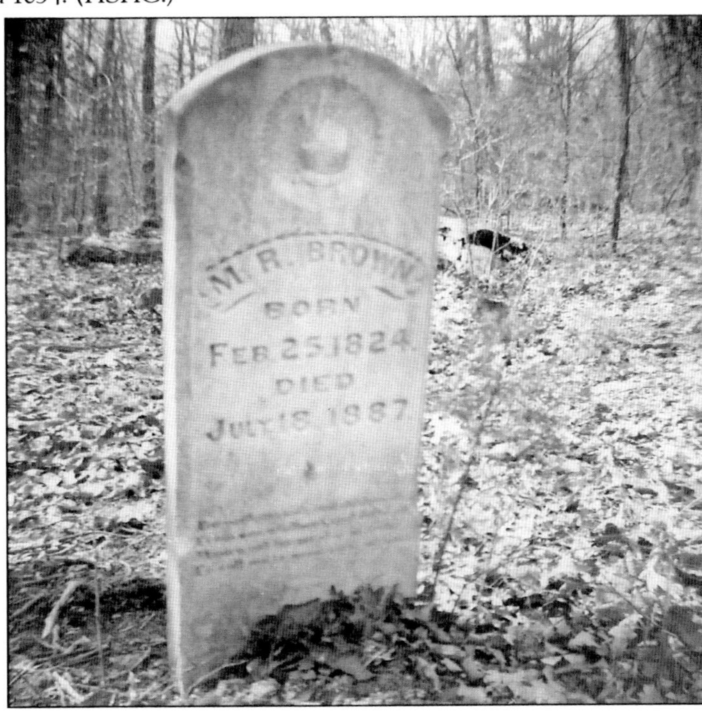

John Lynn was considered to be a drinking, fighting, likable Irishman. Lynn was being carried in a hand-hewn coffin when a red bird reportedly lit on the casket and whistled twice. The mourners believed this to be a sign of bad luck. The cemetery became well known for horror stories. In addition to the property being used for picnicking, it was also used for political speeches, refreshments, and music. (HSHC.)

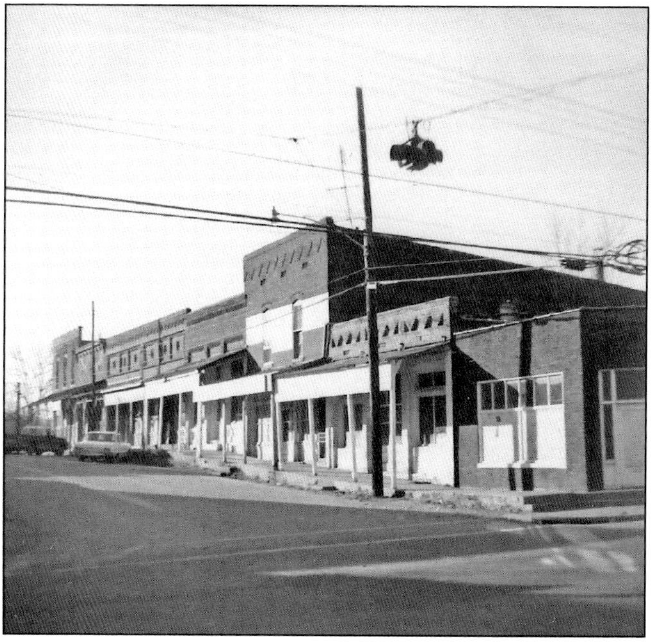

The city of Hanson came into being in 1869, when the railroad was being built. The city was named to honor Henry B. Hanson, an engineer of the company building the railroad. The photograph here shows the north side of West Main Street in Hanson on February 4, 1974. The last building on the left and to the middle of the photograph is the E. L. Parish store. (HSHC.)

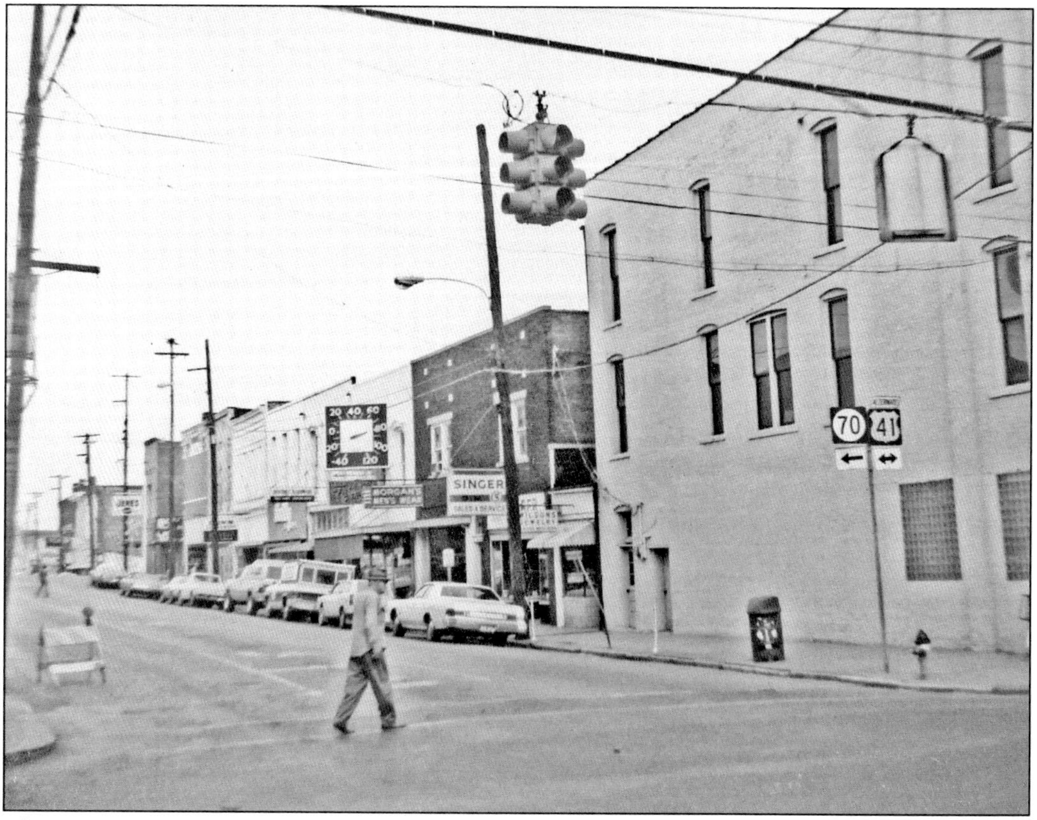

This is a view of the north side of West Center Street in Madisonville about 1974. The Wilson Watch Shop building is now gone. The next two buildings are now Blackwells and Difabio's Restaurants. After that is the law office of Pat Day. (HSHC.)

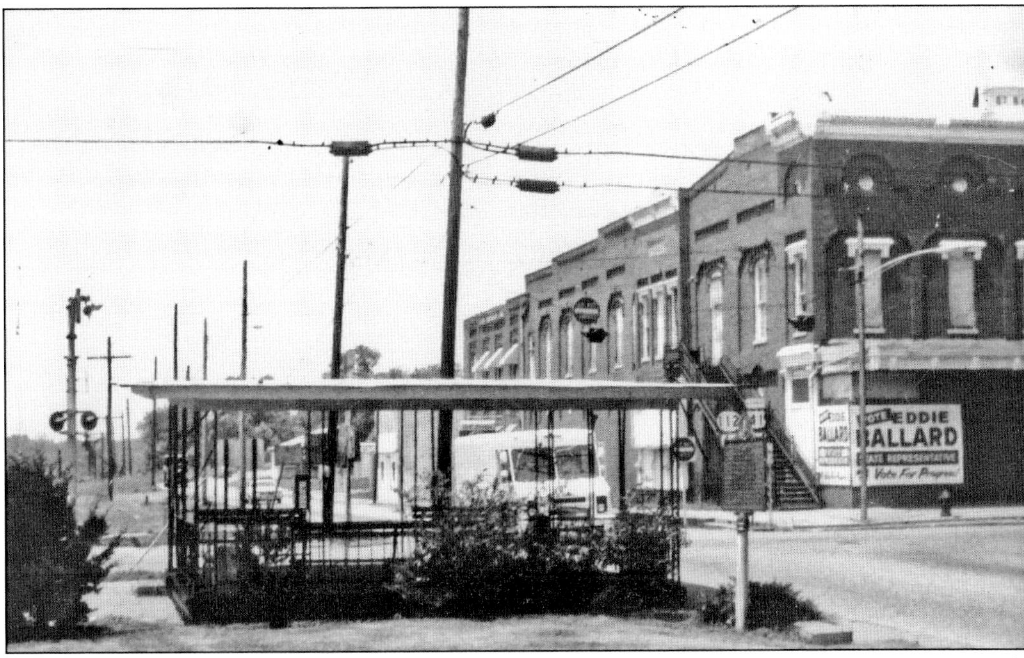

A railroad station was built in 1900 in Earlington on the southeast corner of Main Street. The station was razed on November 1, 1963, and in its place was erected this mini-park. The mini-park was destroyed by a coal truck on June 6, 1987, and has never been replaced. (HSHC.)

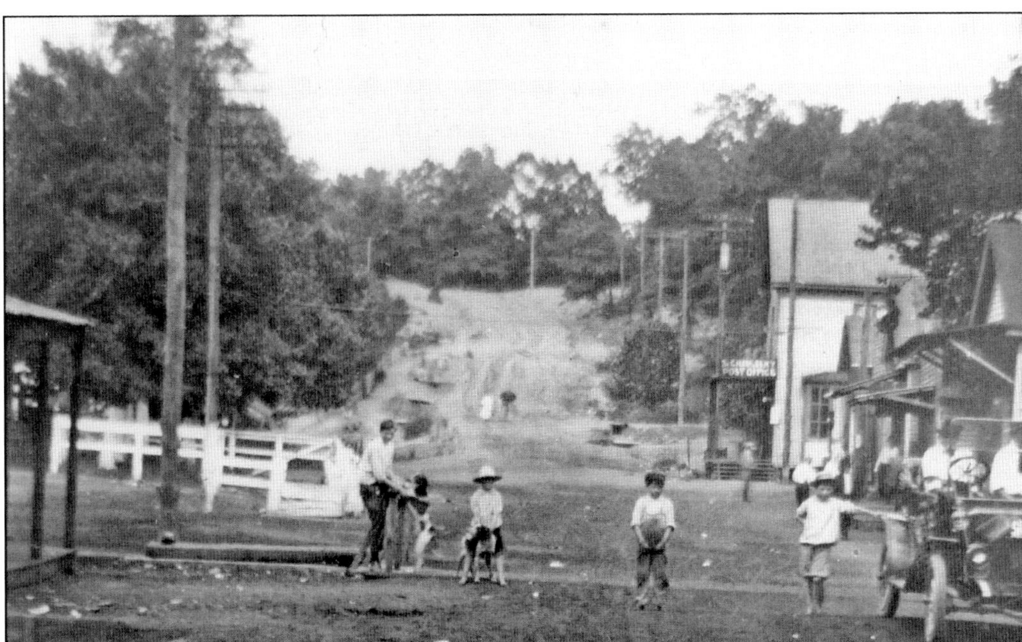

This undated photograph was taken just east of Buck Creek and pointing west in St. Charles. The sign on the building reads "St. Charles Post Office." The building to the extreme left is Smith Chaney's Barber Shop. In the early days, this road was a buffalo trail that led to Greenville. Note the old car at the right. (HSHC.)

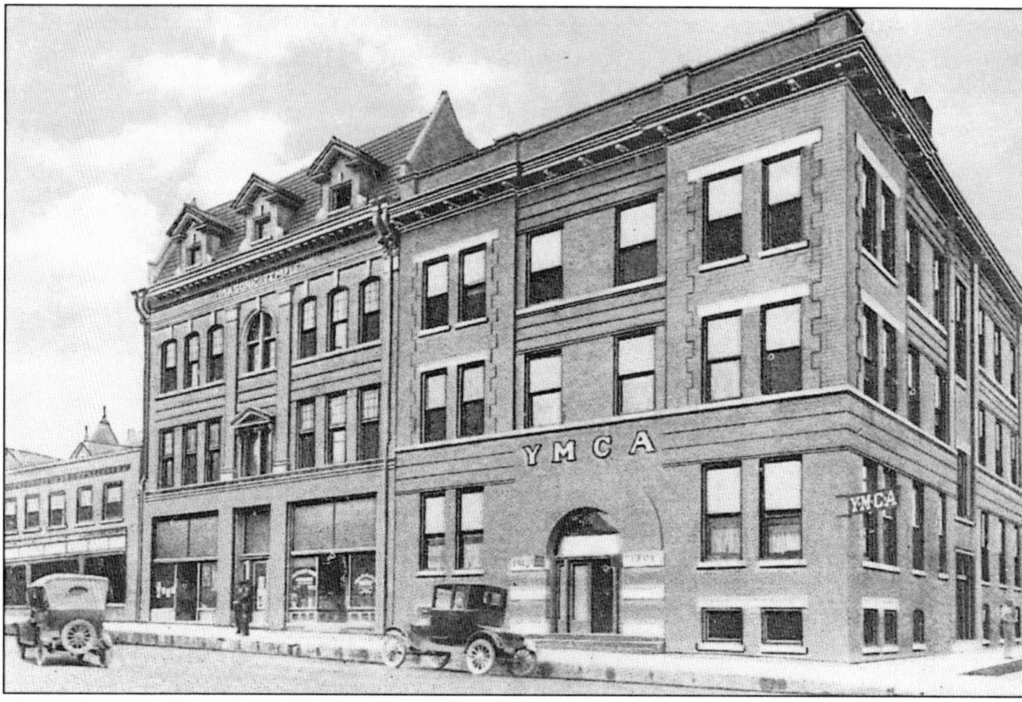

Shown here is the YMCA building in 1906. Madisonville was the smallest town in the country to have a YMCA. Inkerman Bailey was responsible for getting the YMCA to the area. When the YMCA stopped using the building, it became the Madisonville hospital from 1922 to 1939. After that, the building was known as the doctor's building. It was damaged by a tornado in May 1961 and torn down a few years later. (HSHC.)

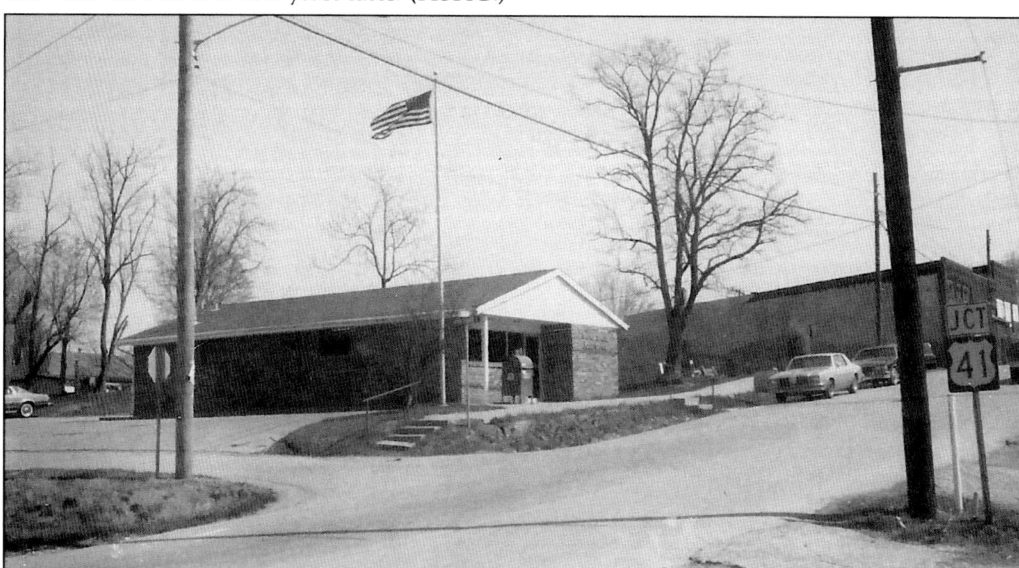

The U.S. Post Office now stands on the site where the Hanson Hotel once stood. The Hanson Banking Company opened an office there in December 1909, but it was taken over by the Kentucky Bank and Trust Company in the early 1930s. The photograph was taken on March 23, 1987. (HSHC.)

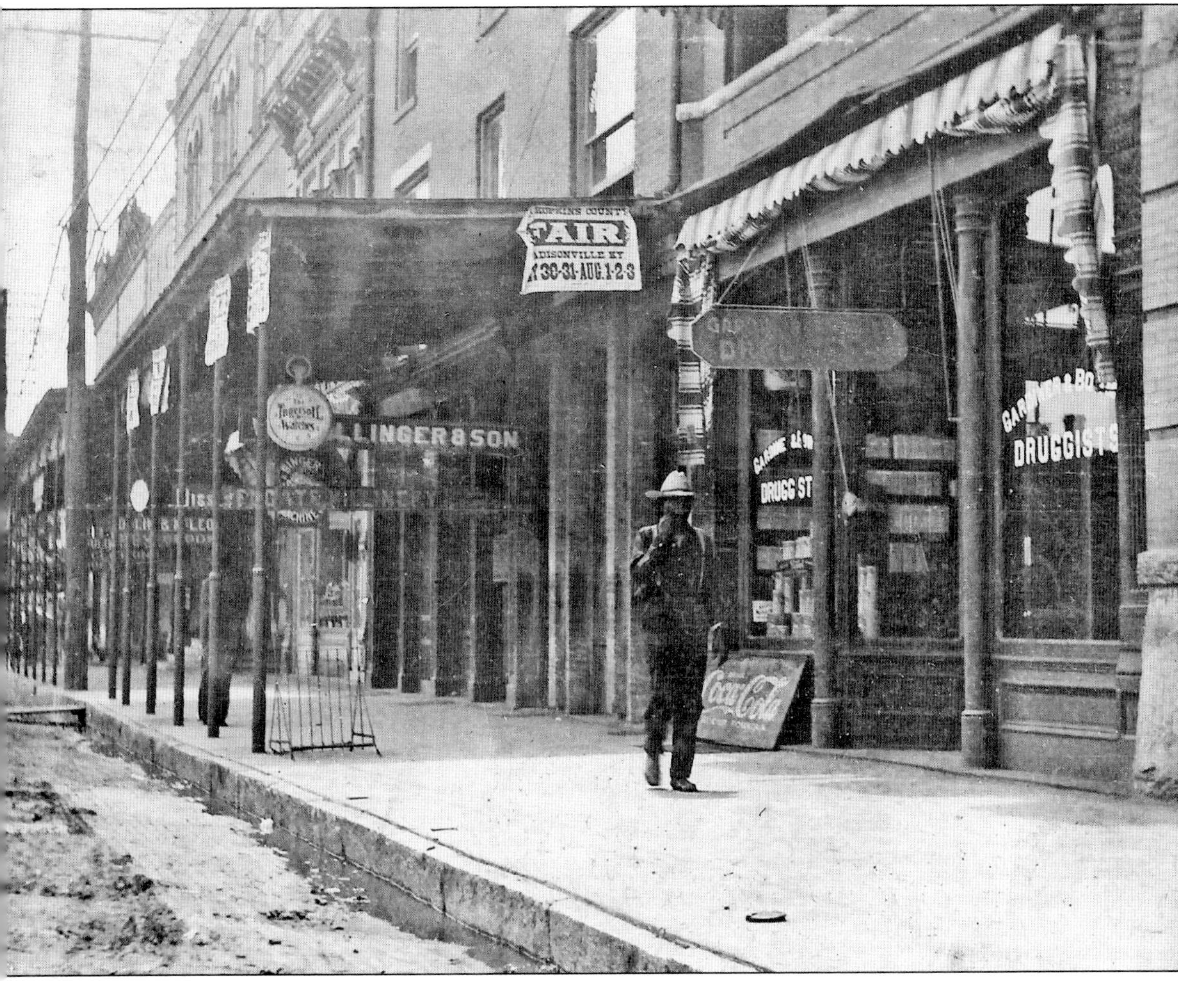

Notice the unpaved streets in this 1902 photograph taken in Madisonville. The businesses recognized are, from left to right, Hollinger and Son Jewelry, Gardiner and Bowmer Drug Store, and Kentucky Bank. Kentucky Bank was built in 1901. On May 19, 1902, Kentucky Bank purchased the adjacent lot and building from N. M. Holeman and his wife, Sadie, for the purpose of enlarging the bank. The buildings were remodeled, and the front facades for the ground floor of the two was made to appear as one building. The building remained that way until 1950, when a major renovation was completed. In the 1970s, the Ben Franklin building was purchased, and the size of the bank was doubled facing Main Street. (HSHC.)

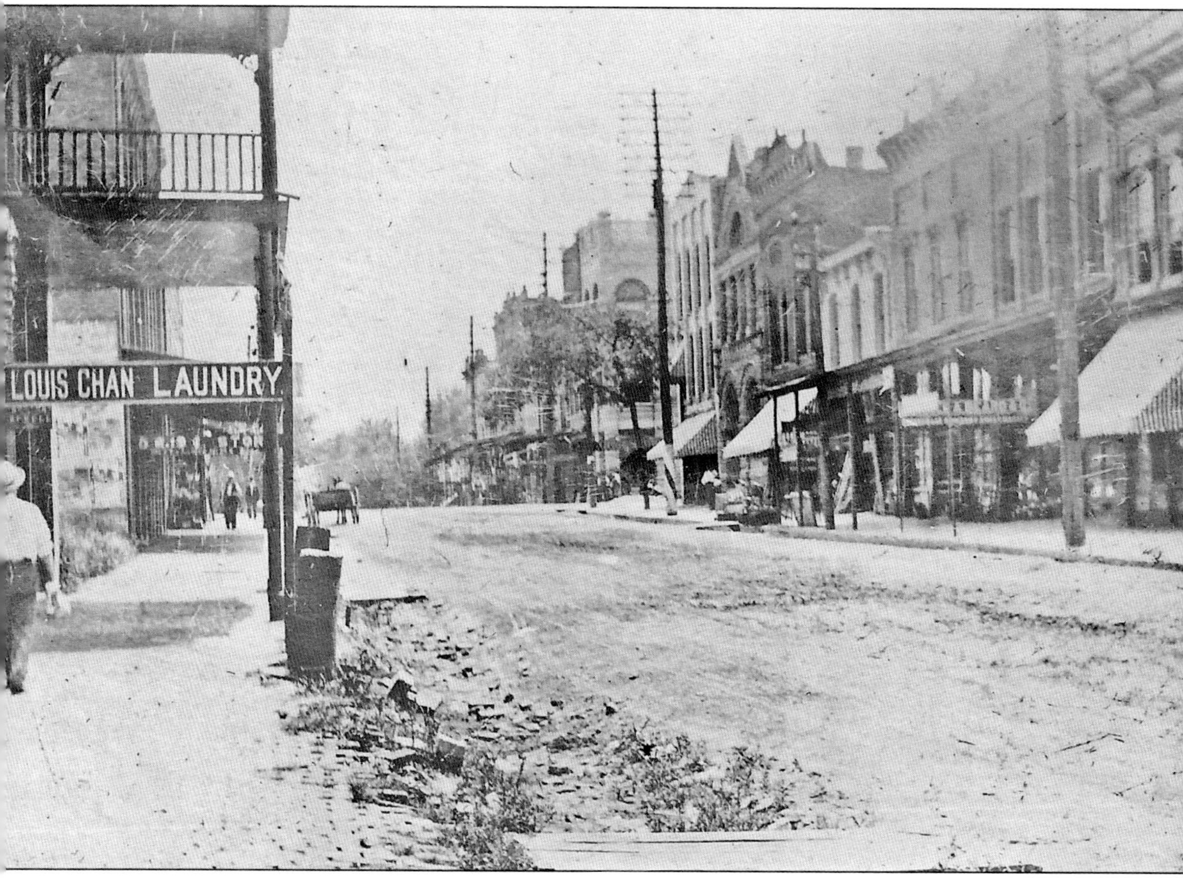

The Louis Chan Laundry was owned by perhaps the only Chinese man in Hopkins County in 1906. Chinese people were some of the earliest immigrants to live in the United States, but the Chinese Exclusion Act mandated that the Chinese be banned from immigrating between 1885 and 1943. Immigration of Chinese was restricted until 1965. Louis Chan's business was located where the TBA Appliance store is now situated. The photograph captures on the opposite side of the street the Morton's Bank, the Kentucky Bank, and Pate's Corner Drug Store. Notice in the picture brick sidewalks, unpaved streets, and ditches with walk boards across. Look at the canopies on the stores on the west side on north Main Street. The telephone poles have nine cross arms to carry the wires required for Madisonville phones. (HSHC.)

Two

Business Ventures

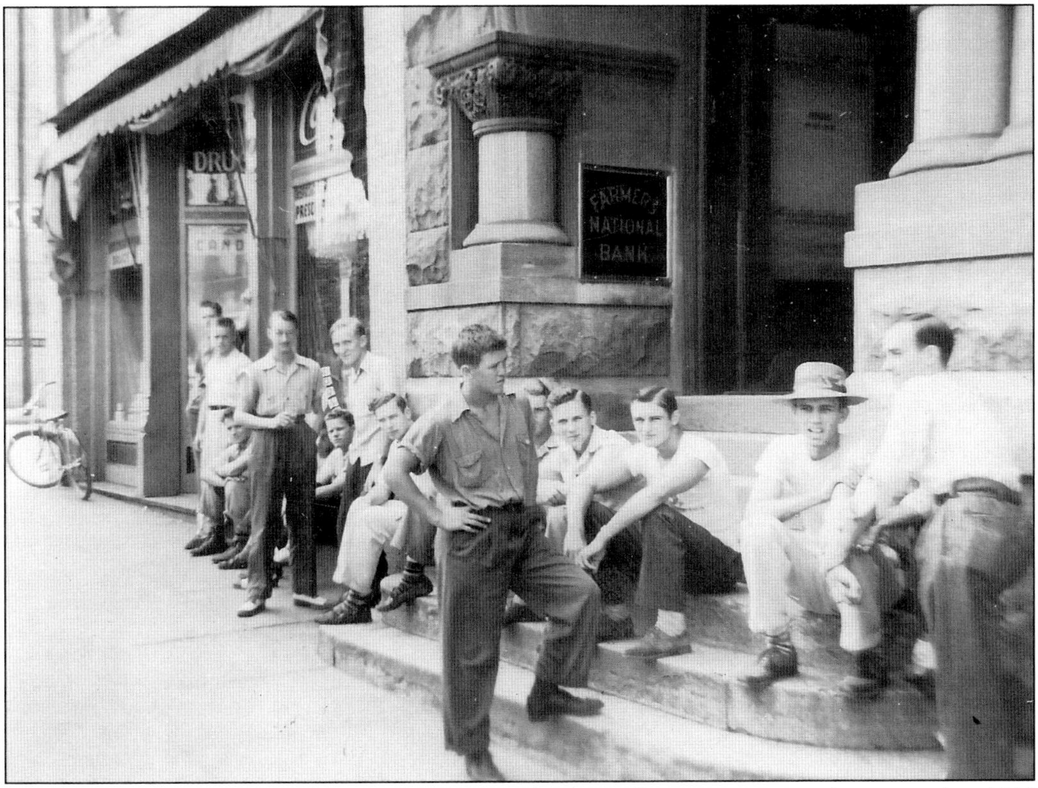

The Pate's Drug Store corner was the favorite hangout for teenagers, as shown in this 1942 photograph. From left to right are John Angel, Otho "Burrhead" Robinson, unidentified, Billy Adams (standing), James "Peaches" Harris (seated), Kenneth Arnold (standing), B. C. Bacon Jr. (seated), James "Shake" Wade (standing), unidentified, C. B. "Bliss" Powell (seated), Jewell Browning (seated), Roscoe Jackson (seated), and unidentified (standing). The extended steps have since been removed. (HSHC.)

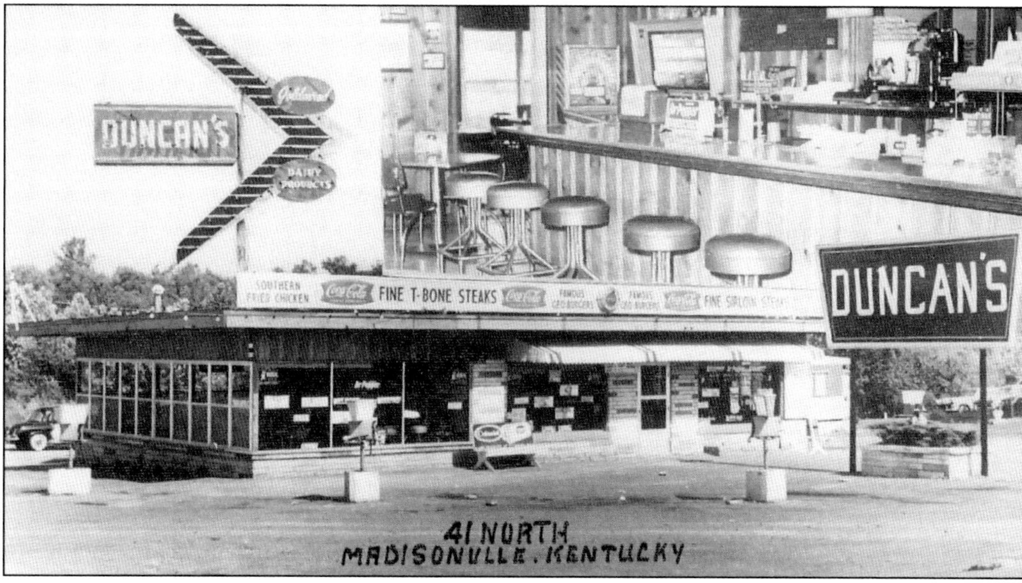

This postcard features Duncan's Drive-In, a favorite teen hangout and restaurant from 1955 until the early 1970s. Teen drivers would race across town at lunch to get a seat. Duncan's was located on North Main Street. It was razed, and a Quick Pick Market was built. Today a BP station stands on the property. (HSHC.)

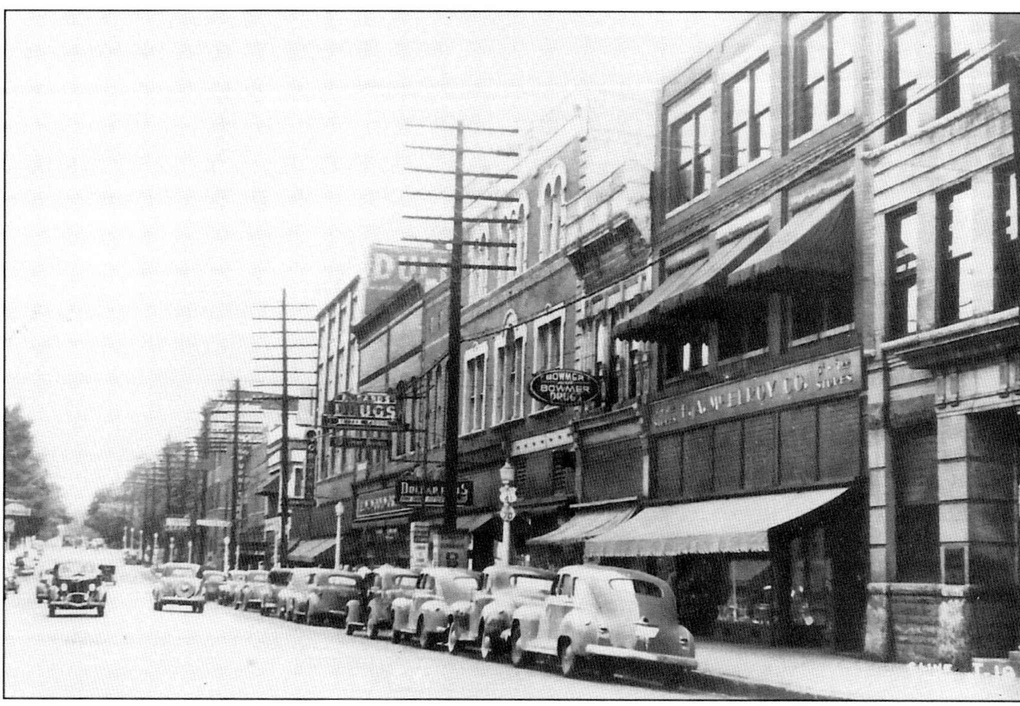

The lampposts on South Main Street in 1947 were the "White Way" posts. The merchant policeman turned the White Way on at dusk and off at 10:00 p.m., except around the courthouse. Buildings from left to right are Jordan Furniture, F. W. Woolworth Store, The Vogue, Dollar Brothers Shoe Store, Robards Drug Store, and Bowmer and Bowmer Drug Store. (HSHC.)

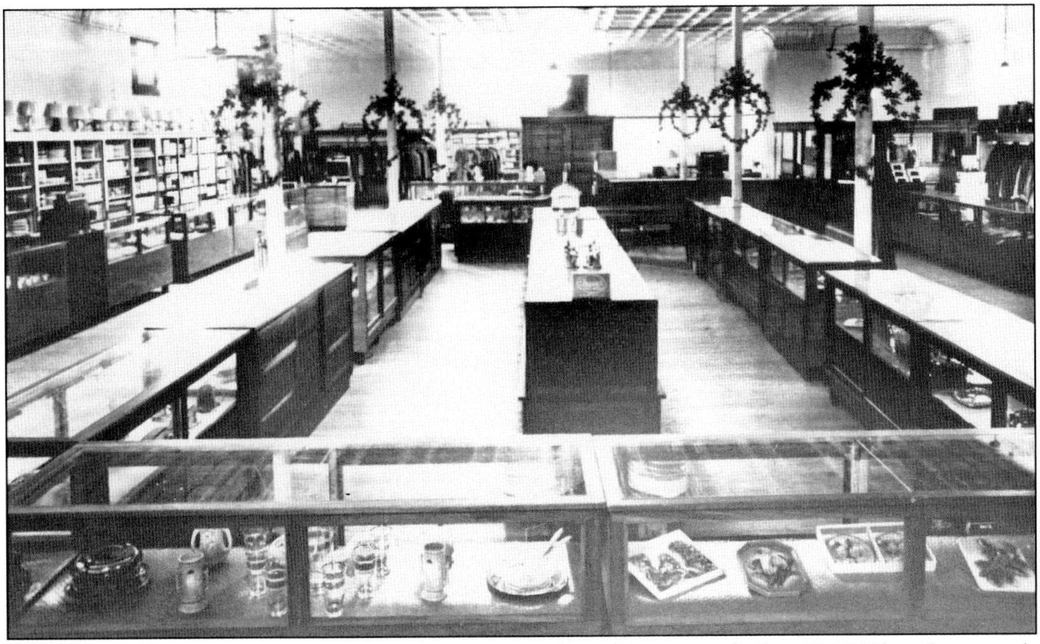

The company store was established by the St. Bernard Coal Company before 1900. This photograph shows the interior of the West Kentucky Coal Company store at Earlington. The company issued scrip, a form of money, to the employees to buy merchandise at the store. This is the origin of the phrase "I owe my soul to the company store." (HSHC.)

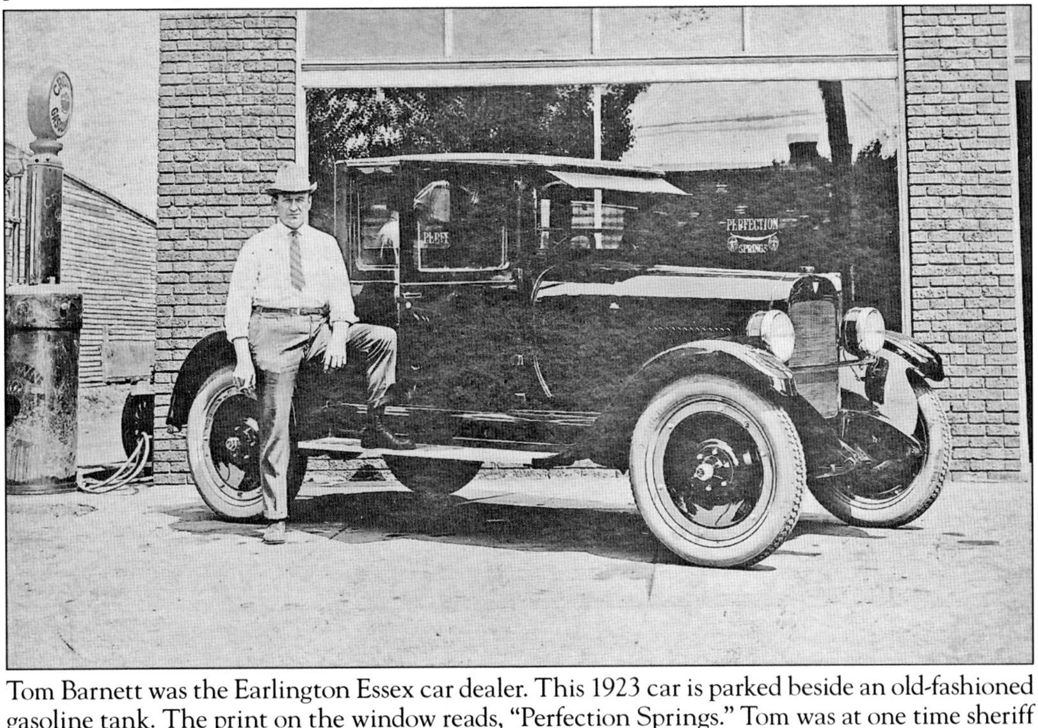

Tom Barnett was the Earlington Essex car dealer. This 1923 car is parked beside an old-fashioned gasoline tank. The print on the window reads, "Perfection Springs." Tom was at one time sheriff of Hopkins County. The back of the photograph has the following imprint: "James A Robinson, Railroad and Farren Avenue, Earlington, KY. Charlie Barnett, Barnett's Garage." (HSHC.)

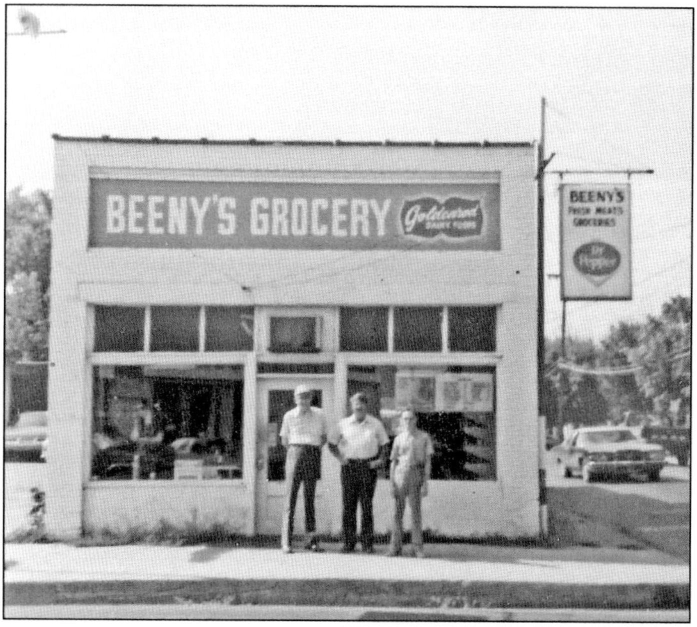

Beeny's Grocery was located on the southeast corner of the intersection of West Center Street and South Seminary Street. From left to right are Bob Beeny, Bill Beeny (grandson of founder), and Virgil Beeny. The store was founded by W. A. Beeny in 1929 and was operated continually by W. A. and his son, Hardy, until closing. (Bob Beeny.)

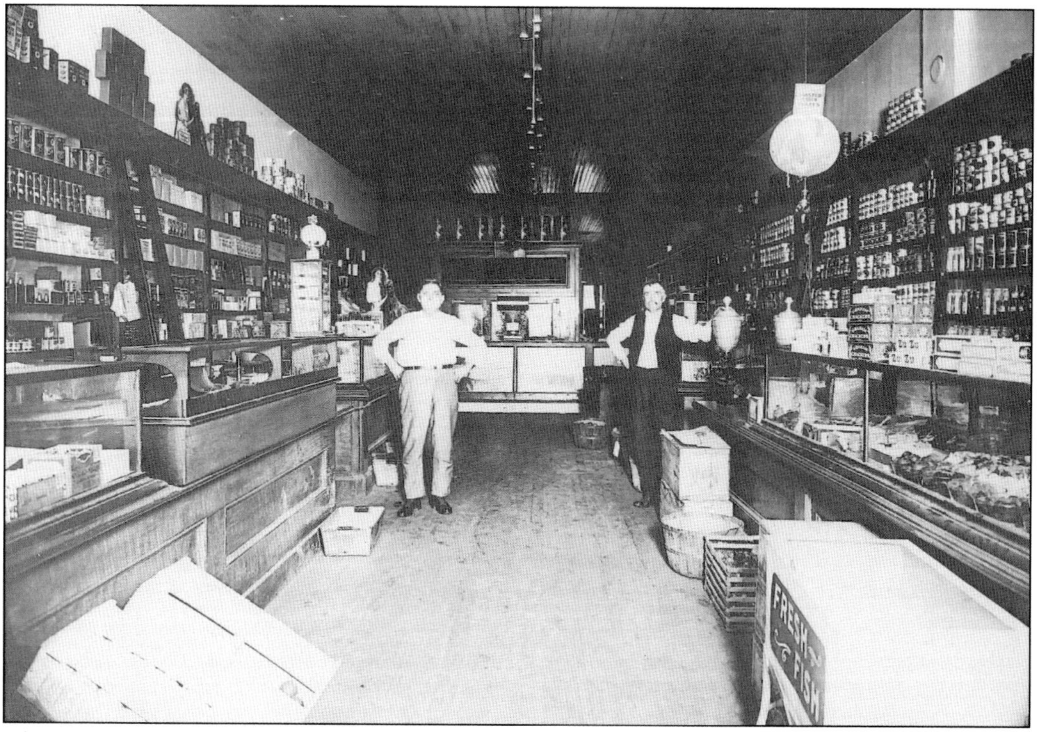

This neighborhood grocery was owned by James A. Thomas and located on Hall Street in Madisonville. He is shown in this photograph around 1920. Some of the items identified on labels are Fresh Fish, Quaker Oats, Toasted Corn Flakes, and Kellogg's Corn Flakes. A grocery store has operated on this corner continually since the first opening. (Gigi Kesterson Smith.)

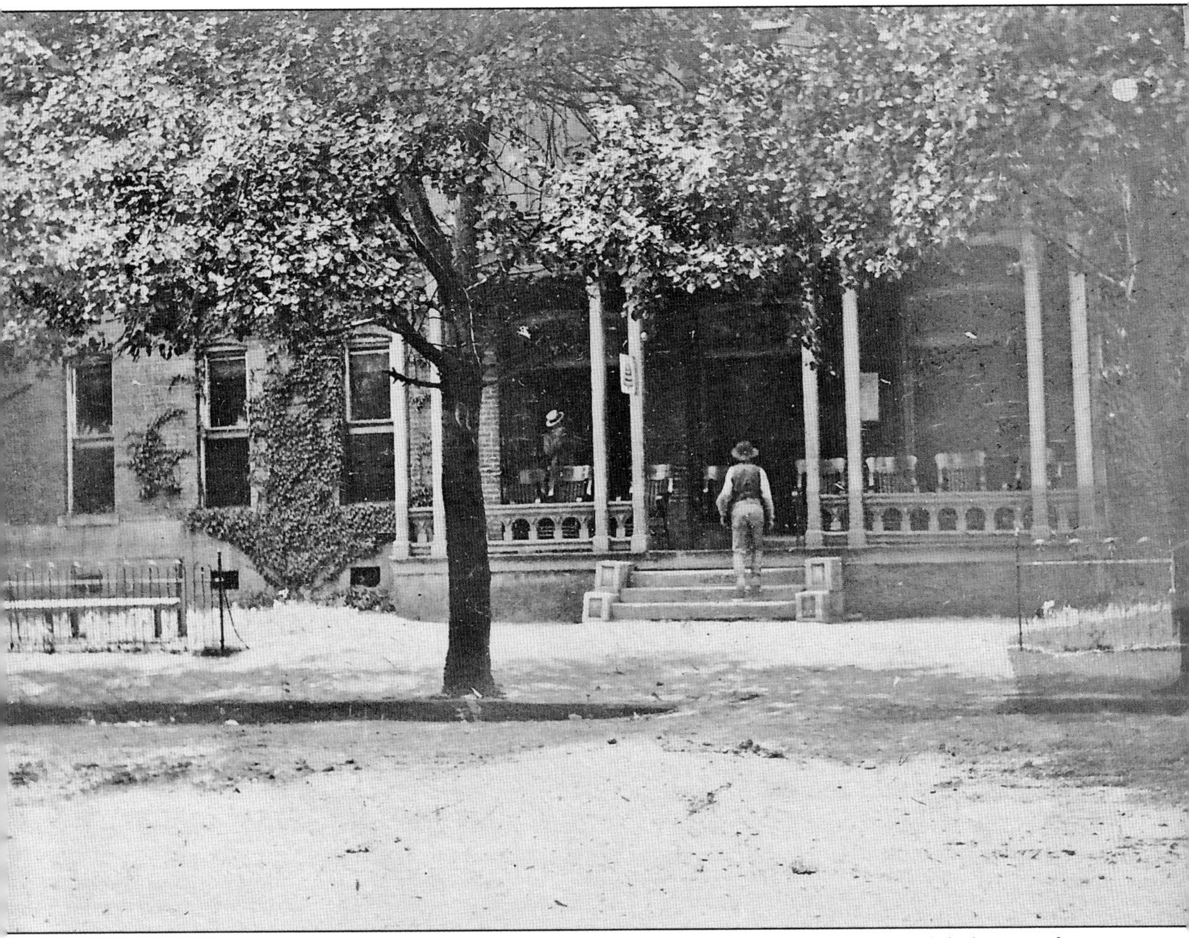

The Hotel Lucile is shown here as it appeared in 1893. The establishment was widely known for its excellent cuisine and genial hospitality. Certain delicacies were ordered from New Orleans for special occasions. The hotel looks like a brick building but was a wood frame with a brick front. The hotel was located adjacent to the L&N Railroad station for convenience of railroad travelers. It burned on December 25, 1906. The owners promised they would build a new hotel on the location, but they did not. Later the Hotel Mary was built on the corner of East Center and Union Streets, then sold a year and a half later and renamed Hotel Madison. The Hotel Lucile was located on the corner of South Main and Sugg Streets. The historical society has a spoon that was recovered from the hotel fire. (HSHC.)

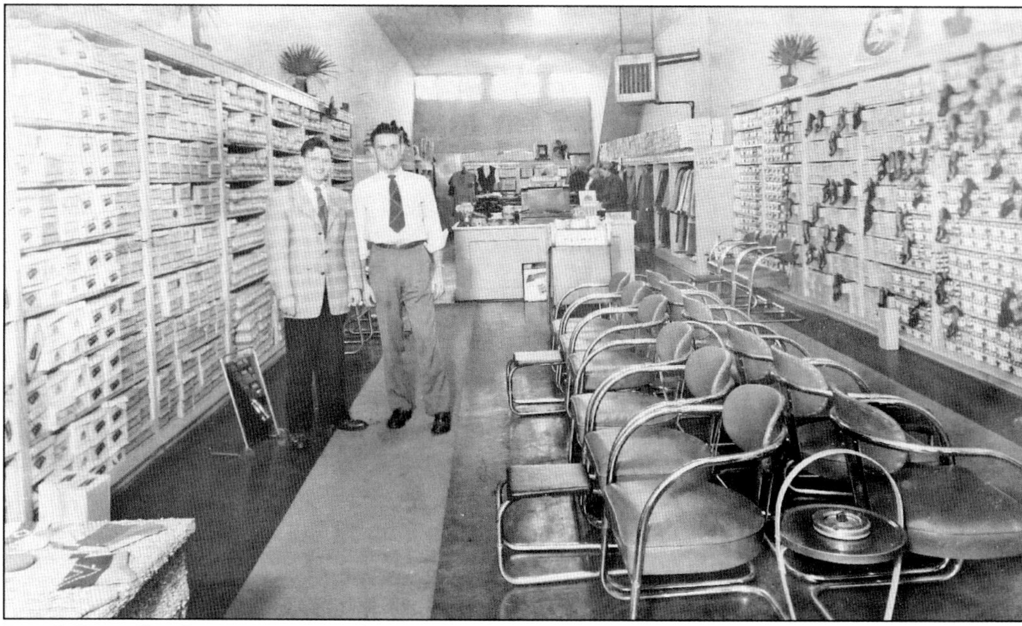

Parish Friendly Shoes was owned by Charles Parish. Shown in the photograph above are Charles Parish (left) and employee Henry Cartwright (right). When the store closed, Parish went to Owensboro, and Henry went to work at Dollar Brothers Shoe Store. Henry later purchased the Dollar Brothers Shoe Store in Hopkinsville. The photograph below is a snapshot of the Madisonville High School basketball team being fitted for shoes at Parish Friendly Shoes. Shown from left to right are Henry Cartwright, Charles Ray, Dickie Strong, Charles Parish (owner), unidentified, Edward Dale Long, unidentified, Bill Coates, Morris Yates (later a doctor), unidentified, and Bill Knight. (Both, Anita Pate Cartwright.)

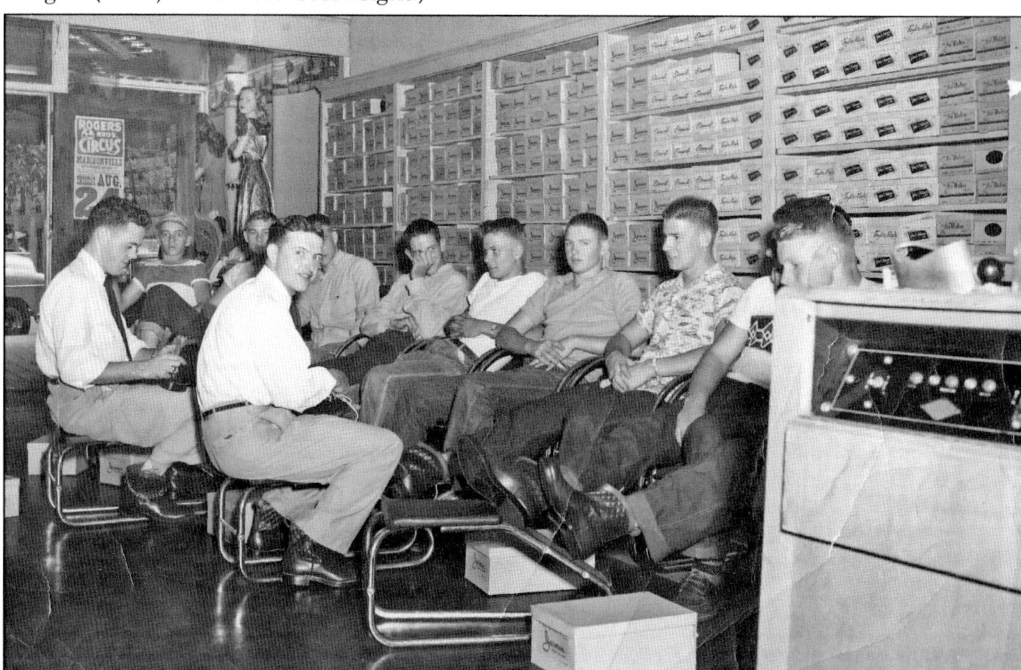

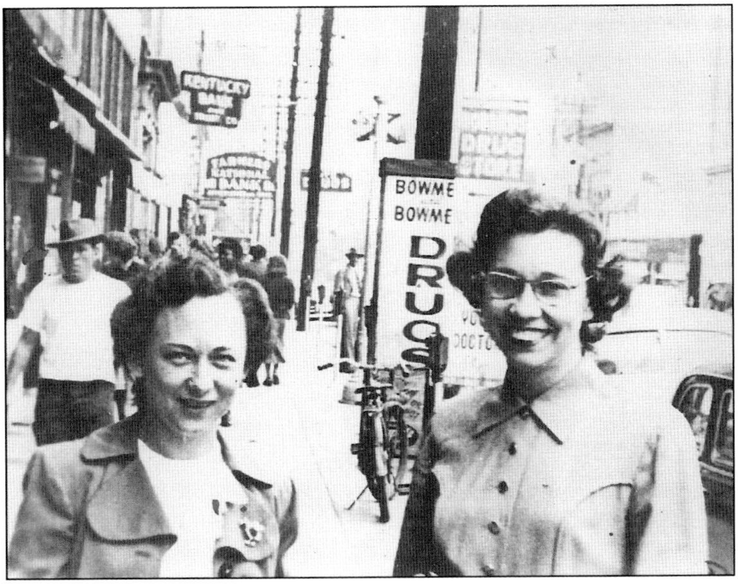

Nortonville neighbors Martha Helen "Margie" Smith (left) and Hazel Whitfield (right) enjoy a shopping spree in downtown Madisonville about 1948. Note the bank and drugstore signs and busy activity in the street. In the 1940s, 1950s, and 1960s, downtown was the hub of activity on weekends. With the creation of shopping centers and malls, downtown is no longer the center of activities. (Gail Warren.)

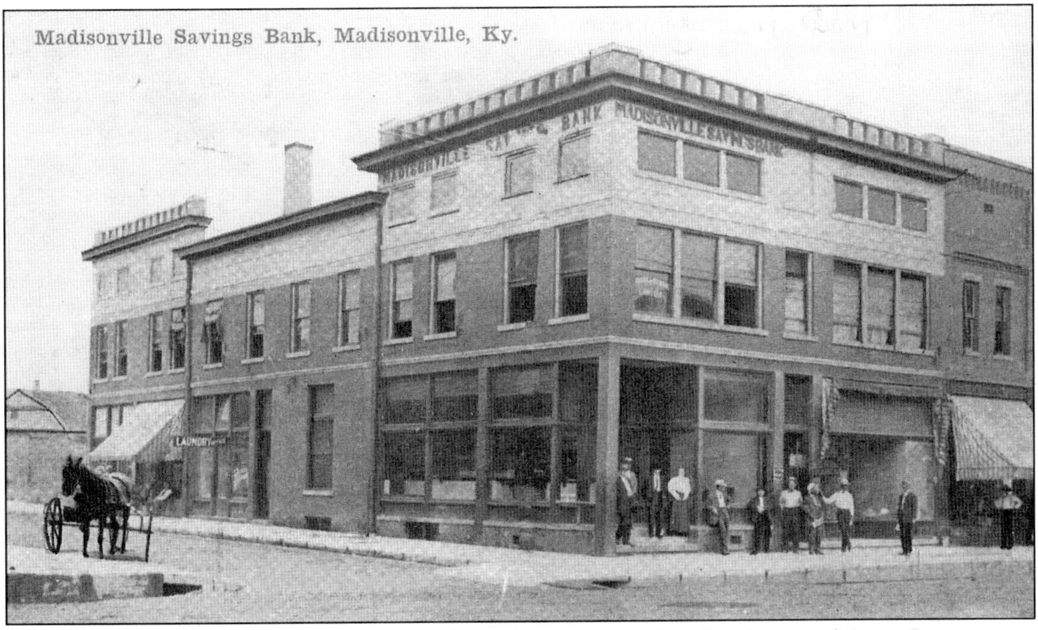

The Madisonville Savings Bank, located on the corner of South Main and Sugg Streets, was razed on October 1991. This postcard is dated 1911. This is now the location of Montpelier Park. A mural of James Madison's home is on the south wall of Bartholomew's Restaurant. The mural is being updated to reflect the restoration of Madison's home. (HSHC.)

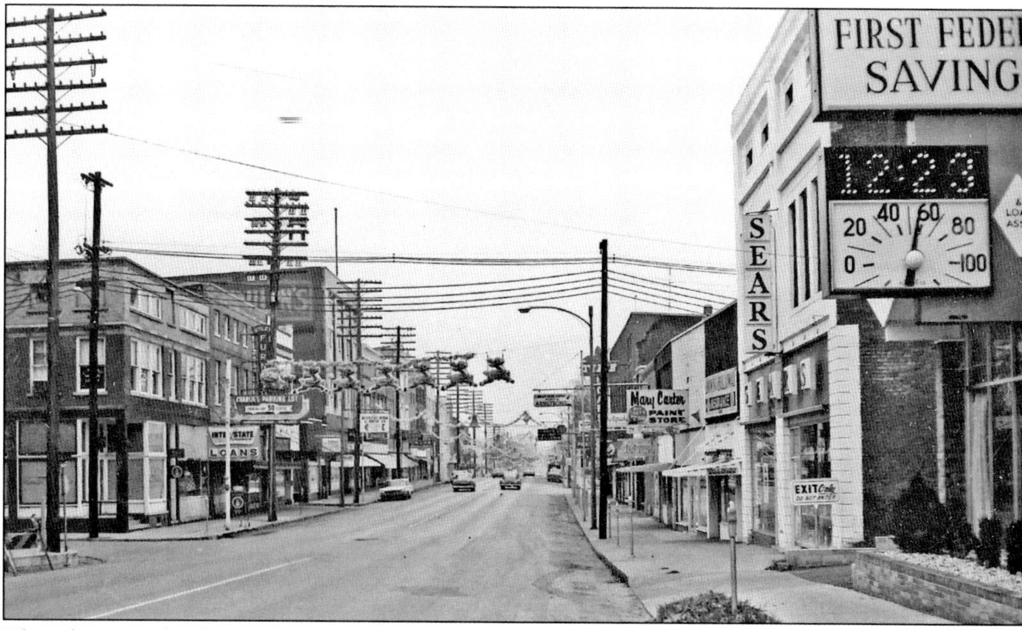

This photograph of pre-Christmas South Main Street, Madisonville, is not dated. The Sears Store is now Happy's of Madisonville. The Happy's building has housed a print shop, coal company store, and appliance store since its erection in 1905. The south side of the building was damaged by the 1961 tornado. (HSHC.)

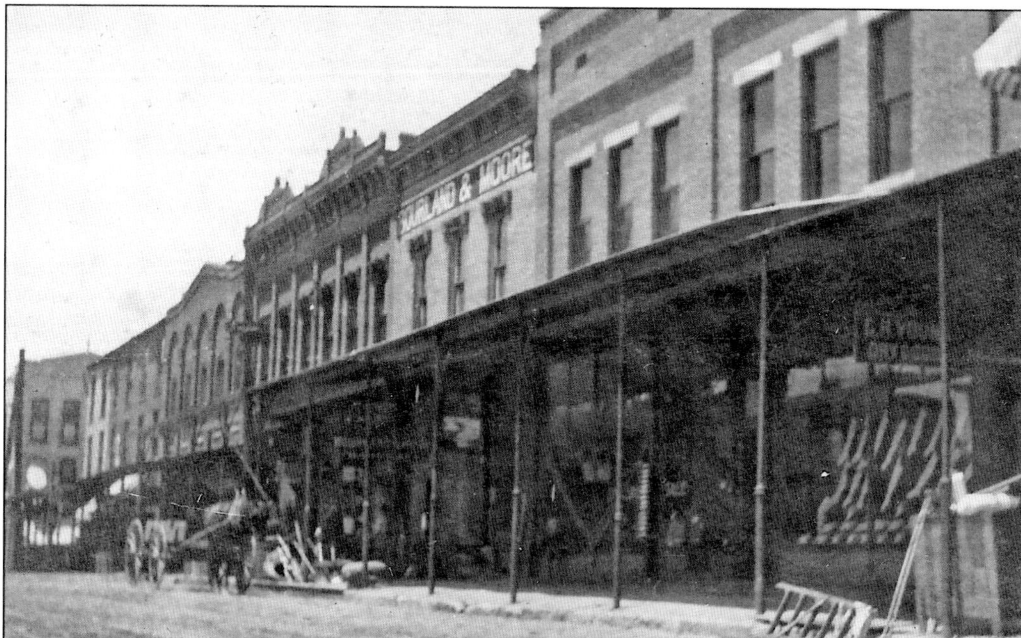

The north side of East Center Street looking west toward Main Street was captured in this undated photograph. Some of the businesses on the street were C. H. Young Dry Goods, Bourland and Moore Hardware, and the old Eagle Hotel. The hotel was demolished to make way for Farmer's Bank. The hotel was in such a sorry state that when it was torn down, townspeople said, "An eyesore is gone." (HSHC.)

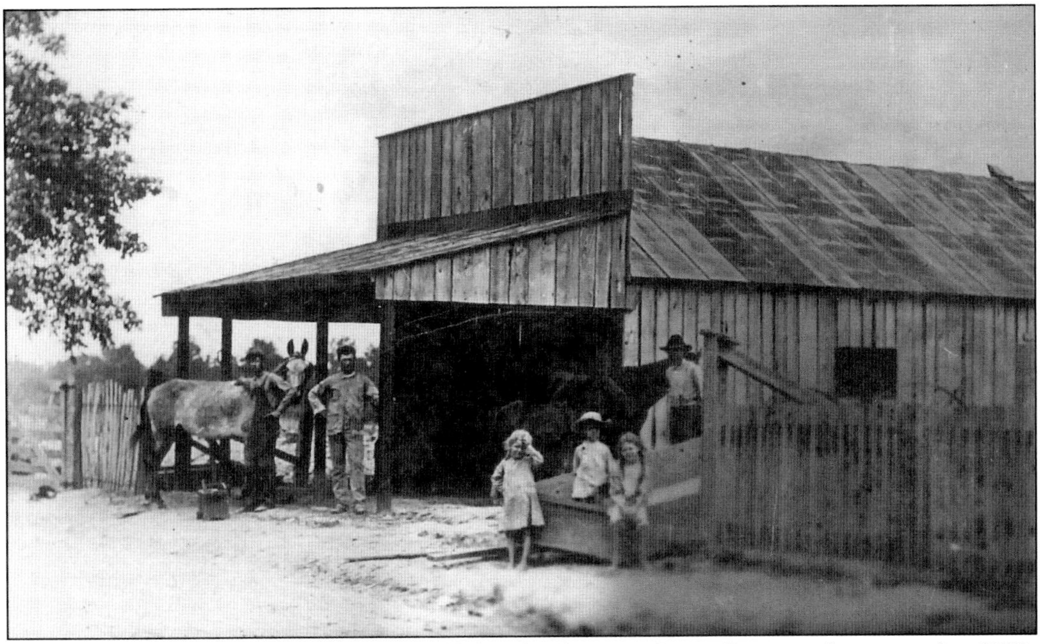

The McCain Blacksmith Shop at the old family place on Green River is shown in this 1920s photograph. The building was special in its construction in that there were two floors. The top floor was used for the mill. William Lee McCain was the blacksmith. The shop was located in Jewel City. (Robert and Audrey McCain Collection, HSHC.)

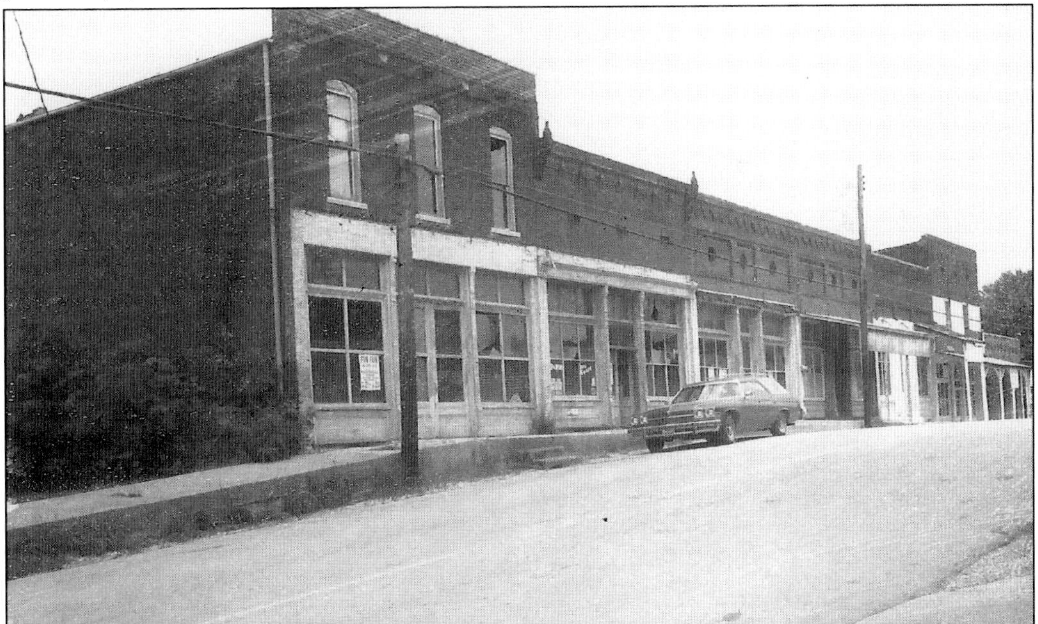

At the time this 1976 photograph was taken, the men on top of the E. L. Parish store building were tearing it down. The building was purchased by Donan Associates, who had it razed to put a grocery store on the land. The old showcases that were used in the store were donated to the historical society. The location of photograph is the north side of Main Street in Hanson. (HSHC.)

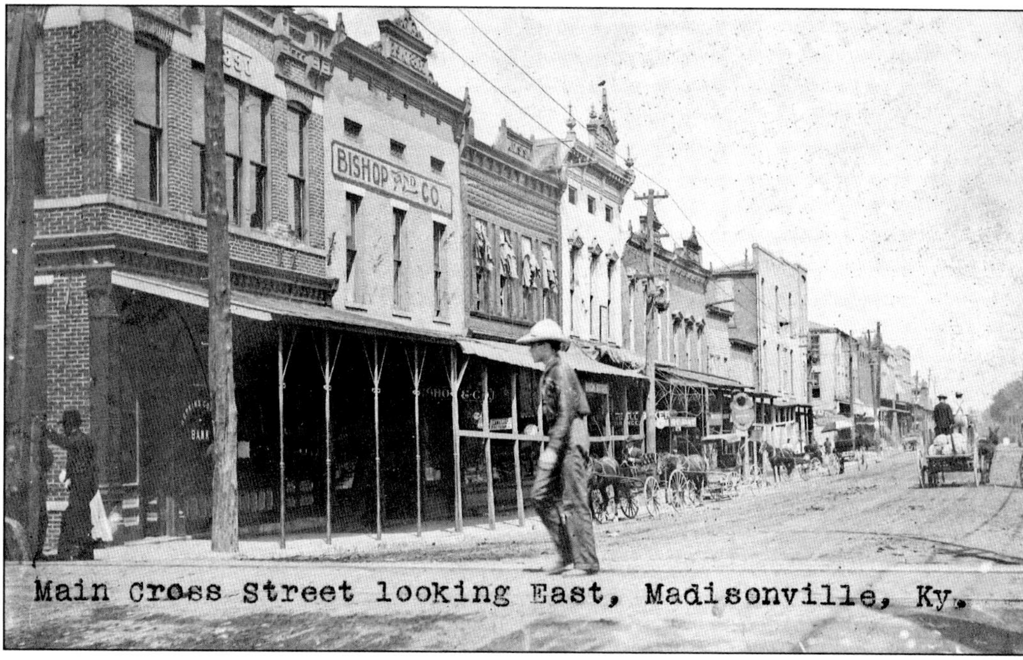

This postcard photograph was taken between 1900 and 1910 and depicts West Center Street looking east across the railroad track in Madisonville. The buildings from left to right are Hopkins County Bank, Bishop and Company, and General Merchandise, which opened in 1879 and closed in 1911. The fourth building is Owen Hardware Store. The three-story building on the corner is the Littlepage Building (Pate Drug Store). (HSHC.)

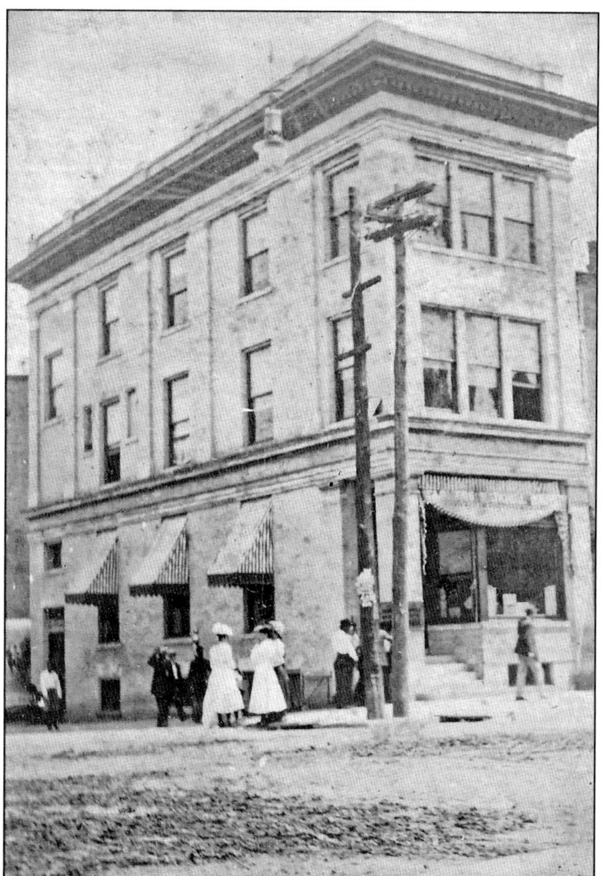

The Eagle Hotel, built in the early 1850s, was razed to make room for this building. Farmer's National Bank's opening day was 1907. The bank occupied this site until 1935, when it moved across North Main Street into the Hopkins County Bank building (originally the Morton Bank). In 1958, the bank moved into its new building at 77 North Main Street. (HSHC.)

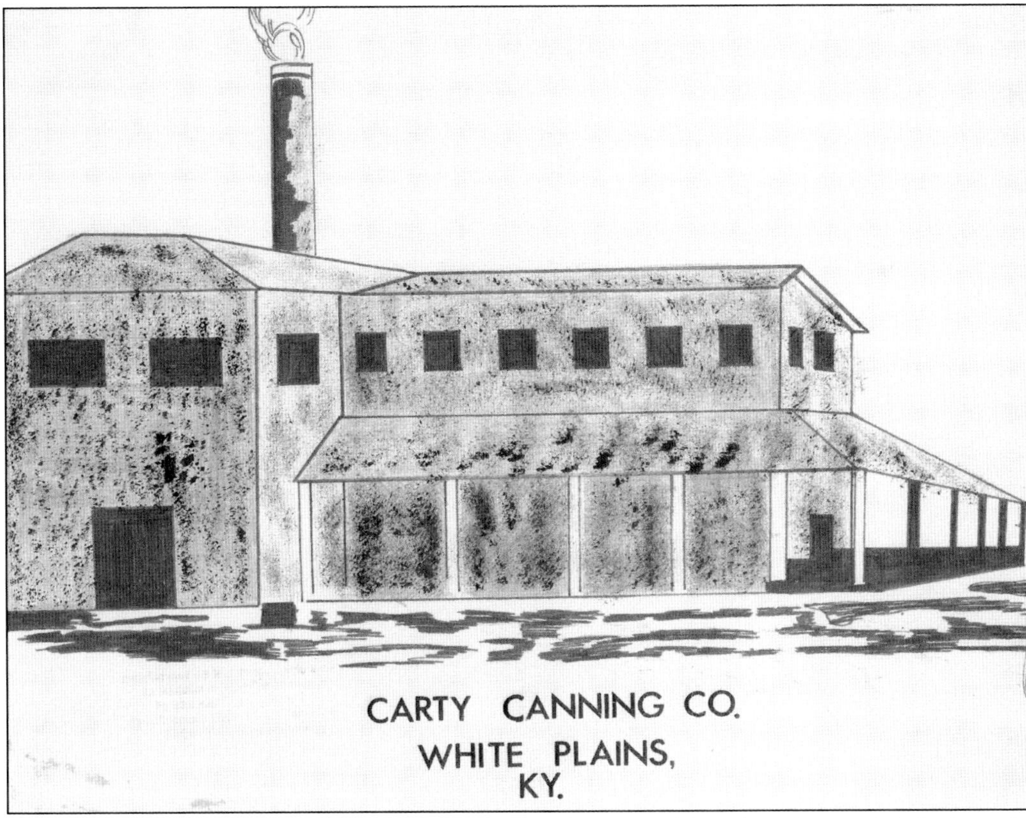

Only this drawing of the White Plains Canning Company (above) and extra labels from the tomato cans (below) remain as reminders of the tomato canning factory that closed in the 1950s. Jane Rogers remembers that her mother worked at the factory and had to bring her own paring knife to work. The Little Prairie text refers to the city of White Plains. White Plains was once known as Little Prairie because of the vast land filled with roaming buffalo. The White Plains symbol today is still the buffalo. The White Plains Museum has several of the labels on display. The back of the labels appear to have been used by a lawyer to make interesting case notes. (Above, HSHC; below, WPM.)

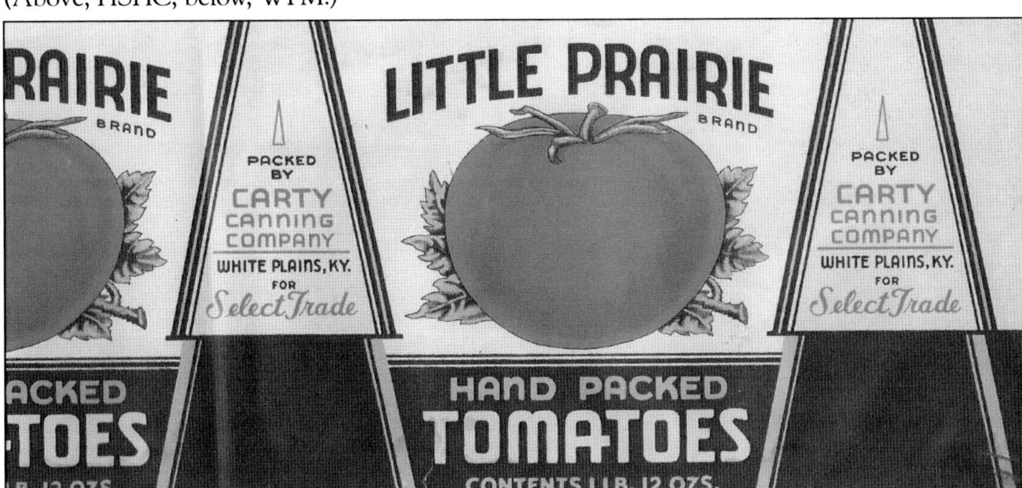

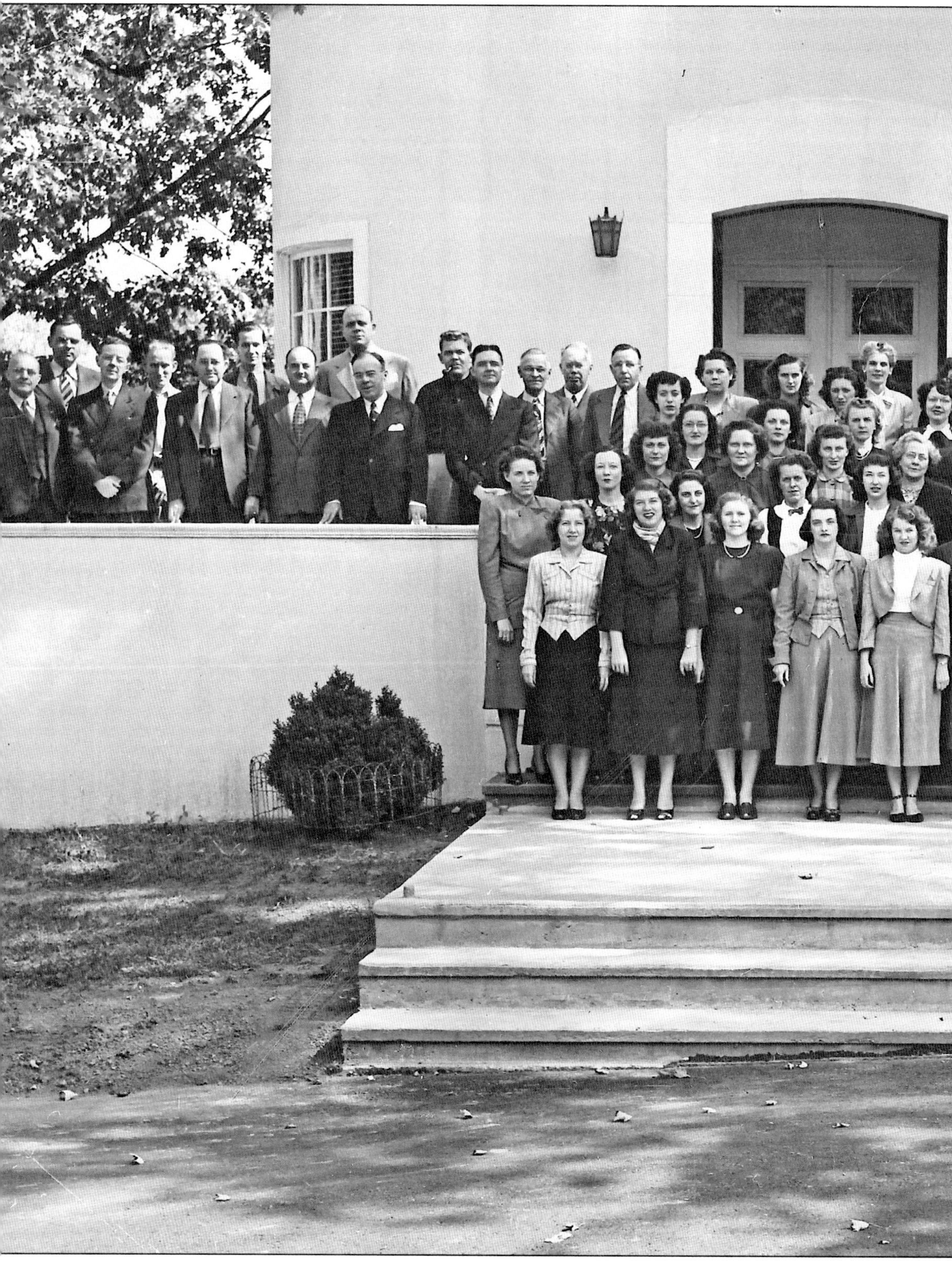

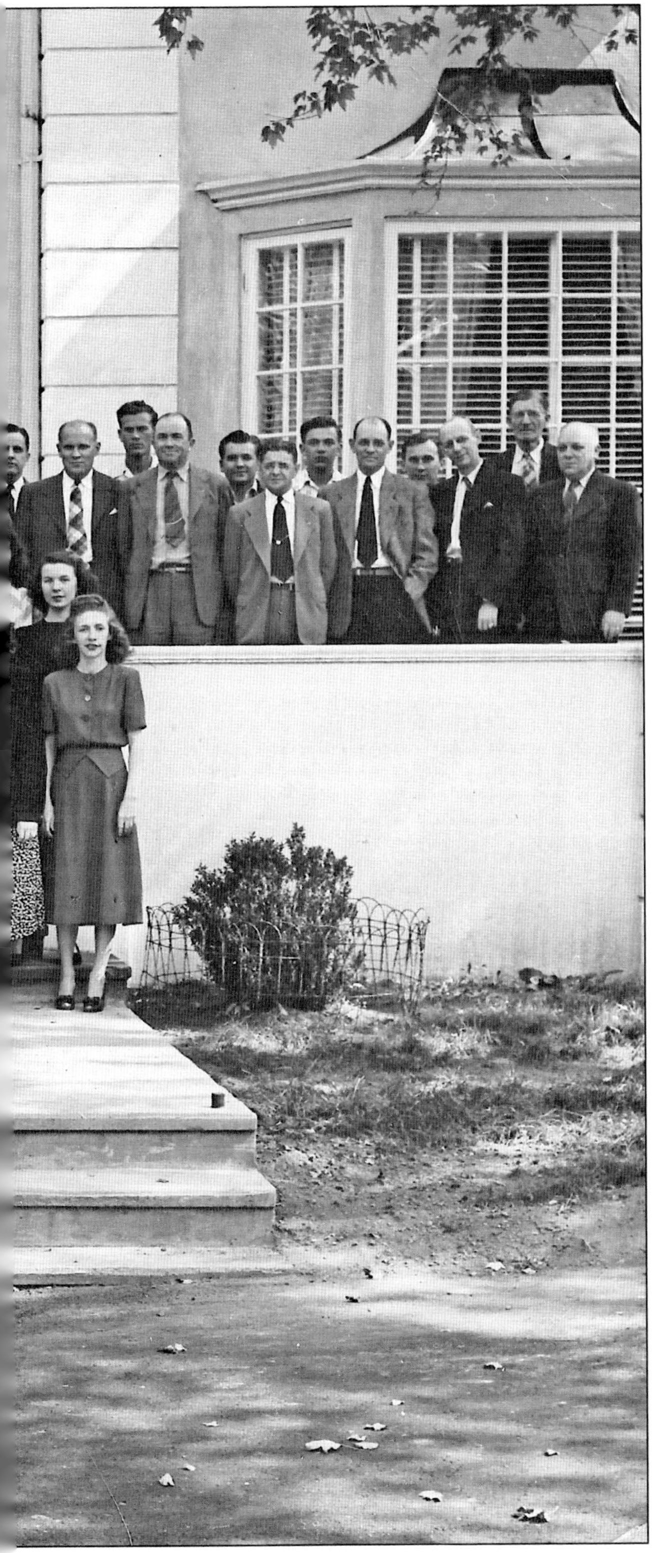

The 1948 West Kentucky Coal office workers included, from left to right, (first row) Cotton Shoulders, Mary Betty Minor, Maxine Davis, Frances Stokes, Edna Shoulders, Pauline Gilkey, Regina Kelly, and Allyne Lansden; (second row) Ethelyn O'Neal, Virginia Donan, Ora Mae Buchanan, Marie Fenwick, Jane Allen, Mary Hagan, and Curtis Bowles; (third row) Leola Blake, Louise Wright, Billie Barnard, Lela Vickers, Nell Wyatt, and Billie Gilkey; (fourth row) Betty McCulley, Agnes Long, Mildred Hammers, and Carolyn Long; (fifth row) Margaret Brooks, Ruth Davis, Dorothy Hight, Irene Corum, Loudene Mitchell, Woody Boone, and Rose Blair; (sixth row) S. G. Collins, Isom Maraman, J. J. Grever, Kenneth Arnold, James Buchanan, D. W. Long, Aubin Higgins, C. M. Hicks, Bob Bowden, George Land, Bob Welch, C. G. Trahern, W. S. Williams, Davis Reed, Mark Eastin, C. M. Dawes, Jimmie Preston, John Fenwick, Garlon Lovan, O. T. Hagan, Herman Stewart, J. W. McMahon, Joe Ratliff, Bob Branson, Sherman Melton, and Ralph Dudley. This photograph was used for the company Christmas card. (HSHC.)

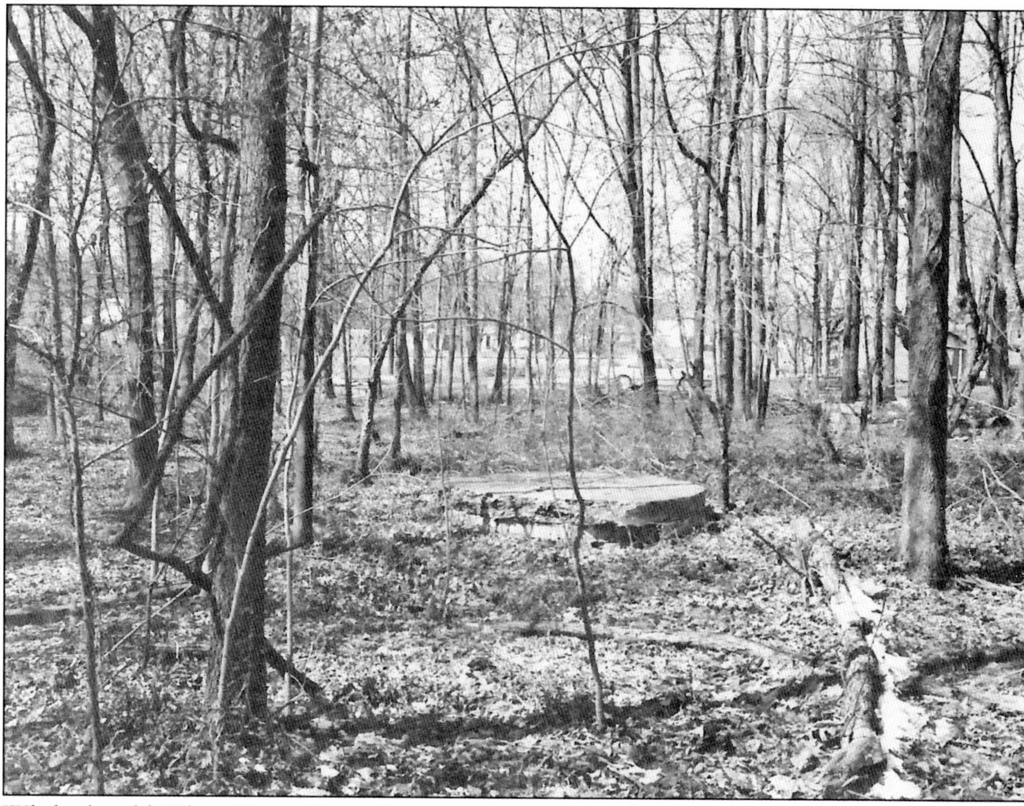

While the old White Plains Carty Canning Company no longer exists, this photograph depicts the property where it once stood. When local farmers would bring the truck of tomatoes, a whistle would blow, letting the workers know to come to work to peel the tomatoes at a rate of 5¢ per bucket. (WPM.)

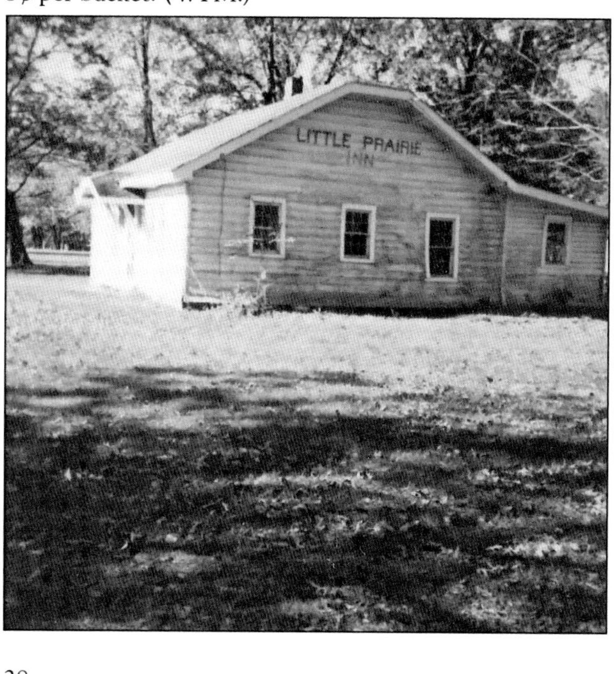

The Little Prairie Inn in White Plains was actually about four little cottages belonging to Bill and Lillian Fox. White Plains was formerly known as Little Prairie. Lillian Fox was a first-grade schoolteacher at White Plains School for over 50 years. It was said that she purchased a 1950 dark-blue Ford with pennies she had saved. She drove the vehicle for 40 years. (WPM.)

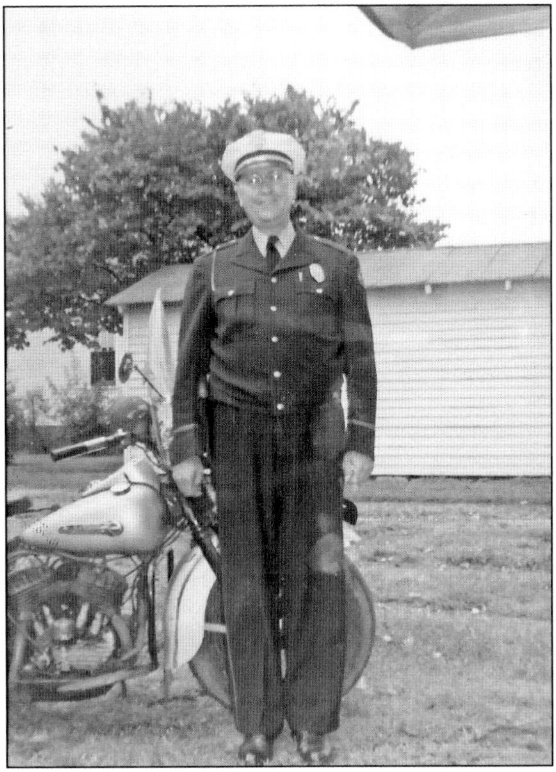

Called by his coworkers "the ice cream man," Harold Ledbetter rode this three-wheeled 1943 Harley-Davidson motorcycle in the late 1940s. He was called this because deliverymen used to deliver ice cream in the late 1940s on a three-wheeled Harley-Davidson motorcycle. He had a serious accident on this motorcycle. The photograph was taken in the backyard of Lewis Payne's home on East Broadway in Madisonville. (HSHC.)

This view of what has been known as Main Street or Sunset Drive in Hanson shows the north side of the street. The little town of Hanson was settled in 1869 when the railroad was built to that point. People from all over Hopkins County came there to catch the train going north. The town was named for Henry B. Hanson, an engineer on the construction of the railroad. (HSHC.)

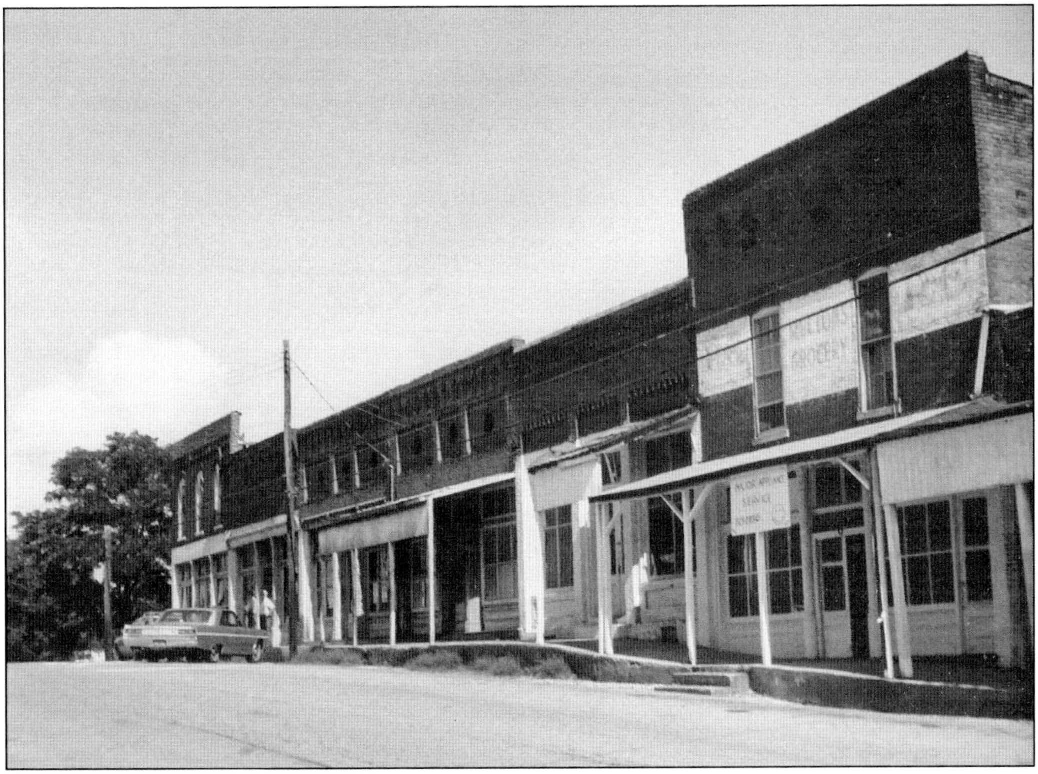

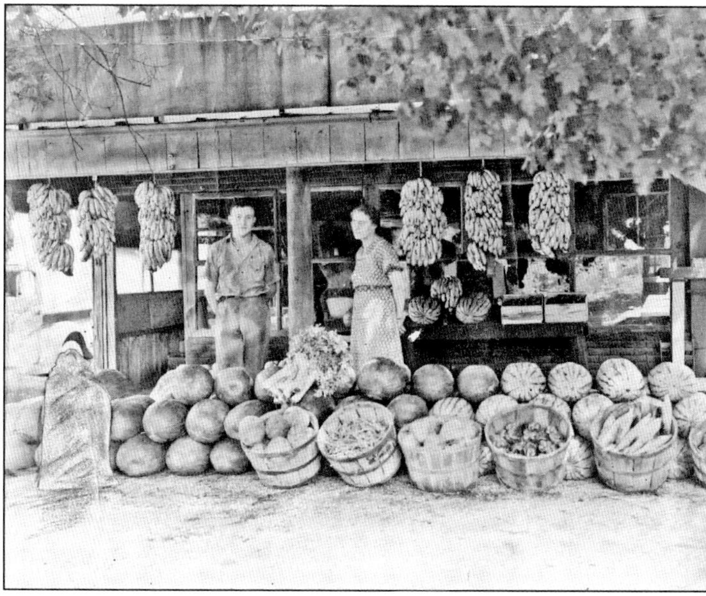

Spencer Melton was injured in a railroad accident and afterwards had to use a wheelchair. Spencer had a great mind for business and, after the accident, opened up this fruit stand and shop at 129 West Broadway in Madisonville. The business was the last building on the north side of the street just before crossing the railroad. (HSHC.)

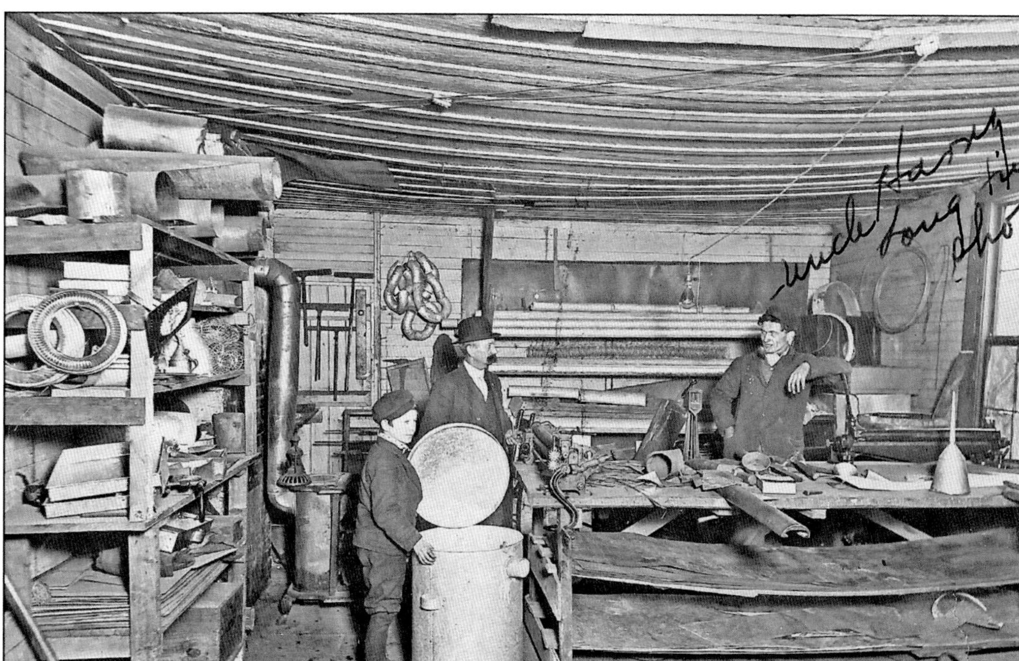

The bowed ceiling inside of Long's Tin Shop has a single lightbulb hanging from a wire. Notice the ceramic insulator in the ceiling through which the wire is run. The insulator kept the wire grounded to deter fires and also kept the ceiling from getting too hot. The photograph is undated. (HSHC.)

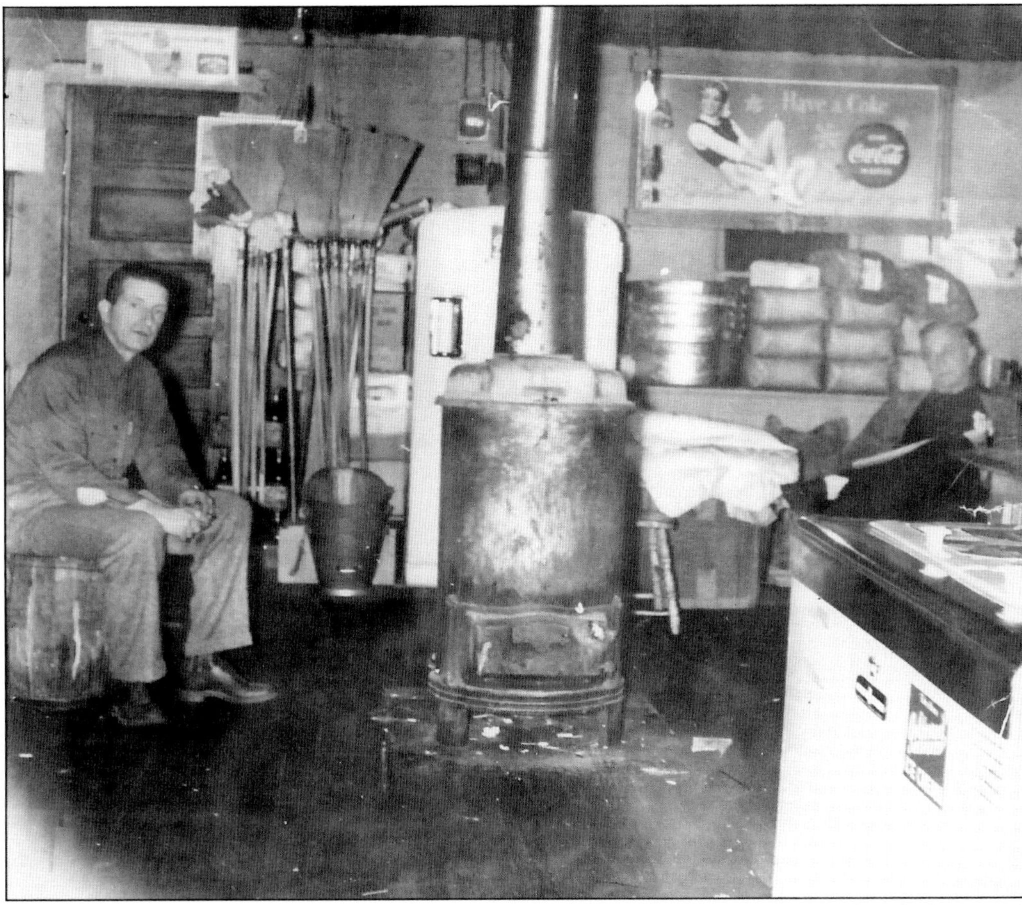

Clarence Hardwick (right) is shown with an unidentified customer in this undated photograph inside of his store, Hardwick's, in White Plains. Among the goods for sale in this photograph are Goldenrod Ice Cream, Coca-Cola, brooms, mops, coal buckets, and blankets. The center stove was a place to gather for warmth and conversation during Kentucky's cold winters. (Jane Hardwick Rogers.)

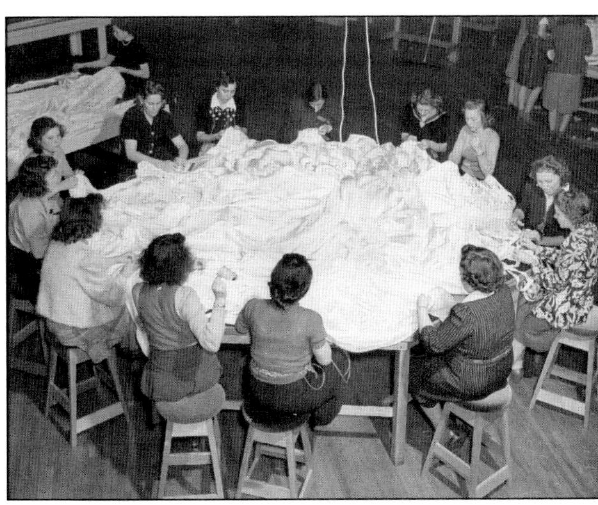

The S. J. Campbell Parachute Factory opened in 1942 during World War II and provided parachutes to the military. The photograph at right shows women sewing during the last stages of the parachute manufacturing process. (HSHC.)

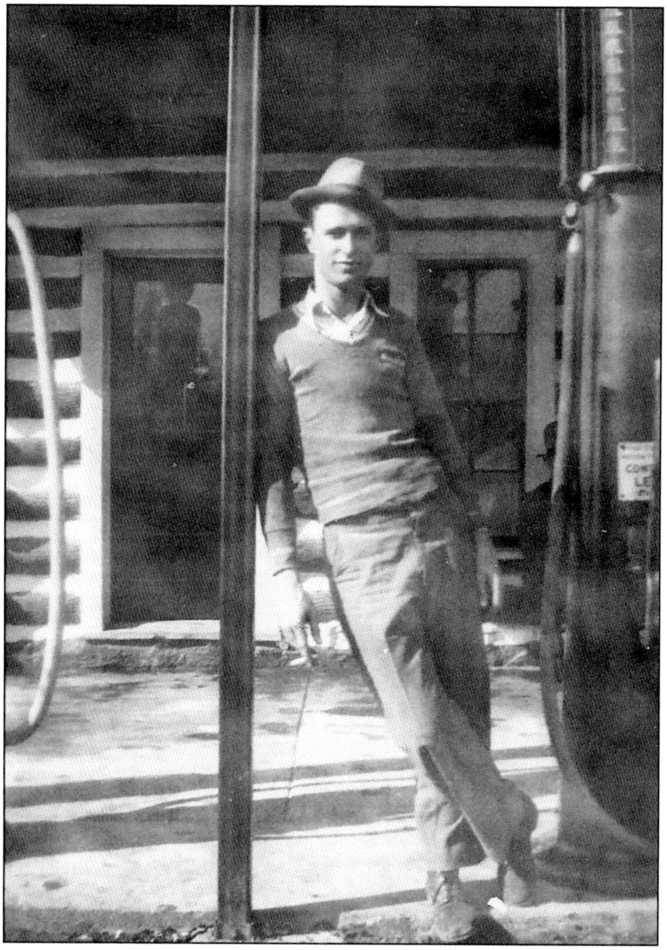

Eugene Lacy stands beside a gas pump at the service station in White Plains in the spring of 1938. The average price for a gallon of gas would have been 10¢. The cost for a new car was about $763. The item in Lacy's right hand appears to be a hand-rolled cigarette. (Jane Hardwick Rogers.)

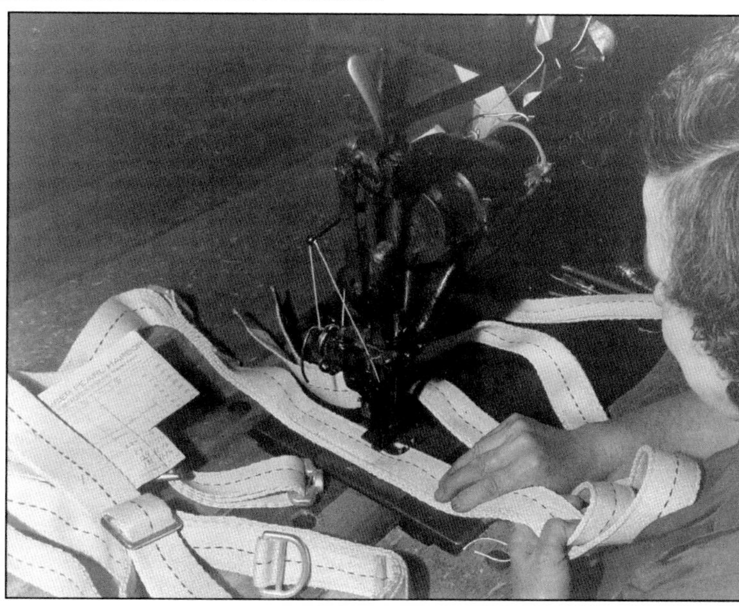

The harness straps are being sewn in the production area of the parachute factory by a seamstress. The order card under the straps has a heading that reads, "Remember Pearl Harbor." Under the heading, some of the words are covered, but what can be seen reads, "a Production Soldier: Minutes Count." (HSHC.)

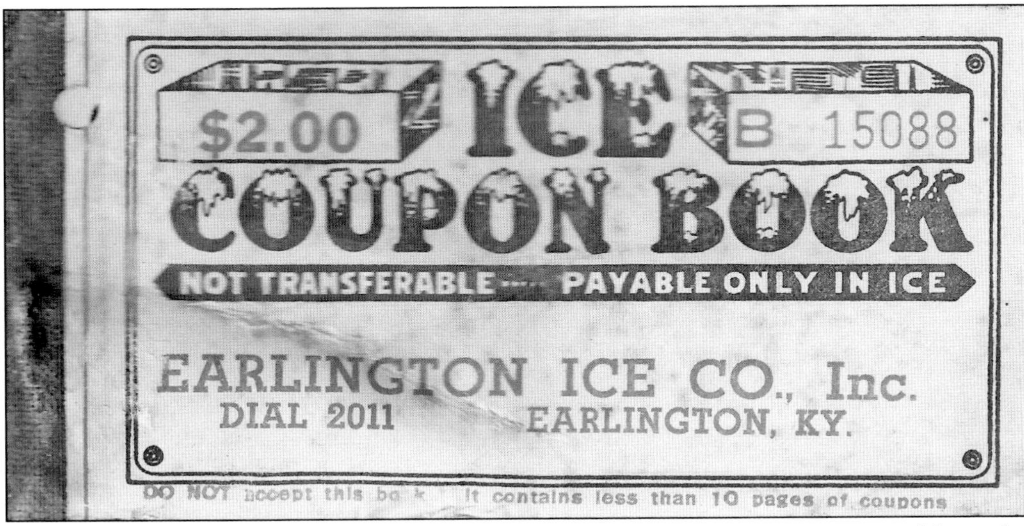

Coupon books were sold by the Earlington Ice Company to customers wanting ice delivered to their homes. When the ice truck arrived, the deliveryman would tear a coupon from the customer's booklet in exchange for the ice. It is unknown when the Earlington Ice Company was in business or where the business was located. (WPM.)

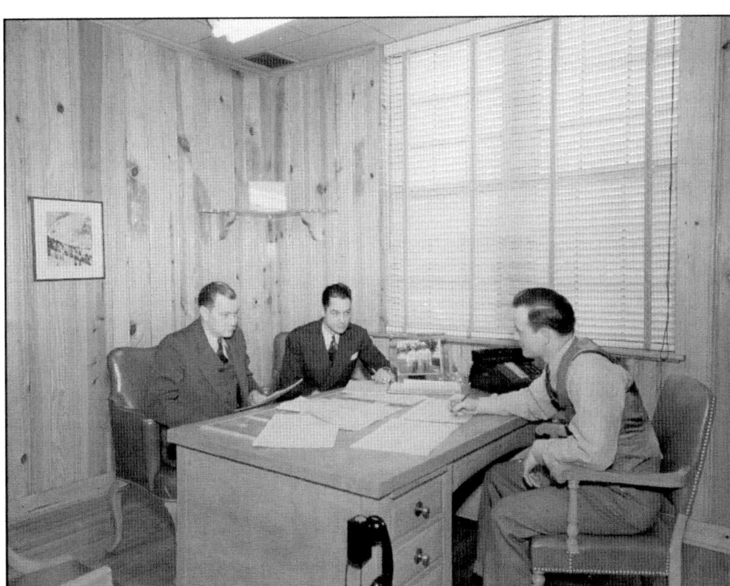

The photograph at right shows Bruce L. Campbell's office in the parachute factory. The two men sitting across from Campbell are unidentified. On top of the desk is a photograph of a man and woman, an ashtray, and an old calculator. Also note the black phone mounted on the side of the desk. (HSHC.)

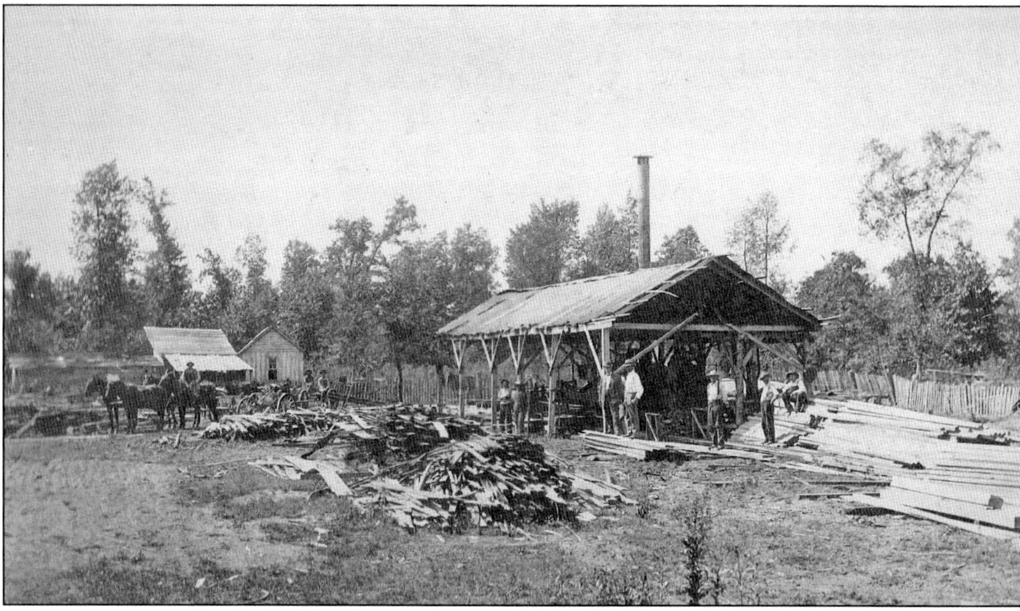

Michael David Hunter owned this sawmill on Brown Road. The photograph is dated 1911–1912. Michael David Hunter is standing at the front of the structure and wearing a white shirt and suspenders. To the right of him stand his sons-in-law, Harvey Cotton (right) and Abraham Lincoln Cotton. At one time, Hunter was the president of Woodsmen of the World. (Jan Dixon.)

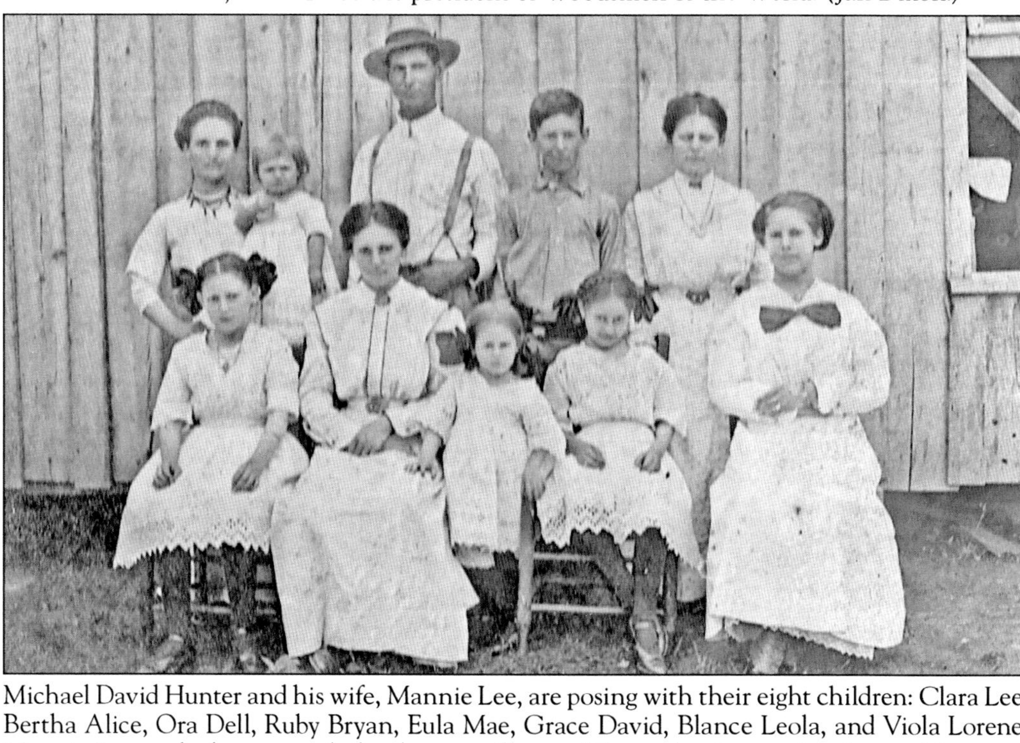

Michael David Hunter and his wife, Mannie Lee, are posing with their eight children: Clara Lee, Bertha Alice, Ora Dell, Ruby Bryan, Eula Mae, Grace David, Blance Leola, and Viola Lorene. Mannie Lee cooked tasty meals for the sawmill crew. The eyelet dresses, jewelry, and bows are evidence of a successful business. Mannie Lee Hunter is the great-grandmother of the owner of Brook Hollow Catering. (Jan Dixon.)

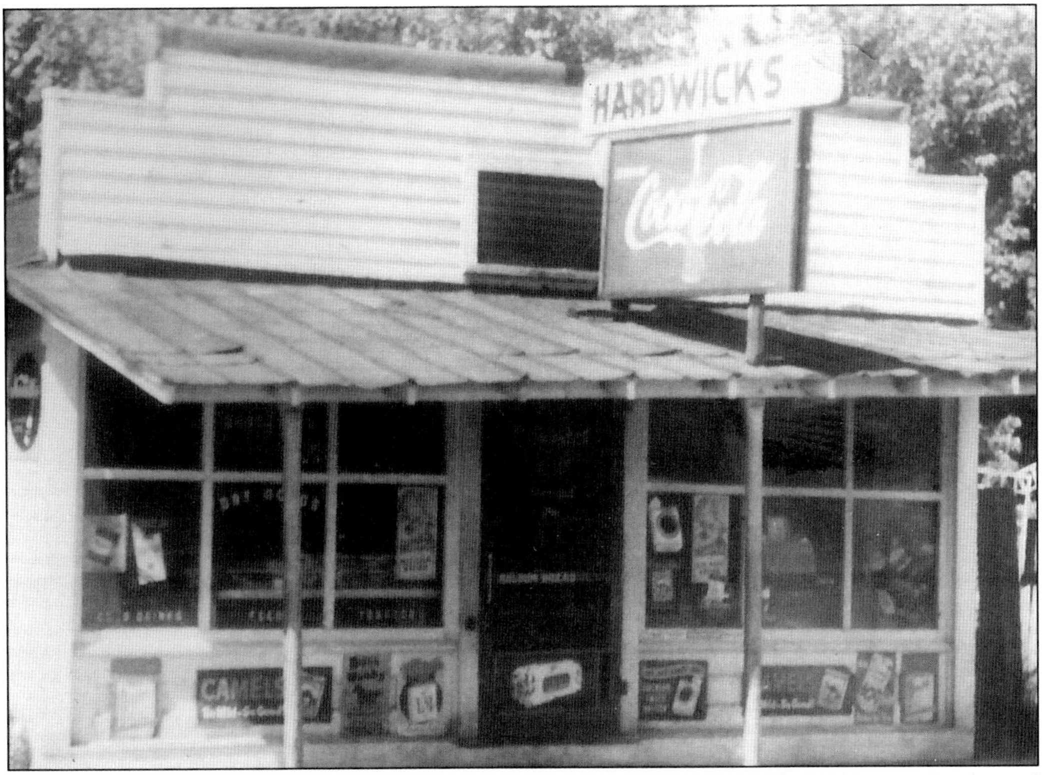

A family from White Plains could go to Hardwick's store and buy everything from washtubs and groceries to shotgun shells. Hardwick's store was owned by Clarence Hardwick, father of Jane Rogers. At one time, Clarence was justice of the peace in Hopkins County. The building burned down in 1980. (Jane Hardwick Rogers.)

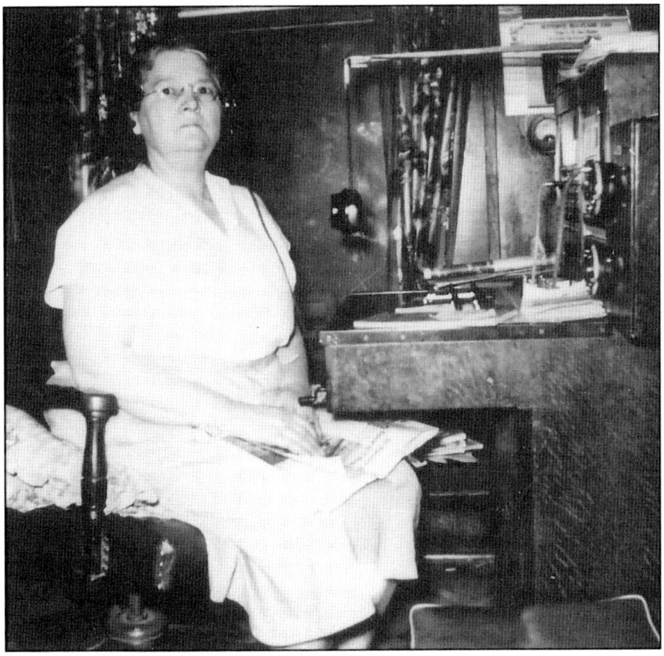

Sylvia Lewis owned and operated the White Plains Telephone Company from the 1930s until 1959. There were only two lines running out of town, so only two callers could call out of town at one time. If a call came for someone without a telephone, Sylvia would send her grandson, Ronnie Lewis, to relay the caller's message. He charged a dime for his services. She sold the company to Bell Telephone for $6,600. (Ronnie Lewis.)

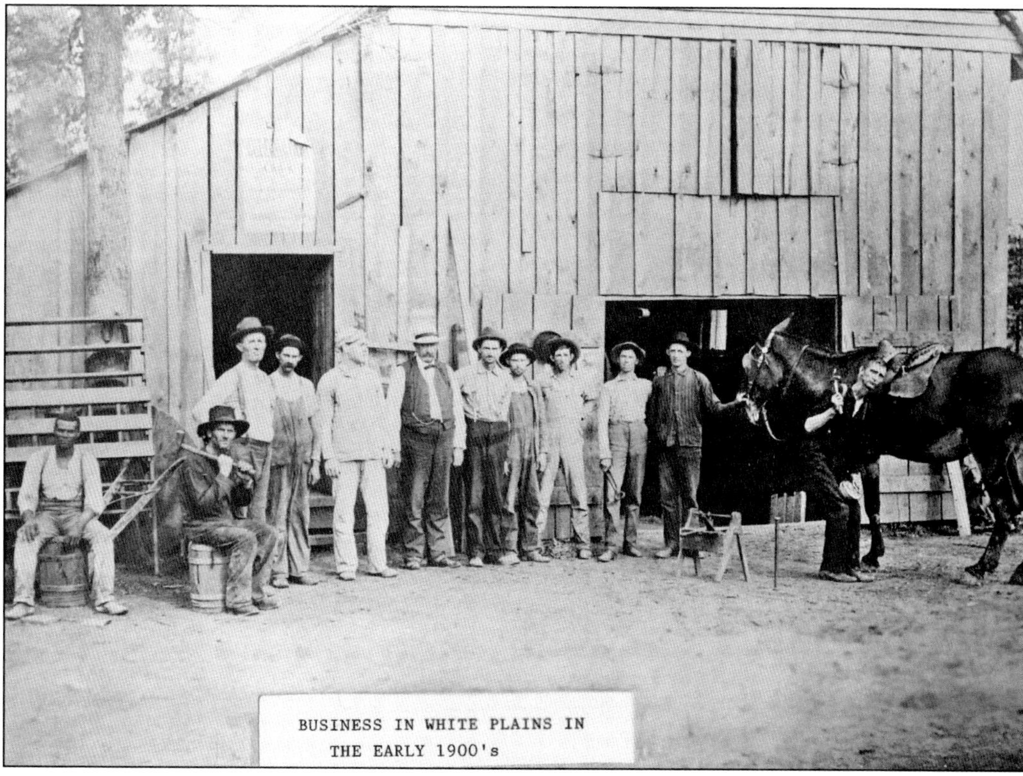

This business was located in White Plains. The men seem to be posing for the photograph, and the farrier is working to shoe a horse. The poster on the building is announcing a celebration picnic. It is believed that the photograph was taken in the early 1900s. (WPM.)

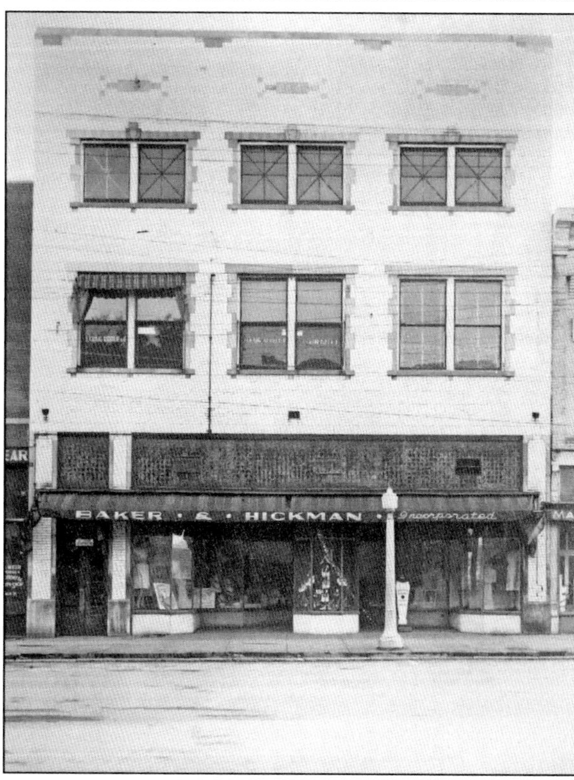

This old building was located in Madisonville at 9–15 East Center Street. The signs in the windows advertise for Baker and Hickman, L. B. Weir Attorney, and the Blondette Beauty Shop. Baker and Hickman opened in this building in 1918. J. Craig Riddle and Sharp's bakery were later located to the right of the Baker and Hickman business. (HSHC.)

Three

EARLY ENTERTAINMENT

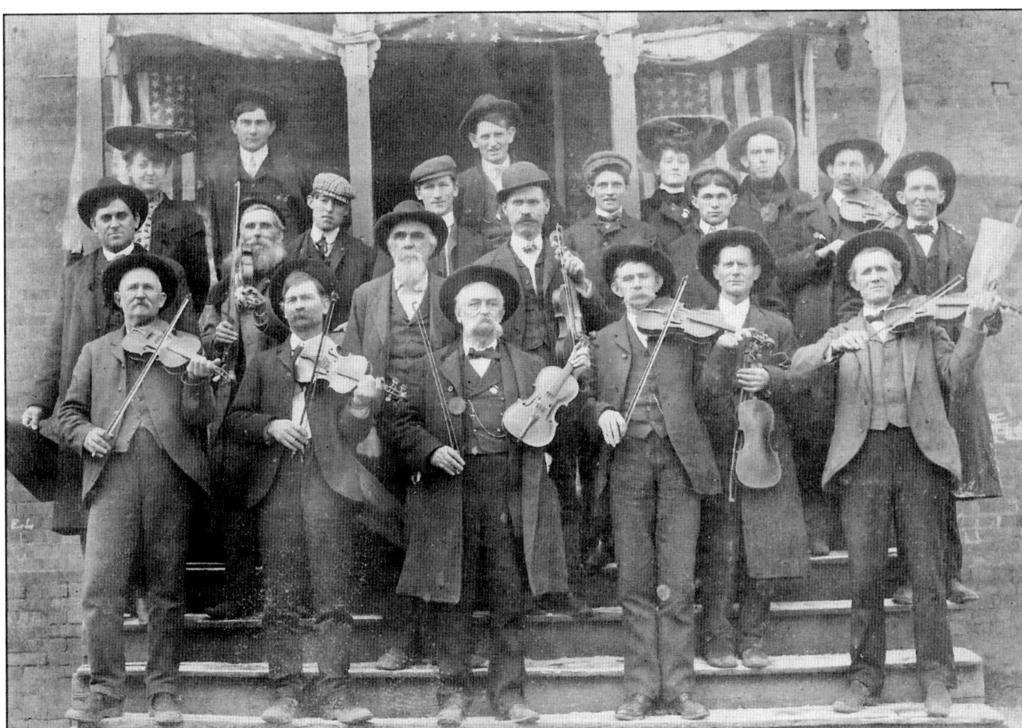

Music, theater, sports, and fellowship have always had a place in Hopkins County. Fiddling contests like the one in this early-1900s photograph were popular. Jane Rogers remembers that her father, Clarence Hardwick, won so many of the contests that he finally just quit entering. Her mother is on the left wearing one of her beloved hats. Note the man with the fiddle in a bag to the extreme right. (WPM.)

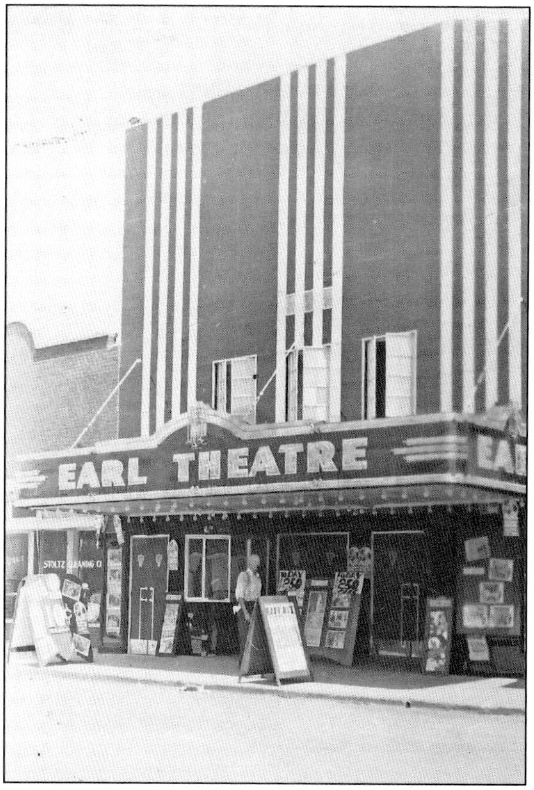

Both of these photographs depict the old Earl Theater in Earlington. Dozens of lightbulbs hang from the top of the entrance. The theater opened November 22, 1949, and had segregated entrances and a balcony. The building to the left of the theater was Stoltz Cleaning. An advertisement outside of Earl Theater reads "10¢ To All." On the two different dates that these photographs were taken, the posters displayed advertise the following movies: "Saturday, *Guns of the Pecos*," "Saturday, *Steele*," and *Varsity Show*. The Earl Theater has not been in operation for many years. There are also advertisements in the photograph about a bank account and a poster that reads "Today $250 Free." (Both HSHC.)

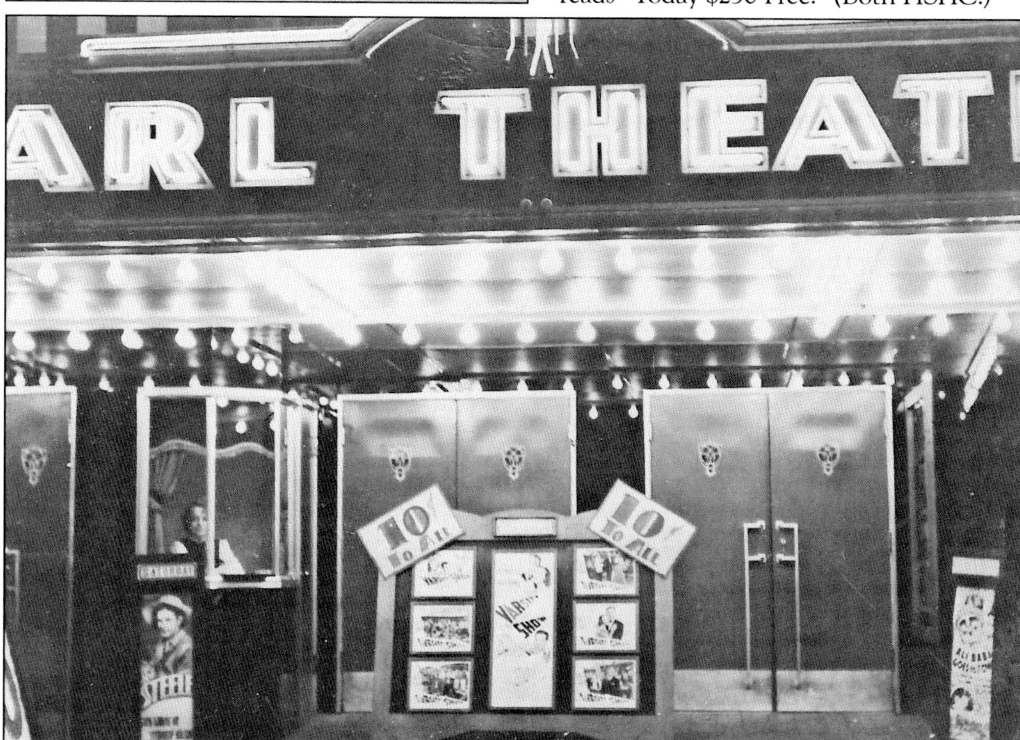

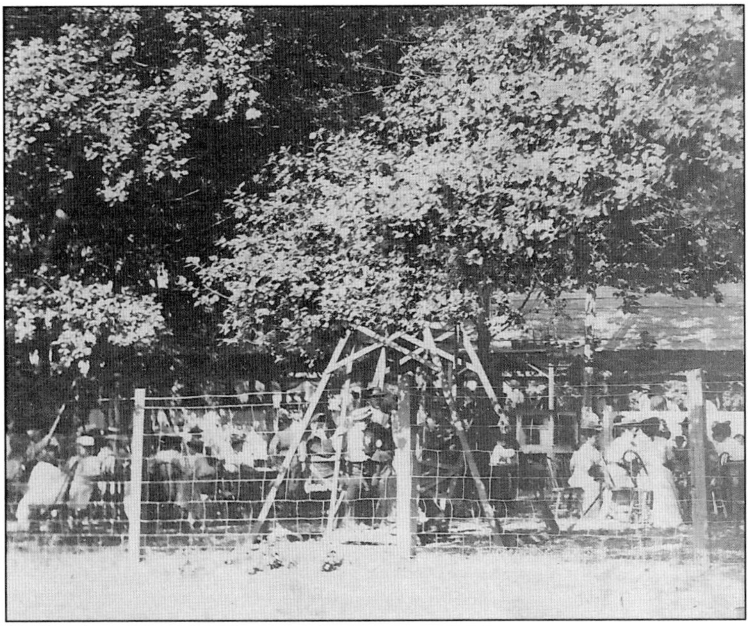

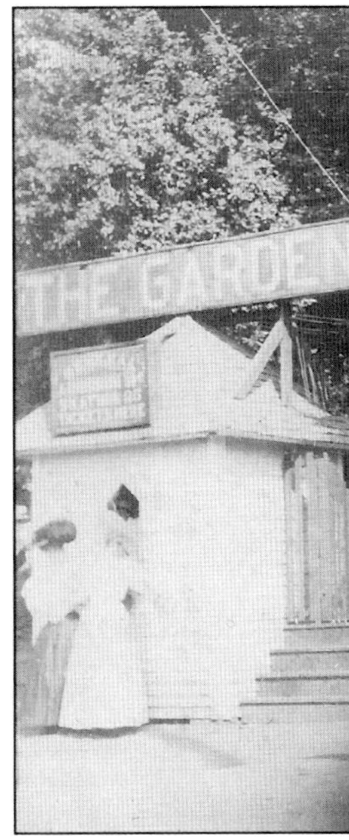

The Garden was a favorite recreation spot, as shown in this 1905 postcard. The Garden was the amusement park of the day. It was located on East Center Street between Franklin and Scott Streets. The sign on the building at right reads, "GENERAL ADMISSION 10¢, SKATING 25, TICKETS HERE." To the left, boys are swinging on a wooden swing while women in long dresses and hats sit around a table. (Both, HSHC.)

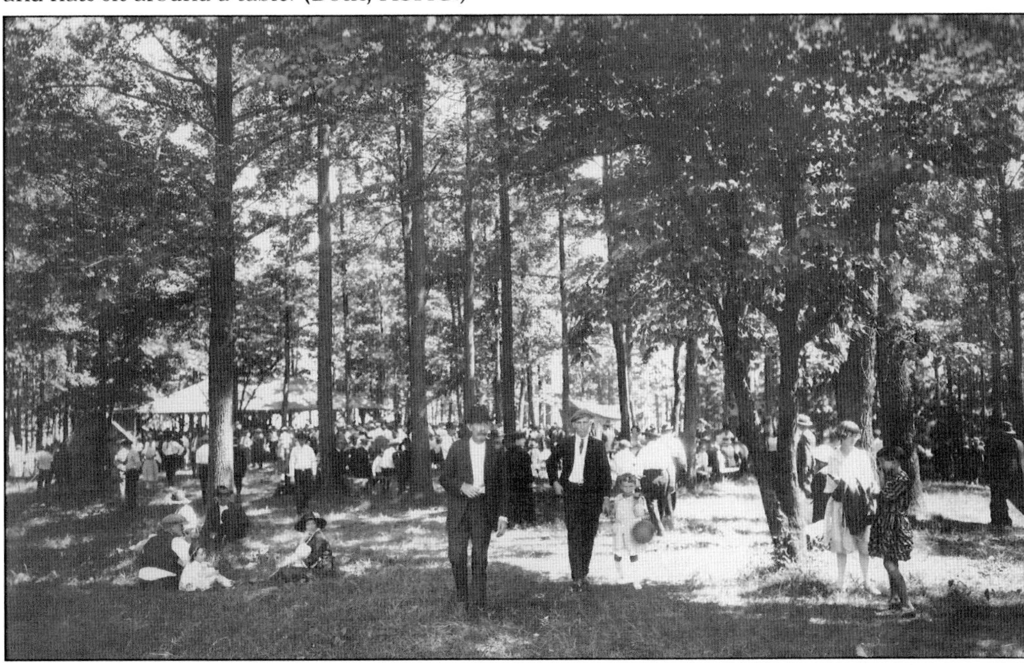

In the 1900s, Earlington was a bustling city with several trains going in and out per day. Six coal mines operated in or near the city. This photograph captured Lakeside Park in Earlington between 1901 and 1924. This scene was probably a coal company picnic for miners and their families. A little girl at the right middle appears to be holding a round toy attached to a string. (HSHC.)

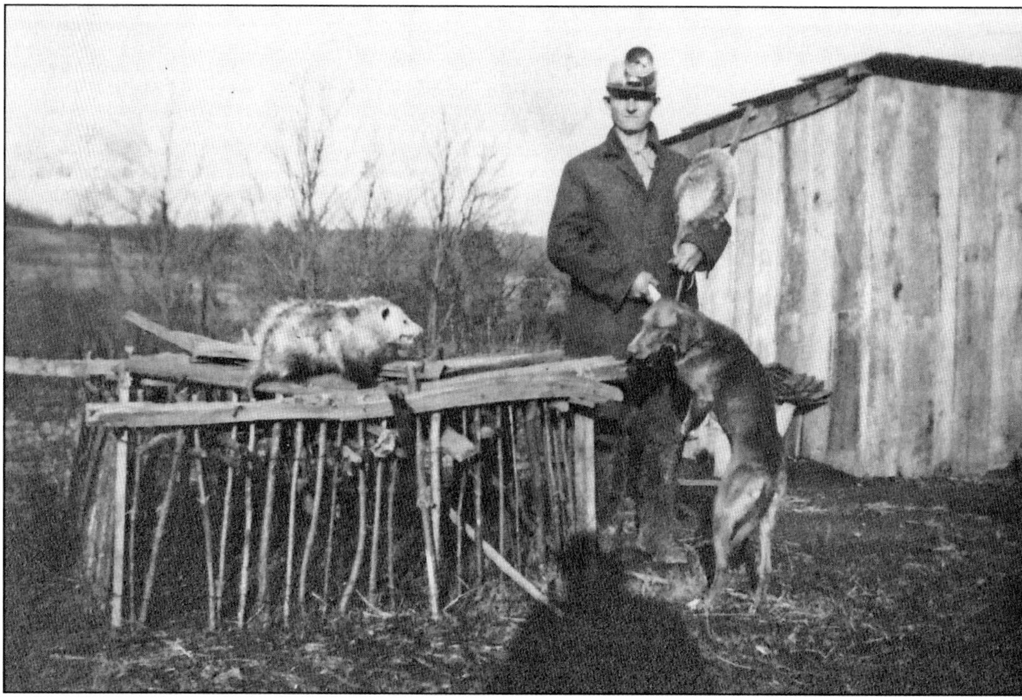

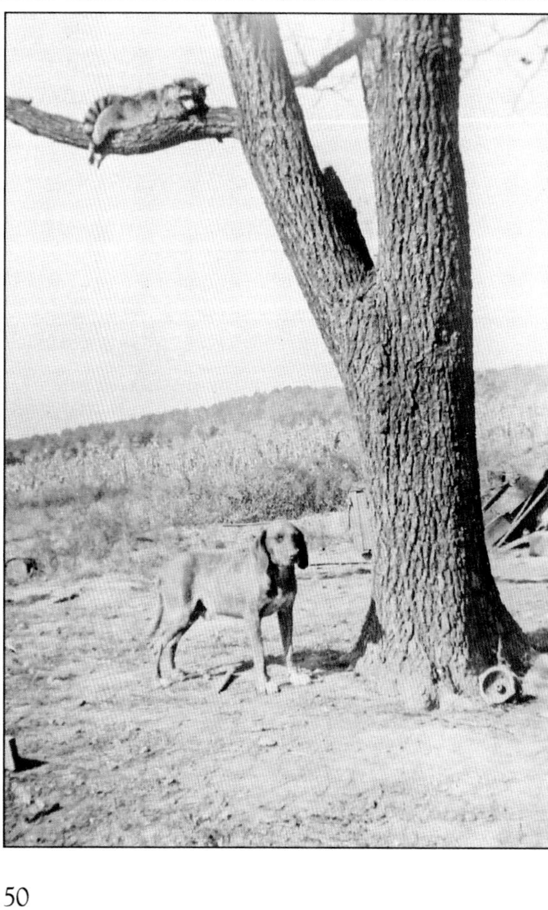

Coon hunting and raising animals have been a love of many Hopkins Countians. To "tree a coon" is to have a great hunting dog companion. The undated photograph above is of Herbert Osborn. He was a prized hunter, a sharp shooter, and an exceptional tobacco farmer. The buyers at the Loose Leaf Floor Company could pick out Herbert's tobacco by sight because it was such good quality. In this photograph, he is training his coon dog. He is wearing a coon hunting carbide light. Carbide and water generate acetylene gas, which burns to make the light. The photograph to the left shows a successful coon dog who has "treed" a sprawled-out raccoon. (Both, Jan Dixon.)

The Oakdale Swimming Pool provided a large swimming area. This 1926 photograph shows boys swimming not only in swimming shorts, but in white or black tank tops as well. The pool was located on the east side of South Main Street. The location is across from the Family Diner. (HSHC.)

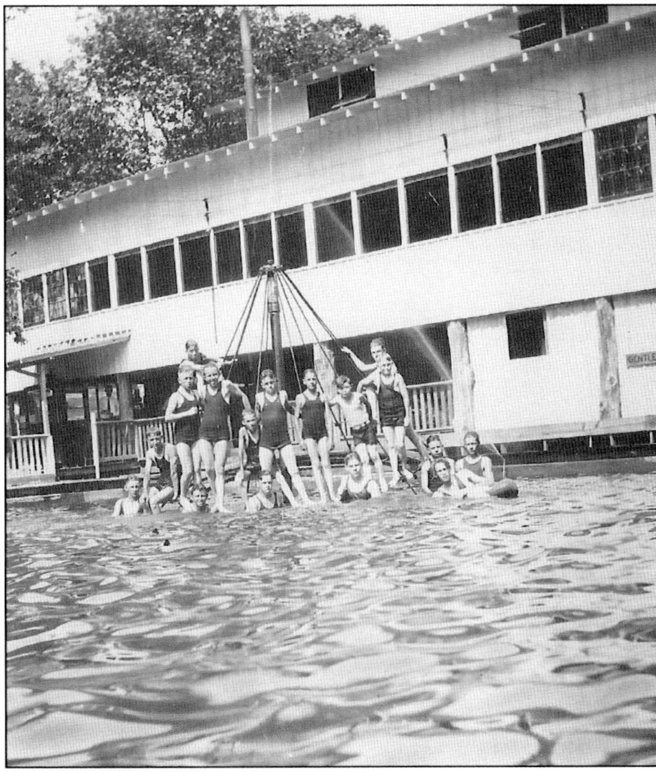

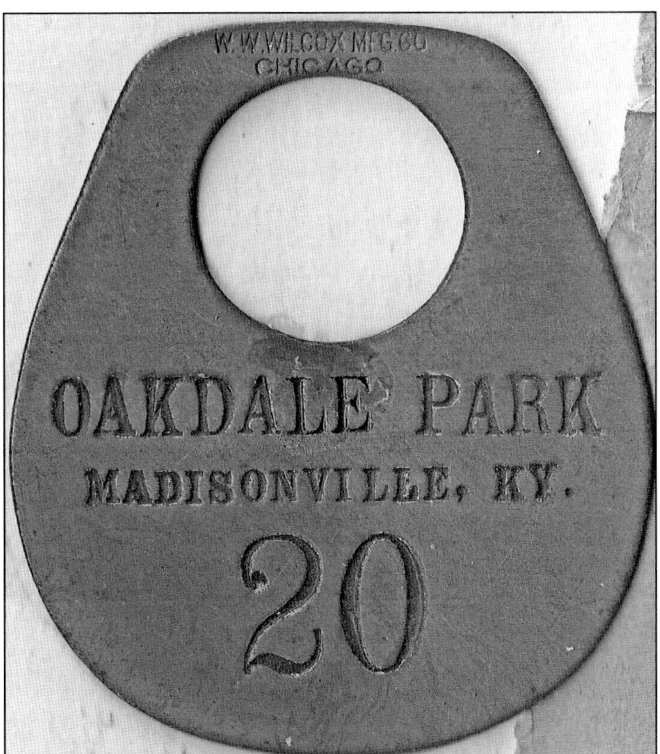

Swimmers at the pool could leave their personal items in the checkroom of the Oakdale Park while they swam. A brass tag, as shown in the photograph, would be given to the swimmer to tie to his trunks so that it would not be lost and he could retrieve his clothing. The Oakdale Park is now known as Young's Tourist Camp. (HSHC.)

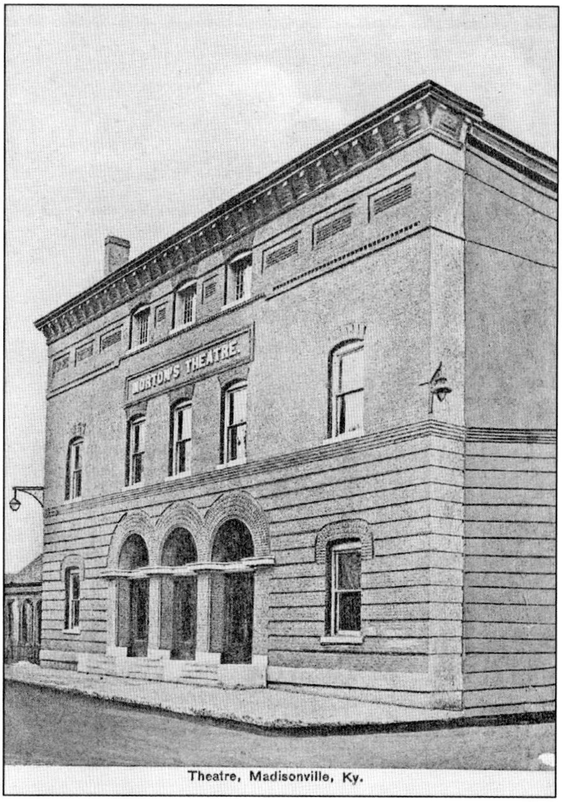

The Mortons Theater (1901–1918) was constructed for $50,000 and was a luxurious opera house. It was located at the northeast corner of Union Street and Cardwell Avenue and was designed by William C. Morton. The brickwork was done by George Stewart. George was a local, well-known brick mason and brick manufacturer. His brickyard was located south of West Jagoe Street and east of South Seminary Street. (HSHC.)

The balcony of Mortons Theater was luxuriously furnished with box seats on the north and south walls and comfortable seats throughout. Opening night was March 8, 1901. The first show was the *Marguerita Sylvas Theater*. First-night attendees were presented with engraved keys to commemorate the occasion. (HSHC.)

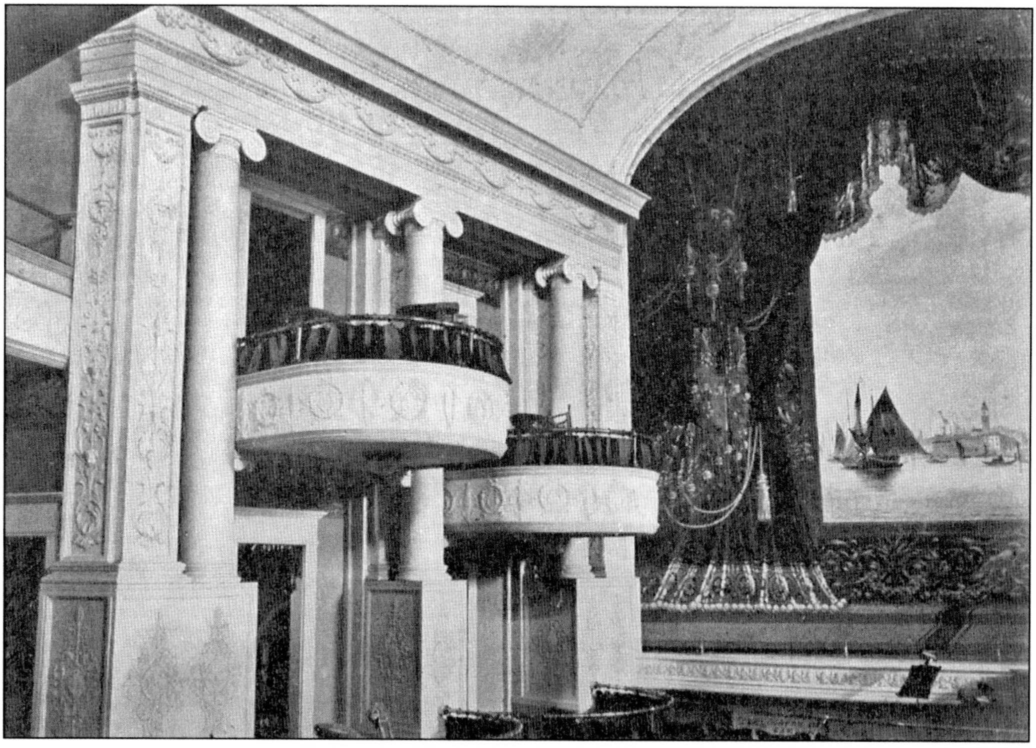

Ampliss Everett "Jake" Wade was born around 1909. For several years, he drove the city bus at a time when the schools did not have their own buses. Jake was photographed in this Open Wheel Racer Midget. It is unclear if he ever raced, but he loved cars and his hobby was trading and collecting vehicles. (Gail Warren.)

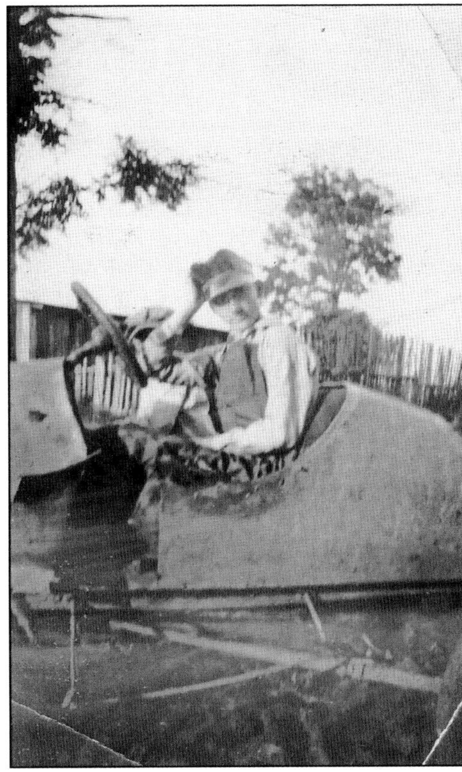

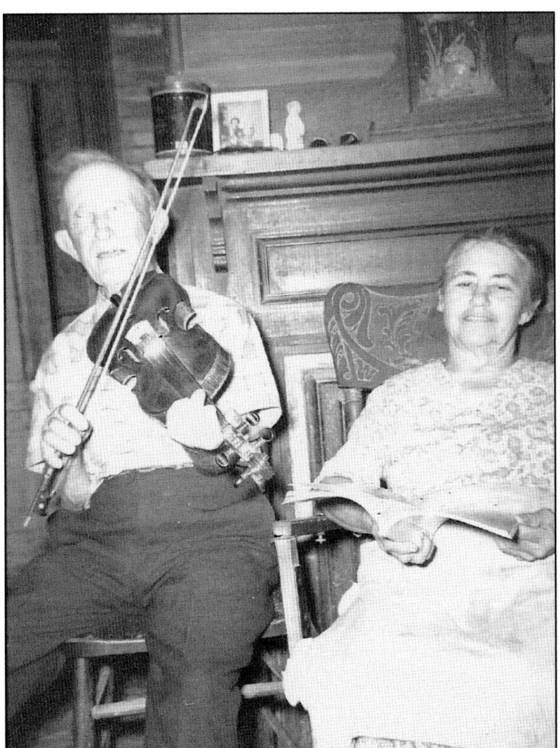

Abraham Lincoln Cotton and Bertha Alice Hunter Cotton sit in their home past Barnsley Loop. Abraham purchased the 1700s Jacobus Stainer reproduction fiddle when he was 20 years old from a young man whom he met when the man was on a wagon train to California. Abraham killed 20 rattlesnakes on his property and kept the tails stored in the fiddle. He passed away at the age of 99. (Jan Dixon.)

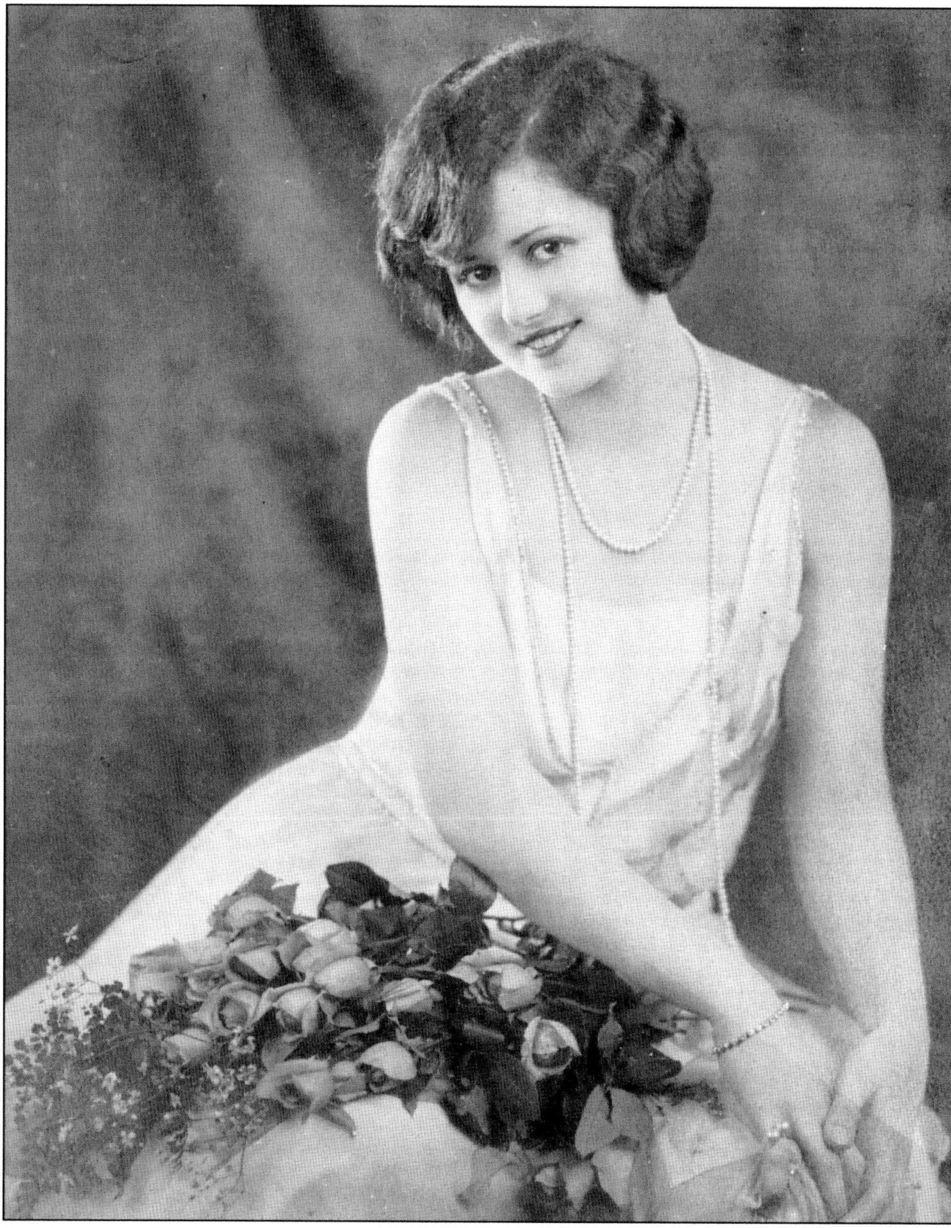

Addie Dukes McPhail was born in White Plains and was once married to the internationally known actor and comedian Fatty Arbuckle. Addie was born on North Railroad Street in White Plains and was the brown-eyed, curly-haired daughter of Van and Cordia Dukes. Her first acting experience was on the stage of the First Cumberland Presbyterian Church in Madisonville in a pageant for the church children. Addie was a singer before an actress. She played leading lady roles with probably a dozen leading men of her time, like Chester Morris, Jason Robards, and Joe Young. She was in the large cast of *Girls Demand Excitement*, which included an actor named John Wayne. Addie was 13 when she moved to Chicago and 19 when she moved to Hollywood. Other movies include *Personal Property*, *Three Sisters*, and *Body and Soul*. In 1932, she and Fatty Arbuckle toured the country. They did a show in Louisville and then visited relatives in Hopkins County. (Taylor Ezell.)

Four

Notable People and Places

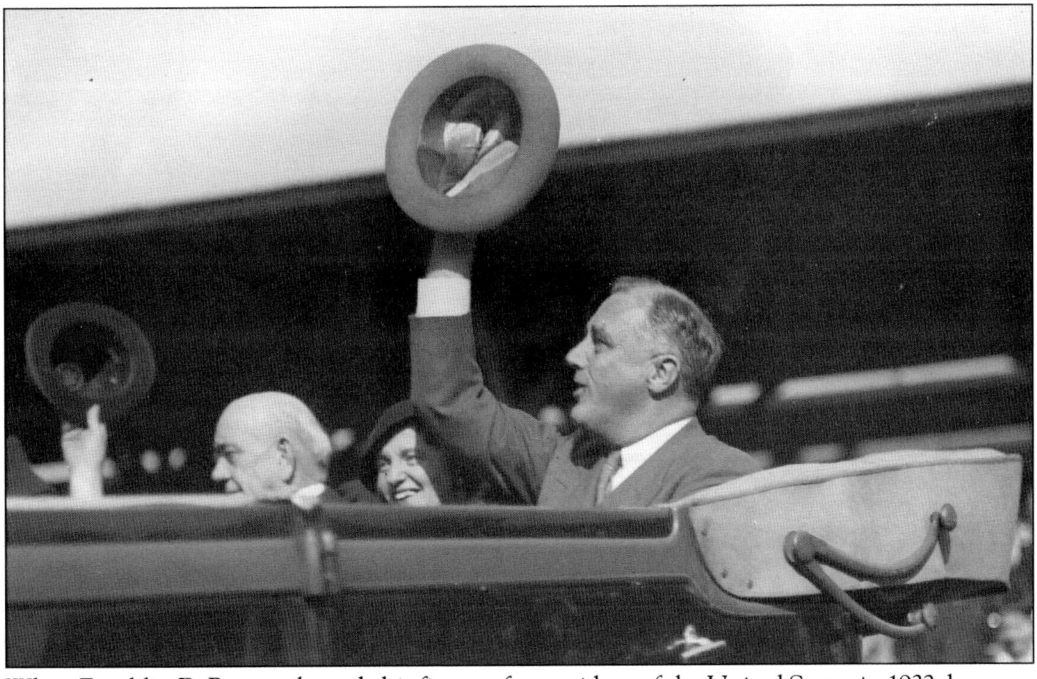

When Franklin D. Roosevelt made his first try for president of the United States in 1932, he came to Kentucky to seek Gov. Ruby Laffoon's support. Governor Laffoon and Franklin D. Roosevelt are shown here riding in a car on a Louisville street. Governor Laffoon is on the left, an unidentified woman in the center, and Roosevelt on the right. (HSHC.)

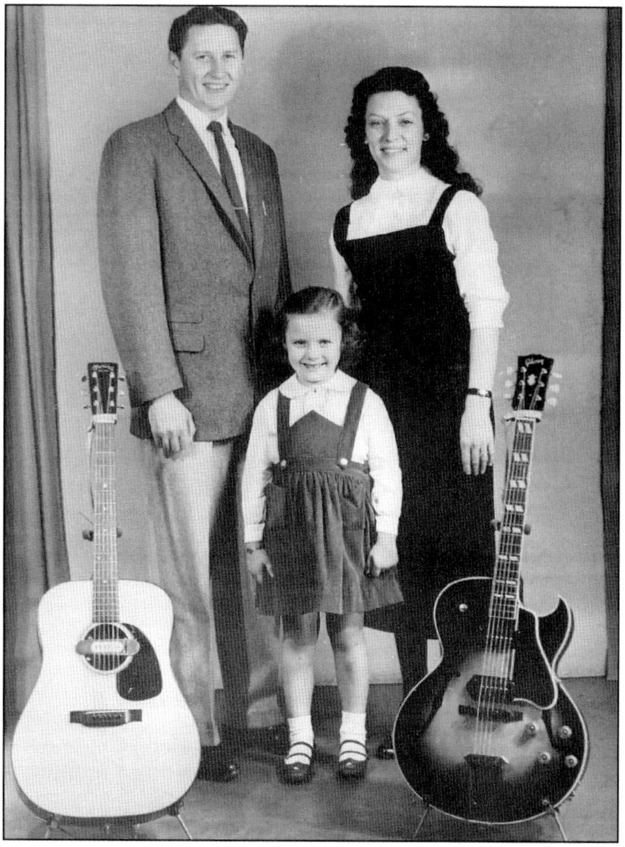

Buck Rambo, Joyce Reba Rambo, and Dottie Rambo were the Singing Rambos. Buck was born in Dawson Springs. Dottie composed more than 2,500 songs, and many were recorded by artists like Elvis Presley, Barbara Mandrell, Carol Channing, Whitney Houston, and Dolly Parton. Reba Rambo married Donald McGuire, and together they now pastor the River at Music City in Nashville, Tennessee. (Gail Warren.)

Buck and Dottie Rambo sang during a tent revival in Hopkins County in the 1950s. From left to right are Jo Russell, Buck Rambo, Dottie Rambo, Mel Daniels, and Rev. Harold Ashby. The woman holding the child in the background is unidentified. Dottie was the 10th female to be inducted into the Nashville Songwriters Hall of Fame. Dottie died in 2008 when the bus she was traveling in crashed. (Gail Warren.)

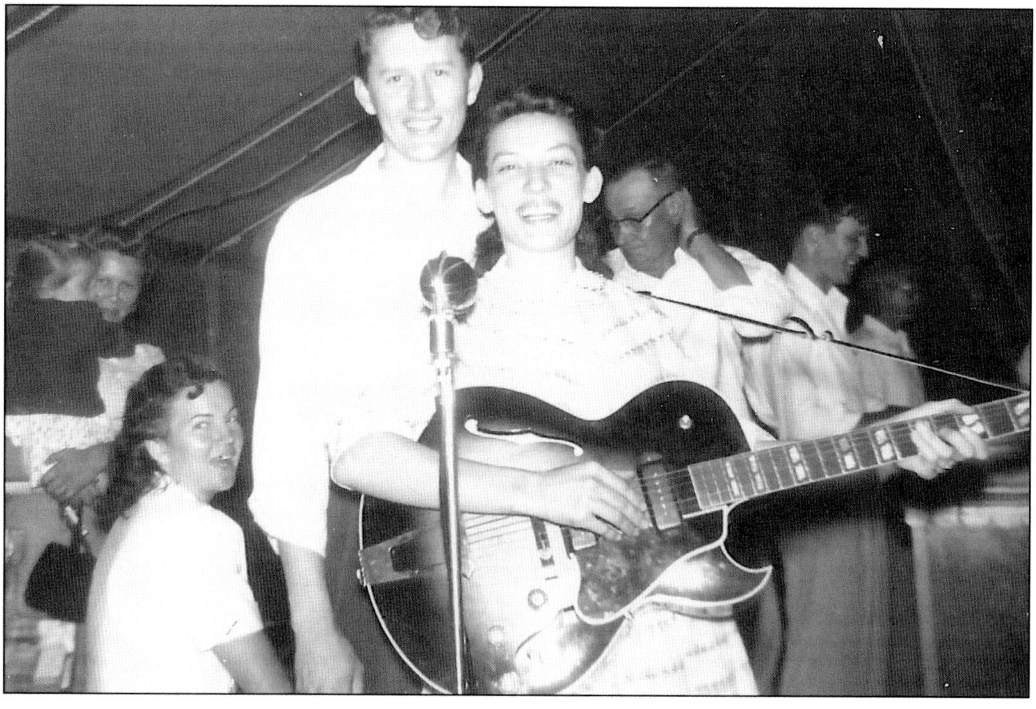

In 1949, Howard Goodman married Vestal Freeman. The two traveled as evangelists before moving to Madisonville and founding Life Temple Church, where they pastored for several years. Howard's brothers, Bobby, Sam, and Rusty, later moved to Madisonville. The family formed the Happy Goodman Family. The photographs on this page were taken while they were still in Madisonville. Vestal Goodman was known as the "Queen of Gospel Music" by her fans. The family sold millions of albums, won two Grammy Awards, and in 1998 was inducted into the Gospel Music Hall of Fame. In 1969, Vestal was named Female Vocalist of the Year at the annual Dove Awards. In 1979, the group performed at the White House for Pres. Jimmy Carter. Vestal Goodman died at age 74 on December 27, 2003. (Both, Gail Warren.)

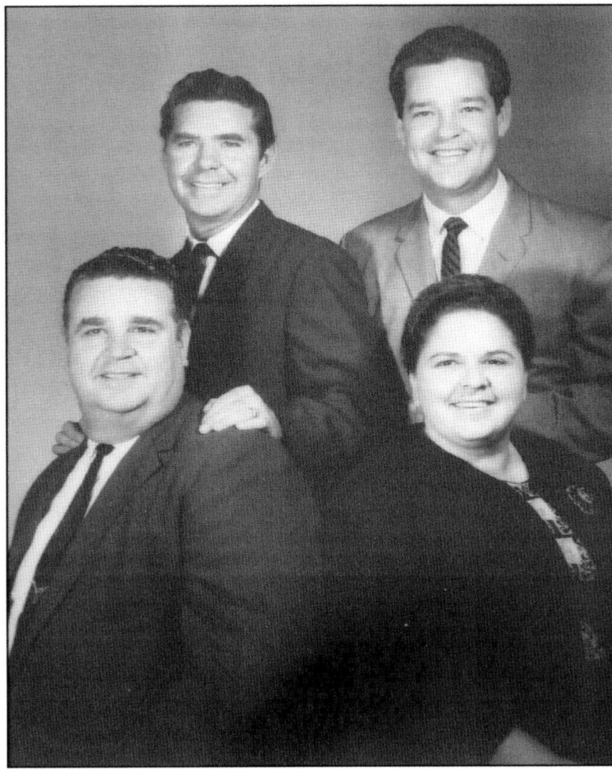

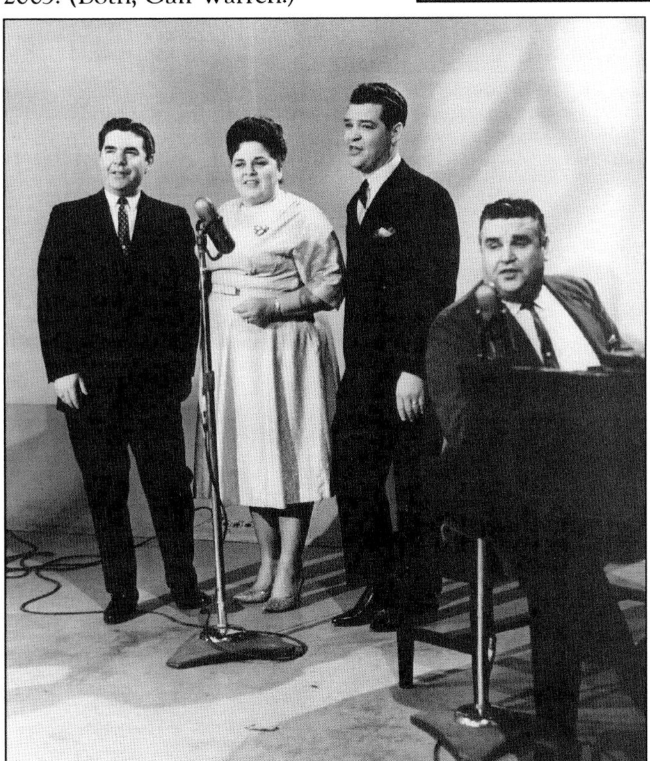

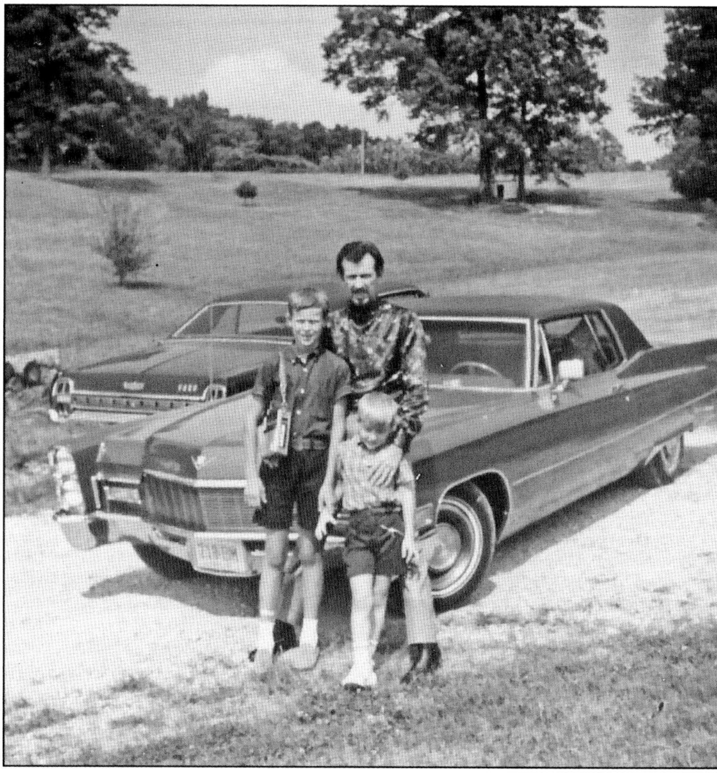

BMI has Buddy Hobgood listed as writing 63 songs. Buddy was raised in Madisonville. Many of his songs were recorded by James Brown. Buddy is shown here with his sons Buddy and Bobby. Note the old radio hanging from the younger Buddy's neck. A few of the songs Buddy cowrote with James Brown were "There Was a Time," "Man in the Glass," and "Shades of Brown." (Debbie Hobgood.)

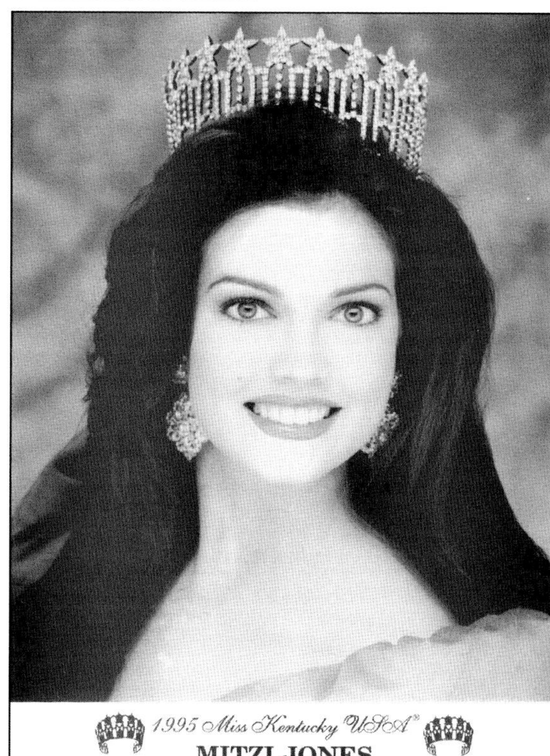

Mitzi Jones, of White Plains, was crowned Miss Kentucky USA on February 10, 1995. Her parents, Donnie and Brenda Jones, still reside in White Plains. This photograph was actually used as a poster for Mitzi to sign autographs while fulfilling her duties as Miss Kentucky USA. (Brenda Jones.)

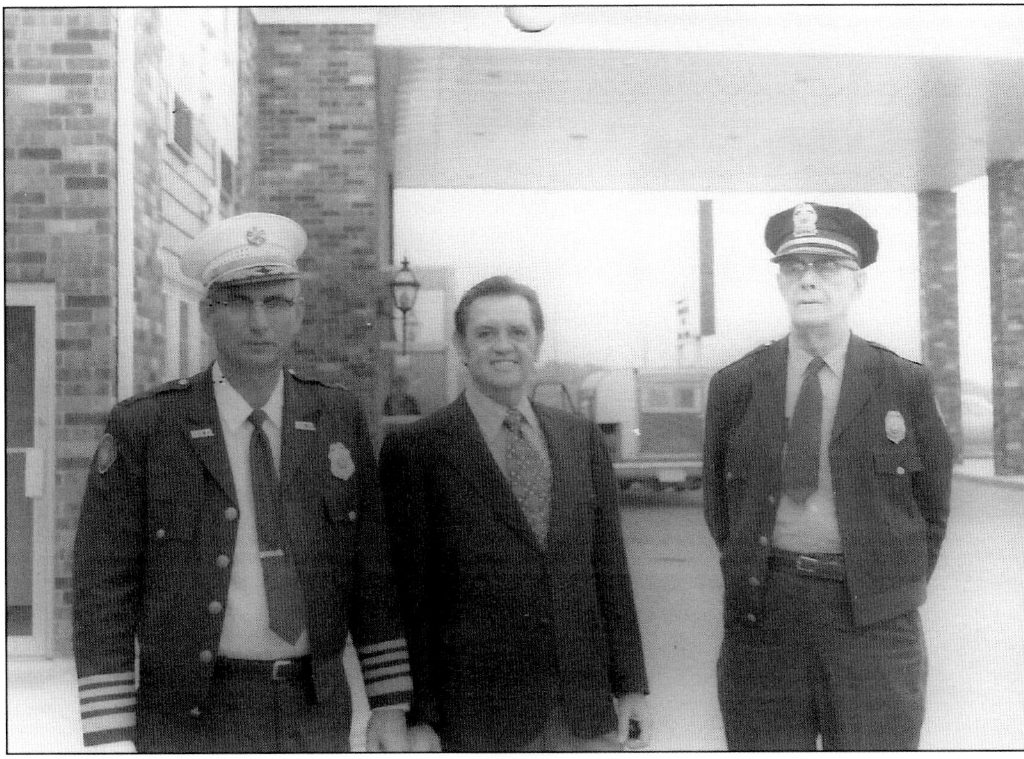

Standing from left to right are Madisonville fire chief Howard Renfro, Merle Travis (famous thumb picker from Muhlenberg), and Madisonville police chief Pat Collins. The building behind the men was the Ramada Inn. Plans for the original Ramada Inn were drawn by J. Harold Utley for Madisonville Contractors. The building is now the Days Inn. (HSHC.)

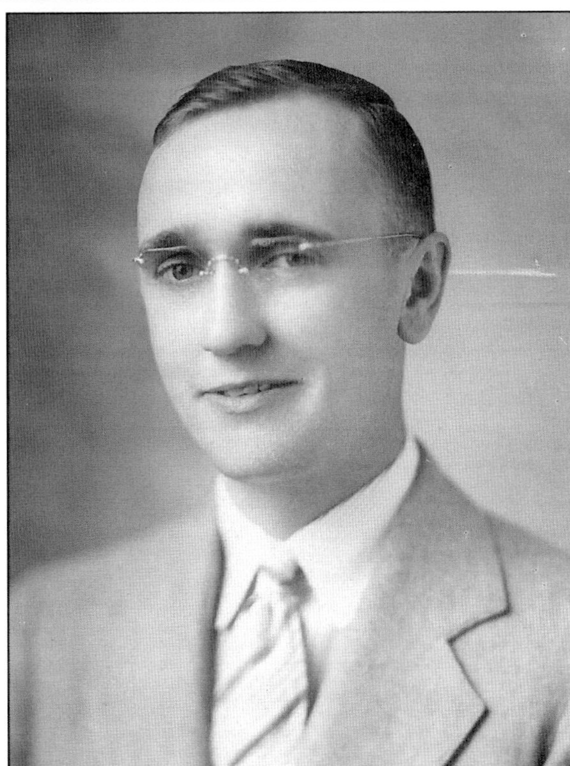

Harold Ledbetter loved Hopkins County and its history. His first job was a night-shift radio operator for the City of Madisonville. He was the first and only person to be elected by the city council as assistant chief of police. Ledbetter had a candy store at one time in the library. He became the first official historian of Hopkins County in 1986. (HSHC.)

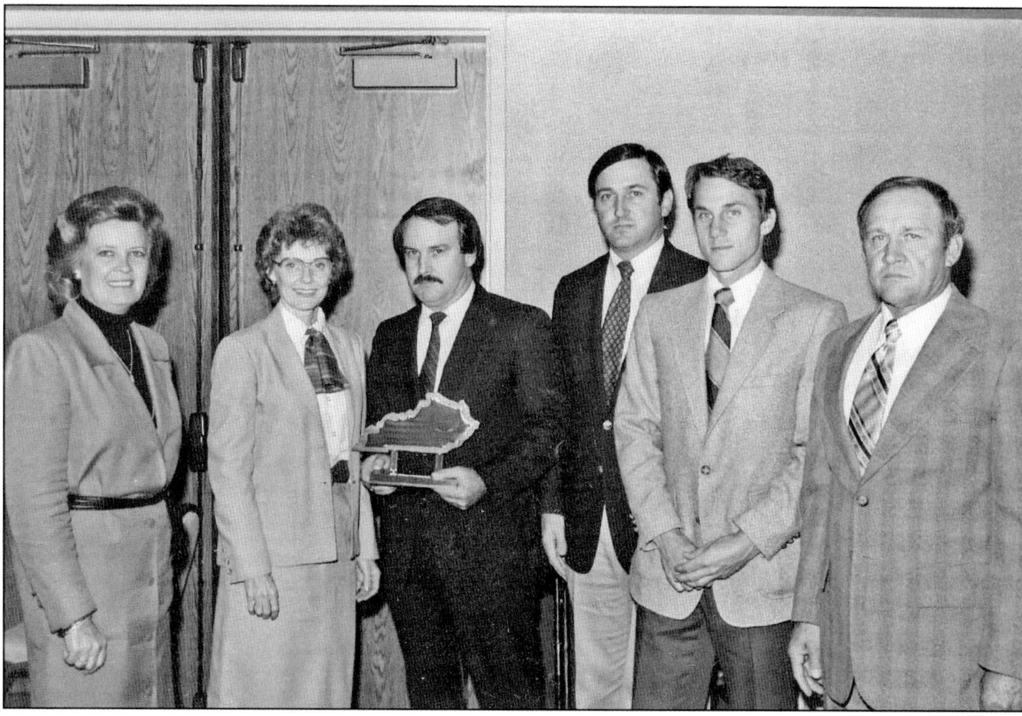

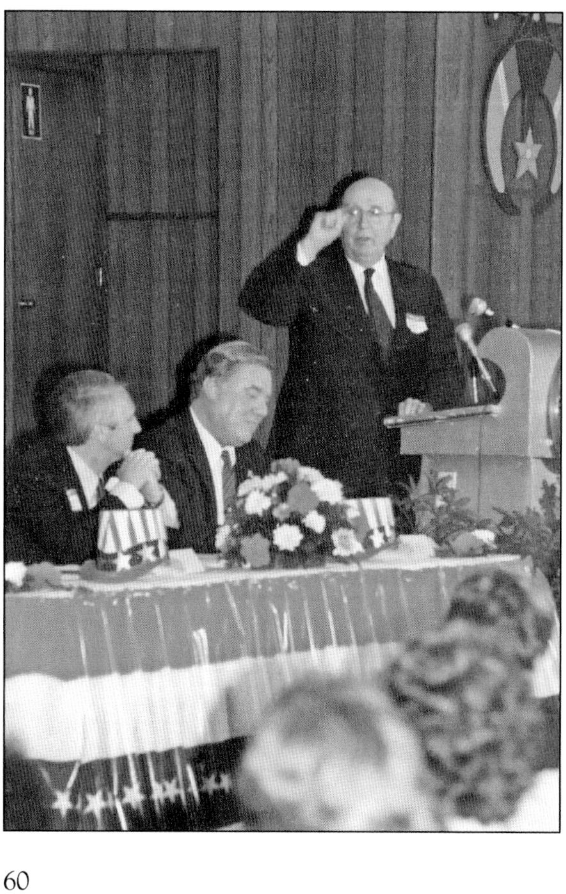

Gov. Martha Lane Collins (far left) is shown presenting a Soil Conservation Award. The award was presented in Frankfort by Governor Collins some time in the 1970s. The governor is shown with Hopkins County representatives: from left to right, Mayor Charlotte Baldwin, Joe Melton, Tom Batsel, Tom Porter Jr., and J. E. Ellis. (HSHC.)

The sixth annual Ruby Laffoon dinner at the Rizpah Temple in May 1987 was attended by Lt. Steve Beshear, First District Congressman Carroll Hubbard, and Harold Ledbetter. Ledbetter is speaking about the Laffoon cabin being restored. Beshear became the second governor from Hopkins County. Governor Beshear is from Dawson Springs. (HSHC.)

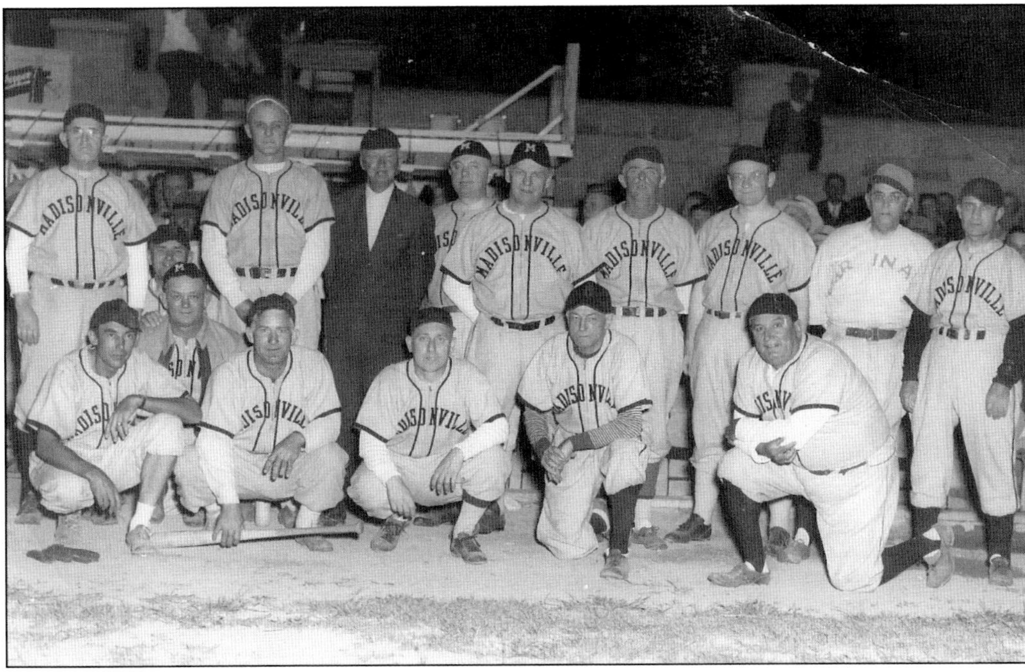

These ballplayers are former members of the Madisonville Miners professional baseball team. The Old Timers played in a game at Municipal Stadium (now Elmer Kelly Stadium) at the city park. The photograph was probably taken in the late 1940s. In the center back of the photograph is Madisonville mayor David Perish. (HSHC.)

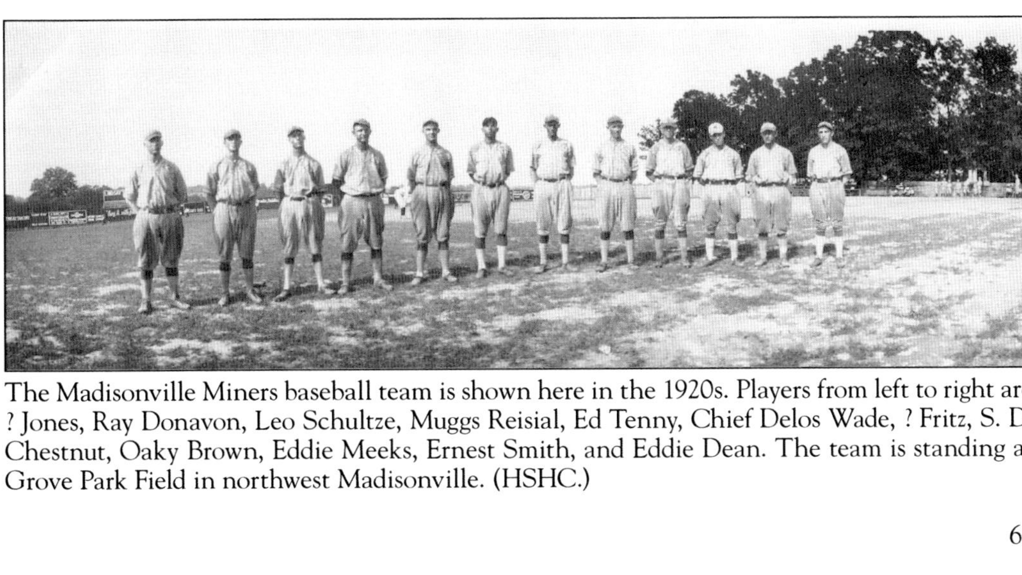

The Madisonville Miners baseball team is shown here in the 1920s. Players from left to right are ? Jones, Ray Donavon, Leo Schultze, Muggs Reisial, Ed Tenny, Chief Delos Wade, ? Fritz, S. D. Chestnut, Oaky Brown, Eddie Meeks, Ernest Smith, and Eddie Dean. The team is standing at Grove Park Field in northwest Madisonville. (HSHC.)

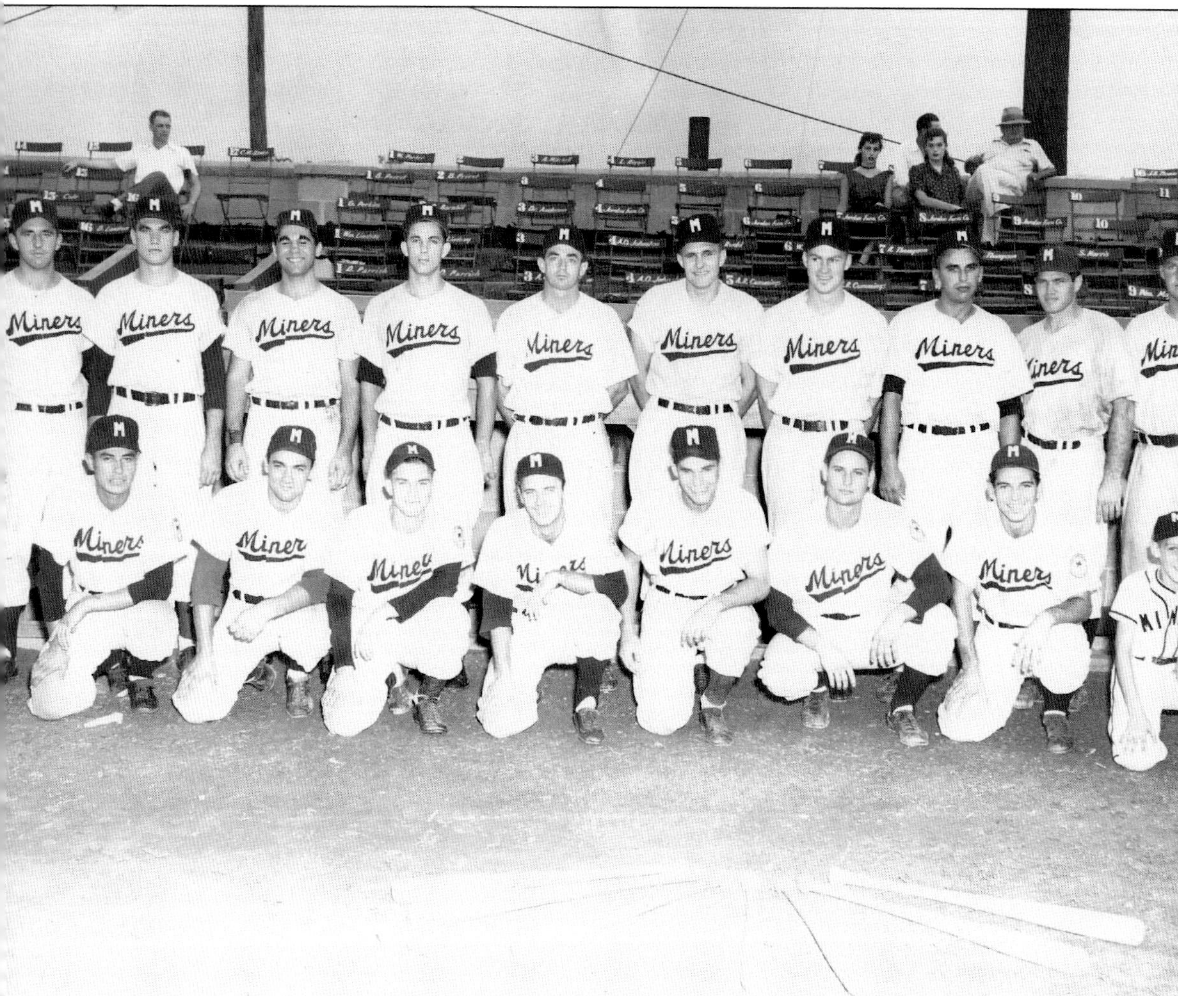

An undated old photograph of the Madisonville Miners baseball team is shown here. The baseball team produced many fans in Hopkins County. After the introduction of television and air-conditioning, the county and the country began to find things to do other than baseball. The Miners baseball team did not survive, and it ceased to exist in 1955. Artie Cummins, a Madison Miners second baseman, was later president of Madisonville Building and Loan, now Hancock Bank. (HSHC.)

Five

Tribute to Military and Public Service

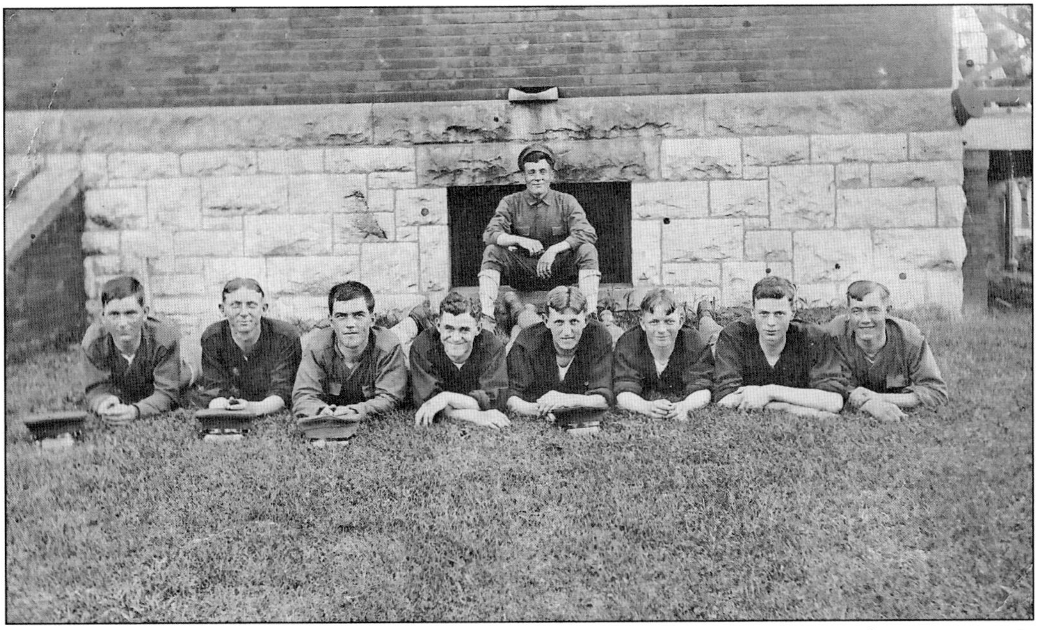

Thousands of Hopkins County men and women have served their country and community. It is bravery, honor, and hard work that have developed the character of the county's people. This chapter is included to honor those men and women who fought or worked unselfishly. Shown in this photograph is a U.S. Cavalry group before or during World War I. (Robert and Audrey McCain Collection.)

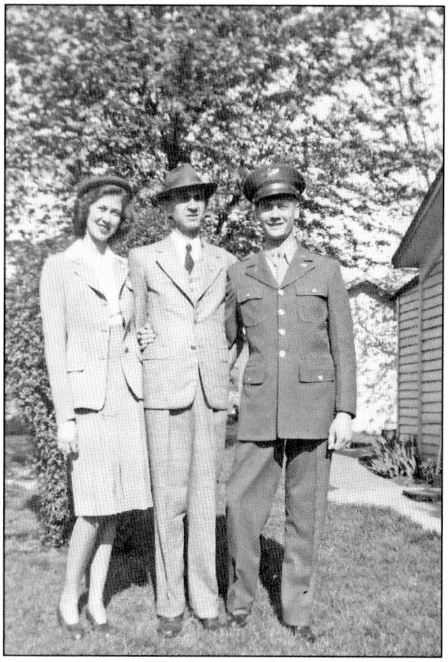

Joyce Jackson is shown in the photograph to the left with her father, Whitnell, and brother, William Jackson. Joyce worked for Kentucky Bank and Trust Company all of her life and never married. Her photographs were about to be destroyed in an old box but were found by accident and donated to the historical society. In the collection was the photograph below of William Weldon Jackson standing in his World War II flight suit. The airplanes of that era were not equipped with heaters. This suit was leather and lined with lamb's wool. The headpiece is an oxygen mask. The photograph was probably taken on South Madison Avenue in Madisonville. (Both, Joyce Jackson Collection/HSHC.)

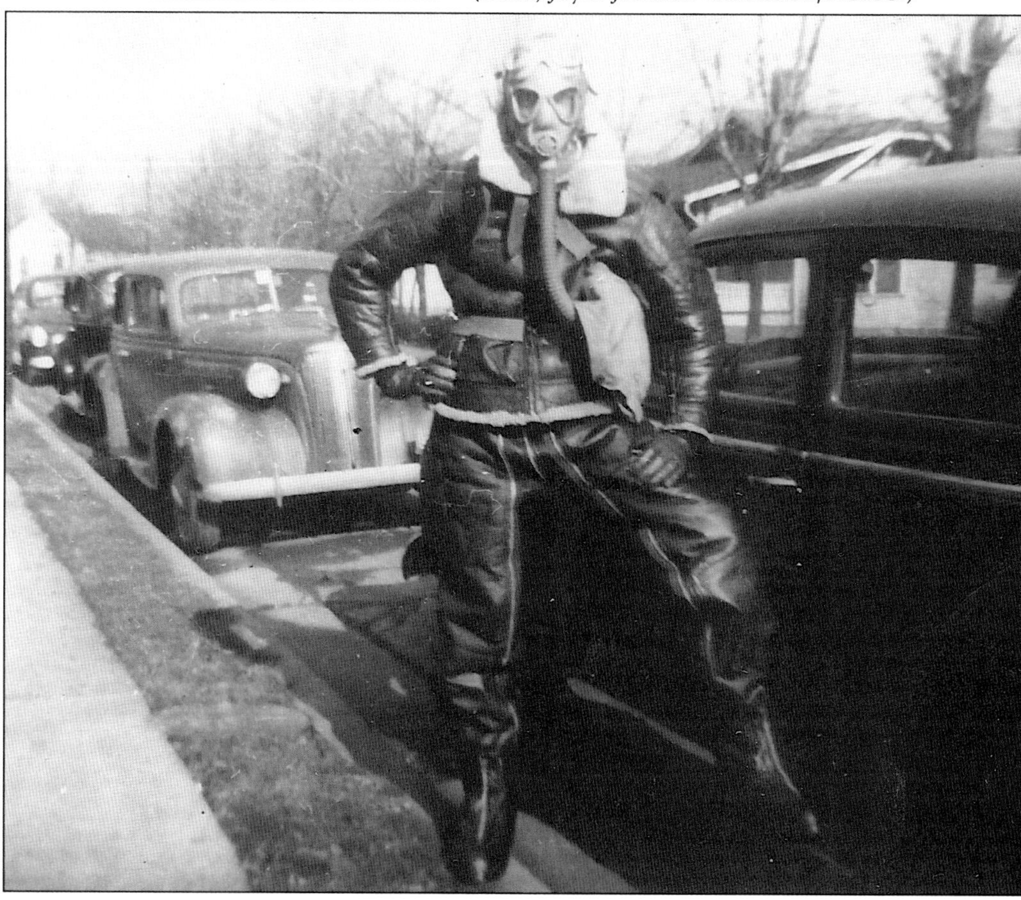

Harold Ledbetter and his brother Roelan served in the U.S. Army in World War II. They were fortunate enough to have leave at the same time. This photograph was made in front of their church, First Christian Church, on South Main Street. The church was struck by lightning on July 4, 1975, and burned to the ground. A new church building was built at the intersection of North Main Street and College Drive. (HSHC.)

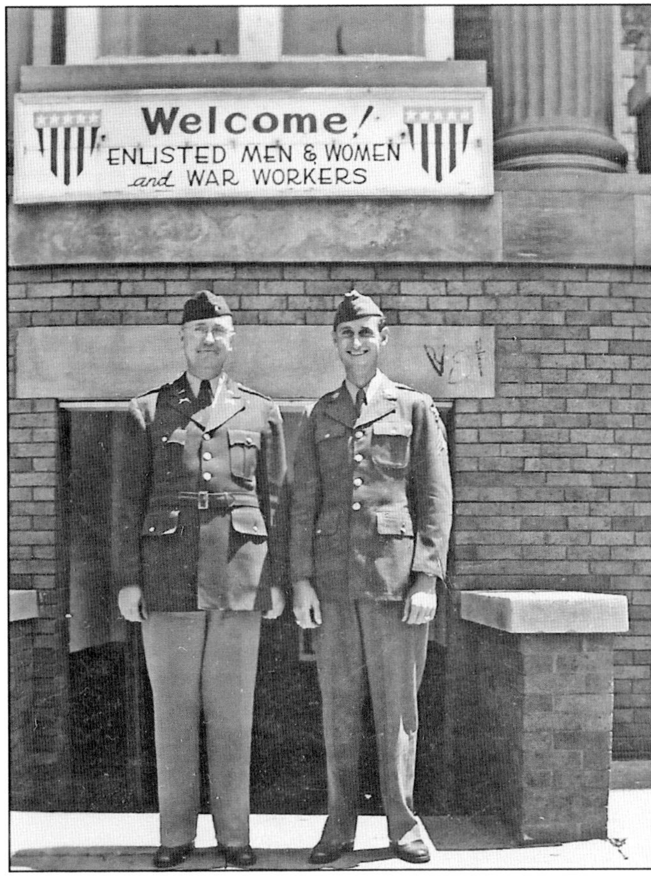

Nevaline Wagoner was an army nurse from 1942 to 1946. This photograph was made in front of the hospital where she was stationed. Written on the back is, "We will soon have caps like Lt. Redmond's. They are better, I think. These are all the nurses that we have here now." Nevaline is the third nurse from the left. (Joyce Jackson Collection/HSHC.)

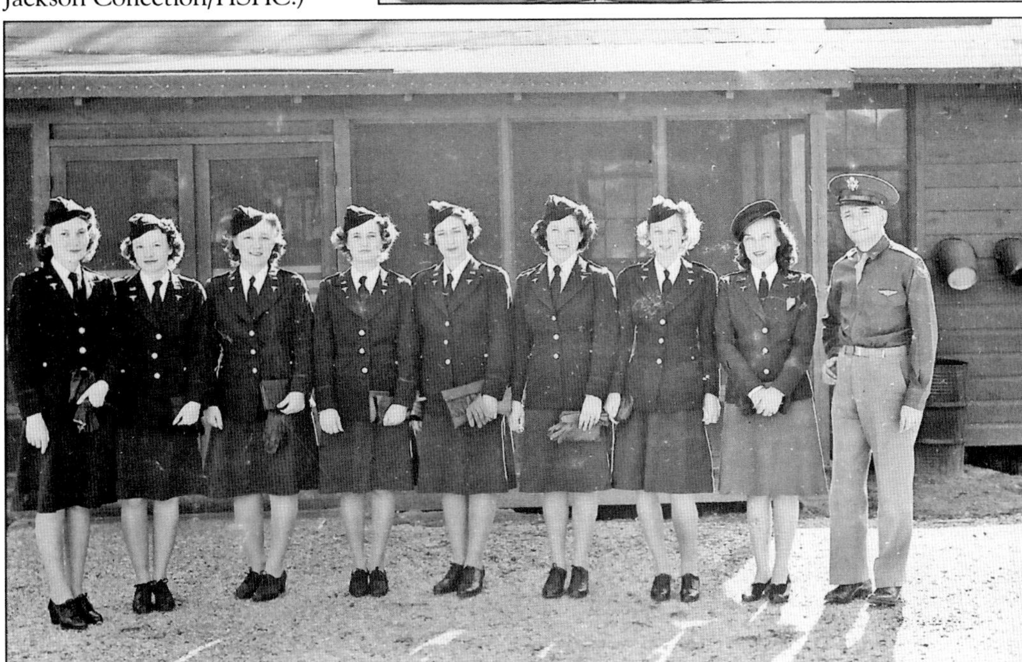

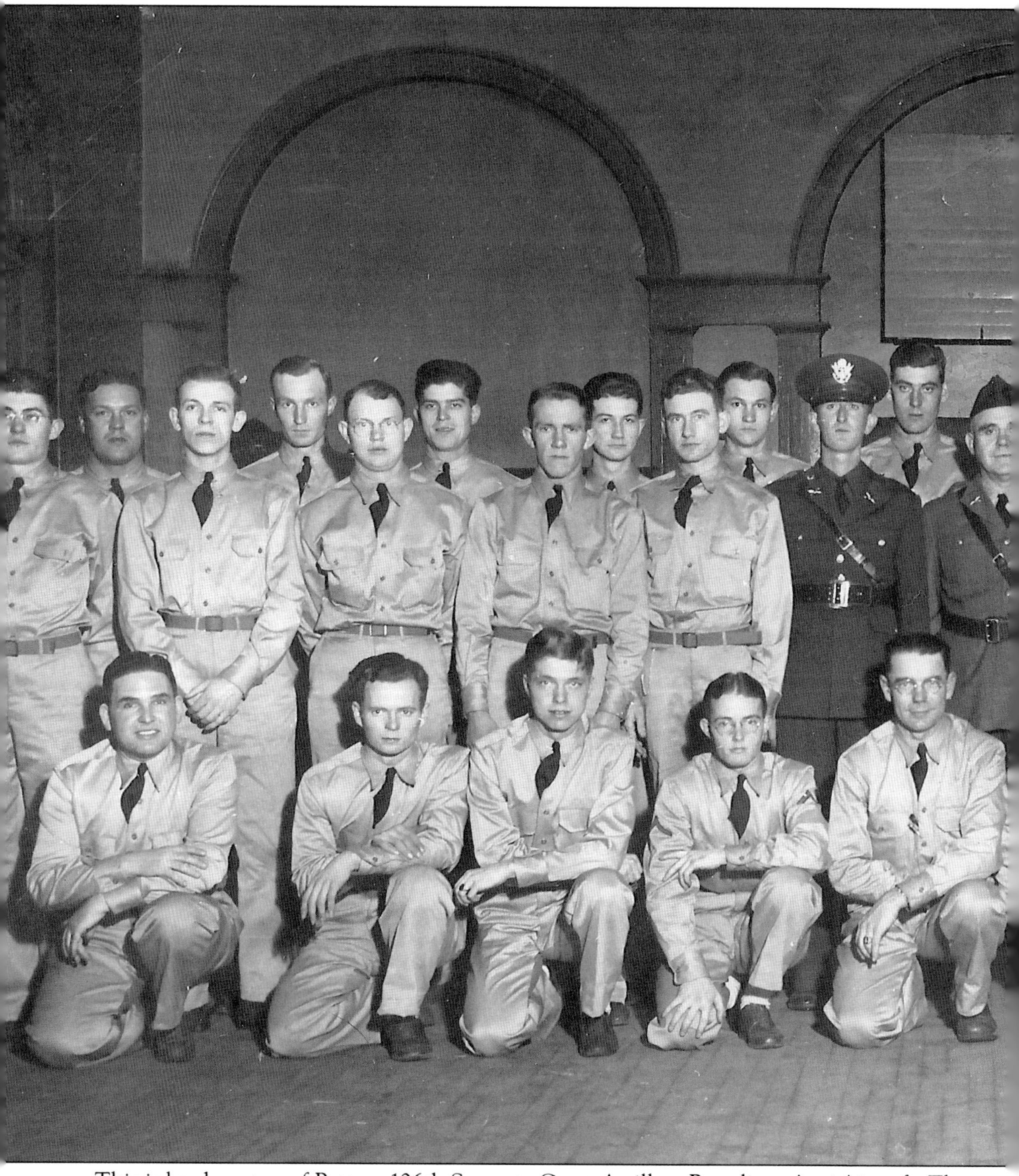

This is headquarters of Battery 106th Separate Coast Artillery Battalion, Anti-Aircraft. The photograph was taken inside the armory on South Main Street. Most of the men shown are from Hopkins County and members of the Kentucky National Guard. From left to right are (first row) Goebel L. Burden, Kenneth C. Tongate, Earl D. Hinton, William R. Howard, Elmer N. Adcock, Welby B. Pritchett Jr., Cecil J. Harris, Albert G. Griffin, Ruby W. Jones, William J. Wyatt, and Fred H. Trathen Jr.; (second row) Jewell F. Hankins, George C. Bennett, Edward F. Ivy, Otis L.

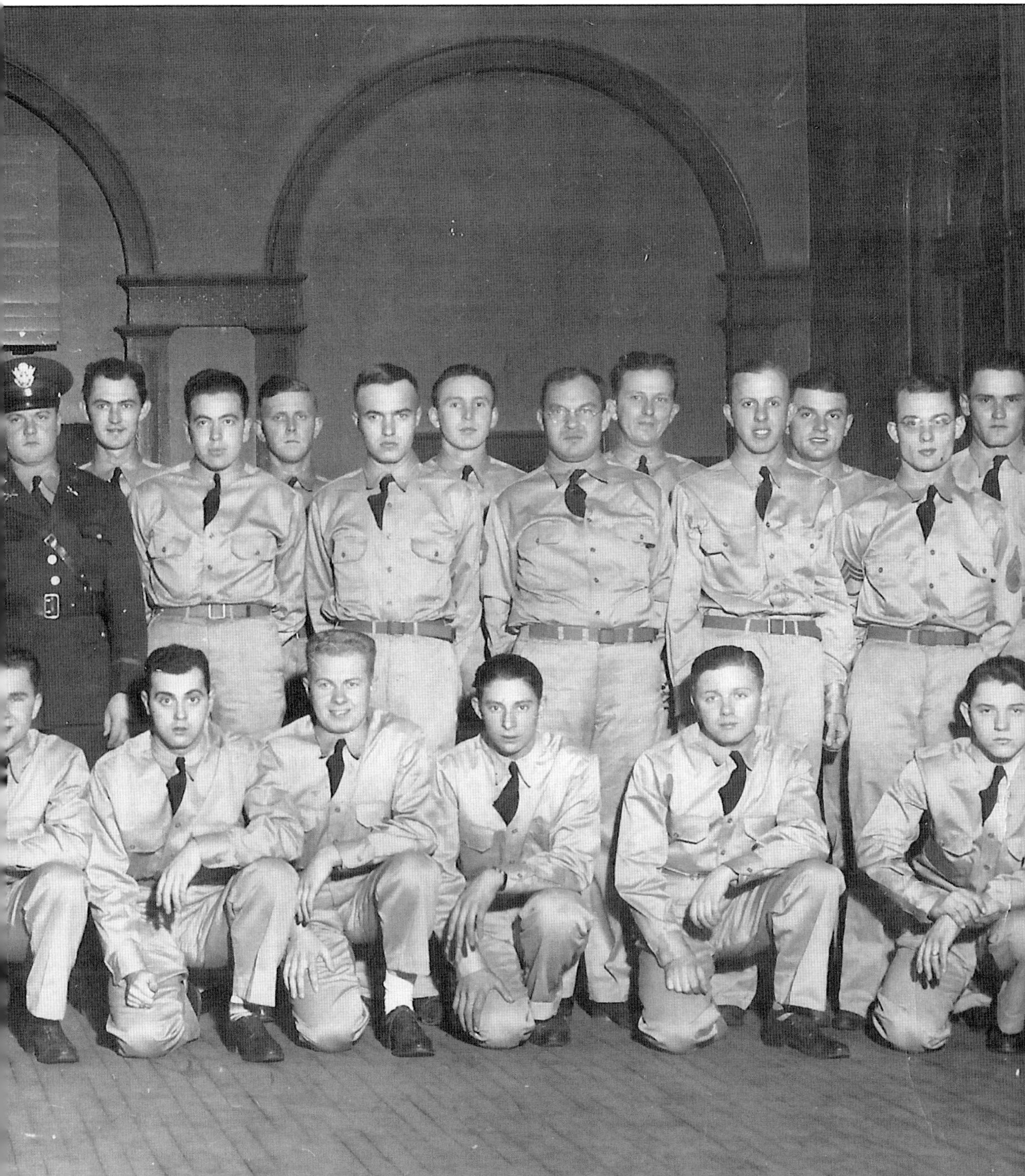

Tillotson, William D. Wilson, Lt. James W. McLemore, Capt. James Karr Ramsey, Lt. Robert V. Hall, Archie L. Payne, James P. Marks, Frank M. Taliaferro, John H. Kirkwood, and Harlan D. Hawkins; (third row) Karl S. Pate Jr., Louis Y. Nisbet, Samuel L. Hawkins, Charles H. Allen, Howard B. Nisbet, William E. Dockrey, J. L. Fuller, Robert P. Hancock, Raymond T. Frazer, Hugh H. Beeler, James U. Adcock, Andrew J. Arnold, and George Reed Frazer. (HSHC.)

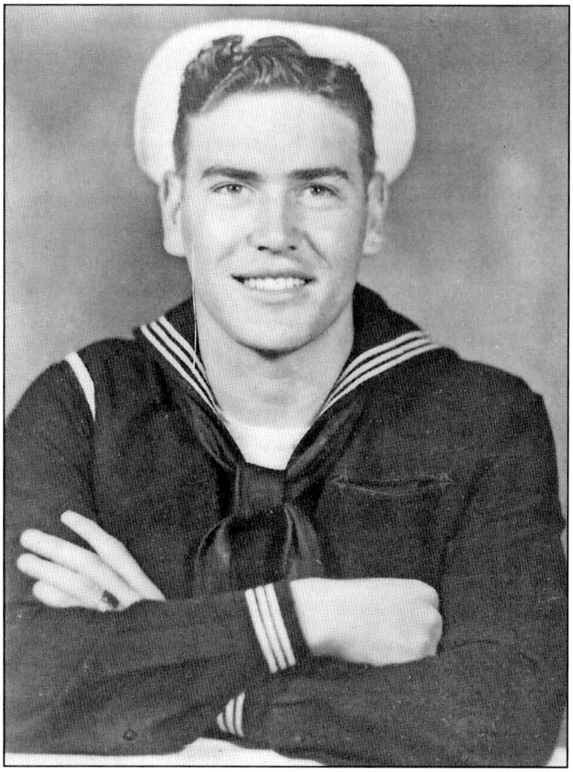

The handsome sailor James D. Hunt is pictured in the photograph to the left. He was born on March 5, 1929. Hunt served in the U.S. Navy from 1942 to 1947. He was stationed aboard the aircraft carrier USS *Kitkun Bay* as a gunner and a second-class mail clerk. After leaving the military, he married Piccola Long Hunt in 1947. Piccola Hunt is shown leaning on a vehicle dressed in her husband's sailor suit. The happy couple lived in what was called "Beanbottom." The area is now known as Little Valley. The Hunts raised four daughters: Teresa Knowles, Lorraine Lynn, Debra Devine, and Kim McPeek. (Both, Piccola Hunt.)

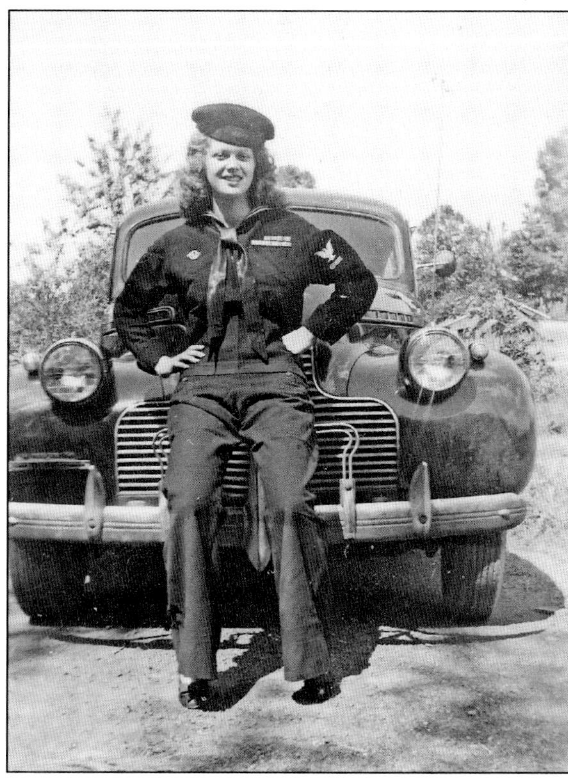

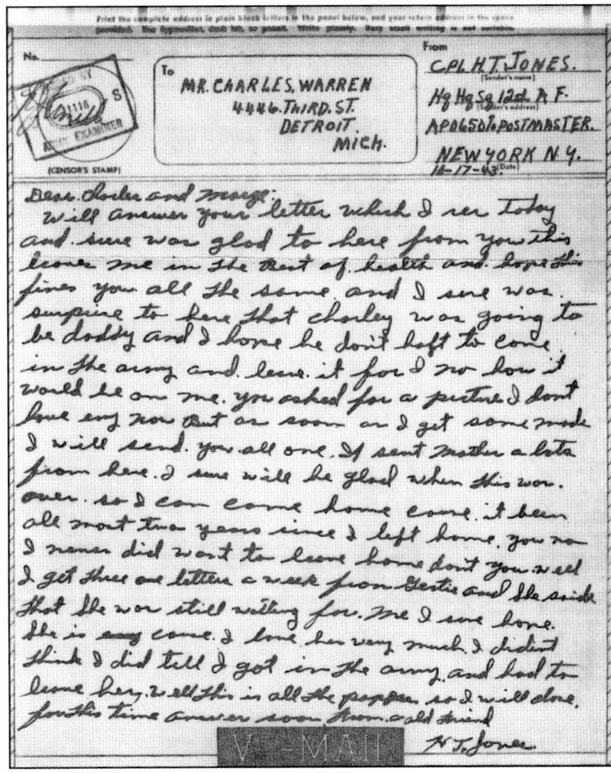

No.

(CENSOR'S STAMP)

To MR. CAARLES. WARREN
4446. THIRD. ST.
DETROIT.
MICH.

From CPL. H.T. JONES.
(Sender's name)
Hq Hq Sq 12d. A F.
(Sender's address)
APO 650 % POSTMASTER.
NEW YORK N.Y.
10-17-43.
(Date)

Dear. Charles and Marge:

Will answer your letter which I rec today and. sure was glad to here from you this leaves me in the best of. health and. hope this fines you all the same. and I sure was. surprise to here that charley was going to be daddy and I hope he don't haft to come in the army and. leave. it for I no how it would be on me. you asked for a picture I dont have eny now but as soon as I get some made I will send. you. all one. I sent mother a lota from here. I sure will be glad when this war. over. so I can come home come. it been all most two years since I left home. you no I never did want to leave home dont you. well I get three are letters a week from Gertie and She saide that She was still waiting for. me I sure hope. She is any come. I love her very much. I didint think I did till I got in the army. and had to leave her. well this is all the paper so I will close. for this time answer soon. from. a old friend

H. T. Jones

Herschel T. Jones penned the letter to the left at age 24 to Charles and Marge Warren on October 17, 1943. Herschel was serving in the U.S. Army during World War II. Herschel and Marge Hartline Warren grew up as neighbors in Barnsley. In the letter, Herschel makes mention that he heard that Charles was about to become a father. The baby mentioned, Roger Warren, was actually born one month and a day after the letter was written. The photograph below shows Herschel T. Jones in uniform as he would have looked when writing the letter. Herschel Thomas Jones married Gertie Lee Henderson on June 20, 1945, in Hopkinsville. (Both, Gail Warren.)

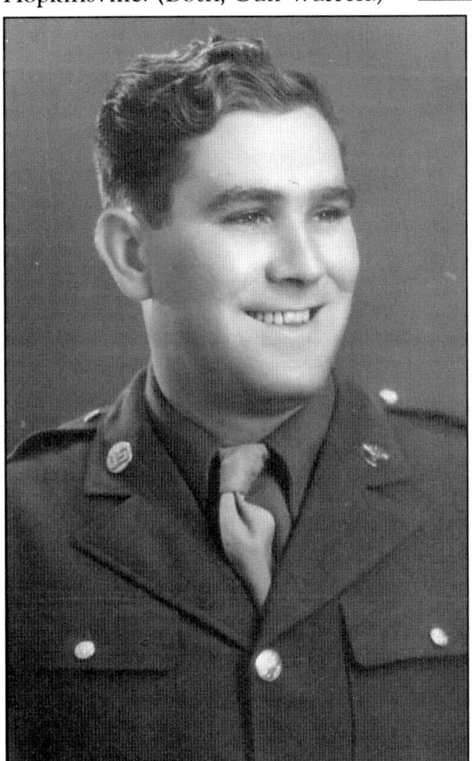

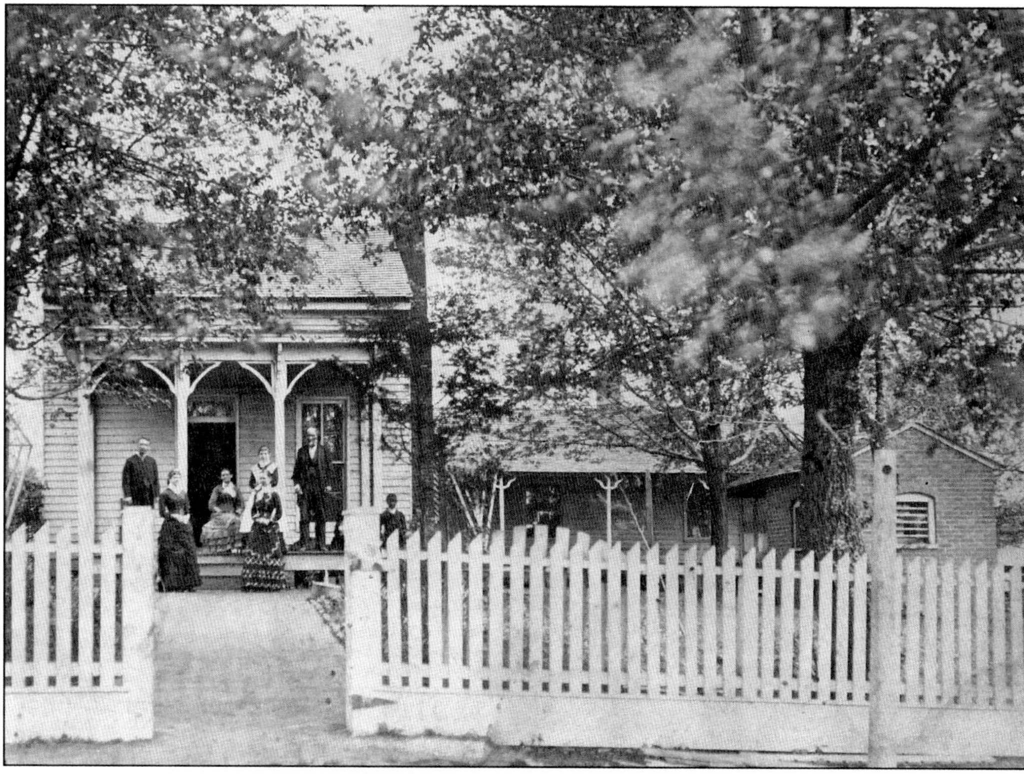

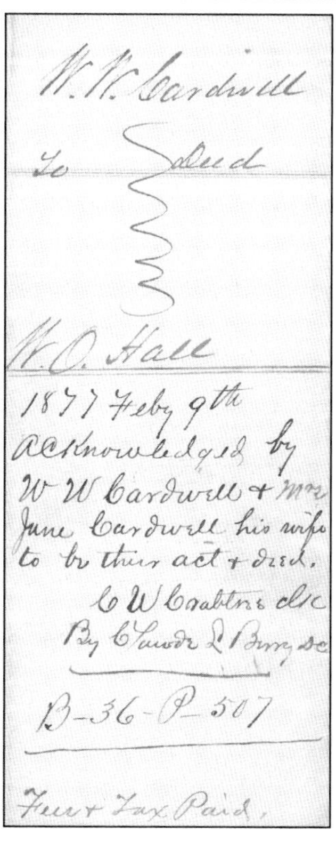

W. W. Cardwell
To Deed
W. O. Hall
1877 Feby 9th
acknowledged by
W W Cardwell & Mrs
June Cardwell his wife
to be their act & deed.
C W Crabtree clc
By Claude L Berry dc
B-36-P-507
Fees & Tax Paid.

The photograph captures the home place of William Orvell Hall, located on the east side of what is now Franklin Street just south of Hall Street. William was born near Clarksville, Tennessee, in 1821. He came to Madisonville as a young man, opened a brickyard, and bought a farm, a part of which became Hall Street. The brickyard remained in the Hall family until it was closed in 1927 by John William Orvell Hall. The African American boy in the picture was called Will Rabbit. He was always a part of the family and lived at the brickyard until his death some time in the 1930s. To the left is a photograph of the deed to the property, which was dated February 9, 1877. (Both, HSHC.)

Lt. William O. Hall was born January 20, 1921, and gave his life for his country as a pilot in World War II. Prior to the war, he was a talented draftsman for an architect. He drafted the Scott-McGaw building, which was built on the northeast corner of Main and Arch Streets in Madisonville in 1939. The building was torn down some time after 1993. (HSHC.)

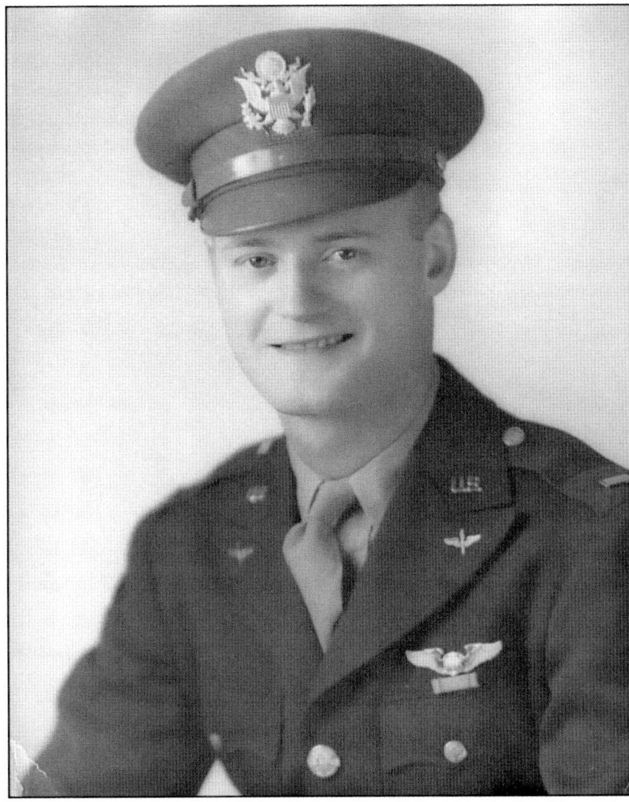

Not only have the soldiers who gave their lives for their country paid a high price, but their families also took part in the cost. This Western Union telegram is the notification that Lieutenant Hall's family received when the lieutenant was killed in action in England on May 2, 1944. His name is listed on the monument of 127 who died in World War II from Hopkins County. (HSHC.)

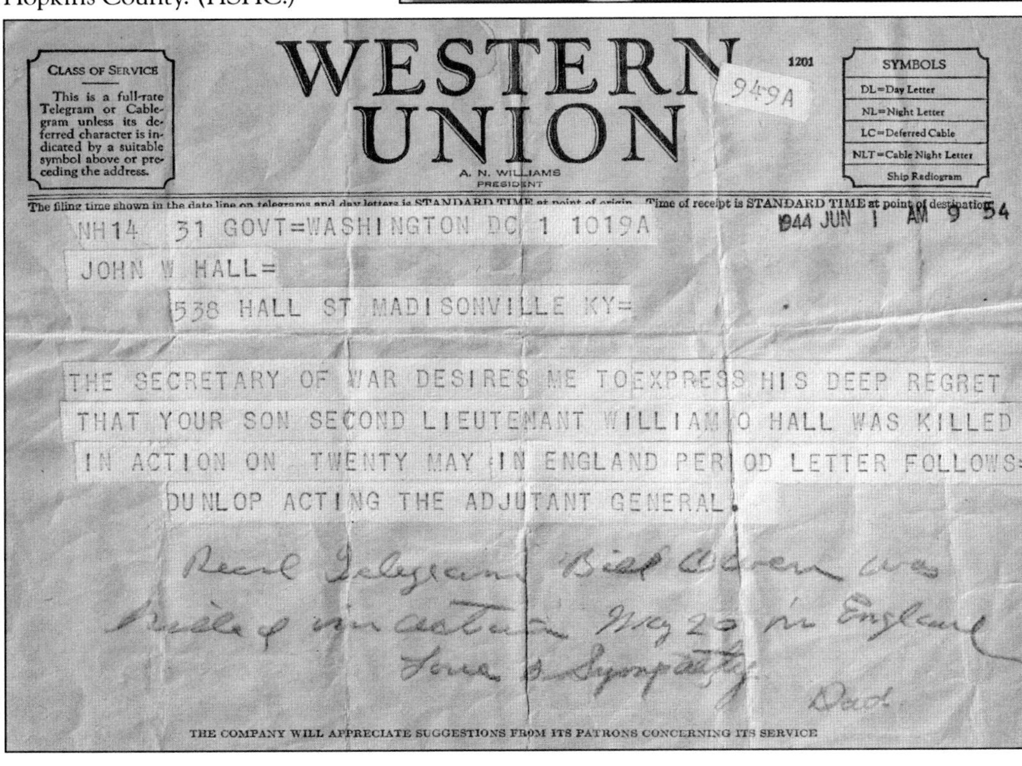

CLASS OF SERVICE
This is a full-rate Telegram or Cablegram unless its deferred character is indicated by a suitable symbol above or preceding the address.

WESTERN UNION 1201 949A

A. N. WILLIAMS
PRESIDENT

SYMBOLS
DL=Day Letter
NL=Night Letter
LC=Deferred Cable
NLT=Cable Night Letter
Ship Radiogram

The filing time shown in the date line on telegrams and day letters is STANDARD TIME at point of origin. Time of receipt is STANDARD TIME at point of destination

NH14 31 GOVT=WASHINGTON DC 1 1019A 1944 JUN 1 AM 9 54

JOHN W HALL=

538 HALL ST MADISONVILLE KY=

THE SECRETARY OF WAR DESIRES ME TOEXPRESS HIS DEEP REGRET THAT YOUR SON SECOND LIEUTENANT WILLIAM O HALL WAS KILLED IN ACTION ON TWENTY MAY IN ENGLAND PERIOD LETTER FOLLOWS=
DUNLOP ACTING THE ADJUTANT GENERAL.

Recd Telegram Bill Oliver was killed in action May 20 in England
Love & Sympathy
Dad

THE COMPANY WILL APPRECIATE SUGGESTIONS FROM ITS PATRONS CONCERNING ITS SERVICE

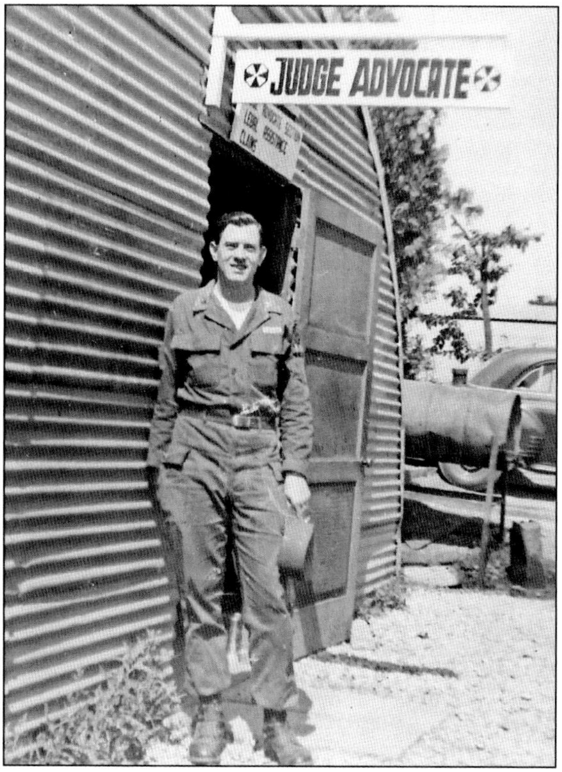

Lt. Thomas B. Spain stands in this photograph for the 8th Army Judge Advocate Section in Seoul, Korea, on June 1953. The sign above his head reads, "Advocate Section Legal Assistance Claims." Judge Spain was a practicing attorney in Madisonville and was later elected to the state court of appeals. (HSHC.)

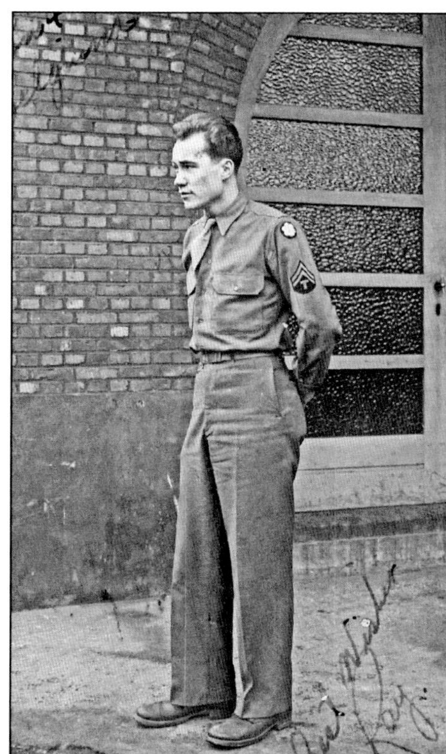

Buddy Farmer, also known as Jaybird, poses for a photograph while enlisted in the U.S. Army. He was stationed at Fort Carson in 1954 and later in Frankfort, Germany, for 2.5 years. After he served his country, he married Wilma Crunk on June 14, 1958. He worked at TVA in Drakesboro, retired from Hopkins County Coal, and continues to live in White Plains. (Jane Hardwick Rogers.)

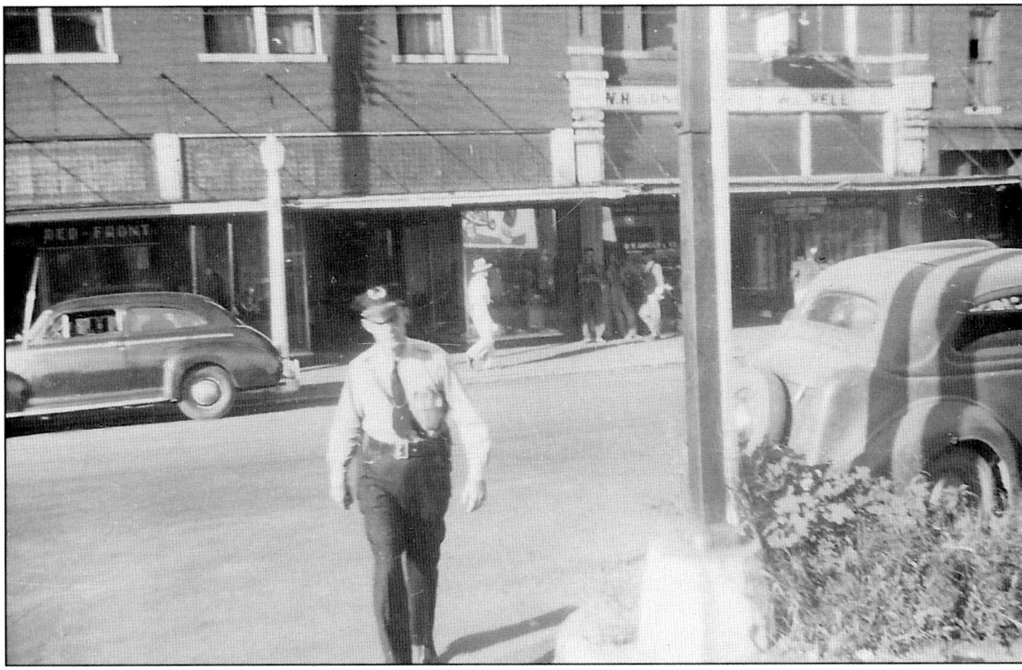

Chief Pat Collins walks across West Center Street in this undated photograph. W. H. Arnold Hardware Store is behind him. The building in the middle is Madisonville Dry Goods Store, operated by Frank Ramsey. Women would walk on the south side of West Center Street for safety. Notice there are only men on the street behind the chief. (Collins Collection, HSHC.)

Before becoming the chief of police in Madisonville, W. H. Collins, also known as Chief Pat Collins, was the constable at St. Charles. This photograph was taken in St. Charles. The vehicle is a 1938 Chevrolet, and the man on the left is unidentified. Constable Collins stands on the right in his crisp-looking uniform. St. Charles was settled in 1872 and incorporated in 1874. (Collins Collection, HSHC.)

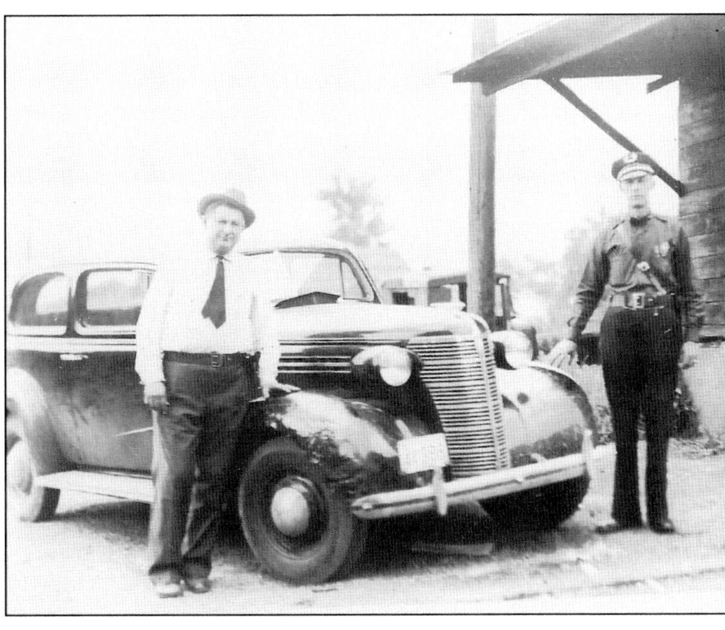

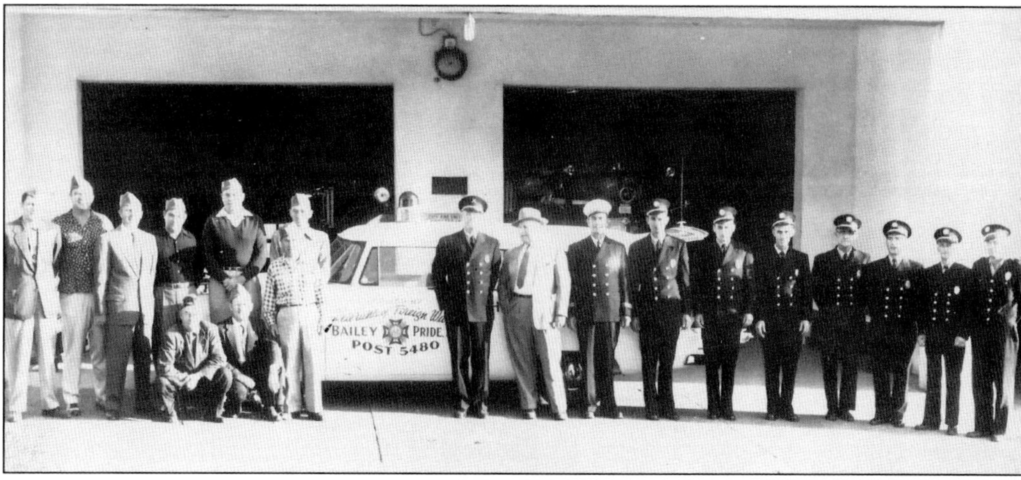

Before 1955, the funeral home operators made emergency runs in their hearses. In 1955, men are pictured standing beside the new emergency vehicle given to the fire department. The writing on the side of the donated emergency vehicle reads, "Donated by Veterans of Foreign War Bailey Pride Post 5480." The sign on the top of the vehicle says, "City Fire Units." (HSHC.)

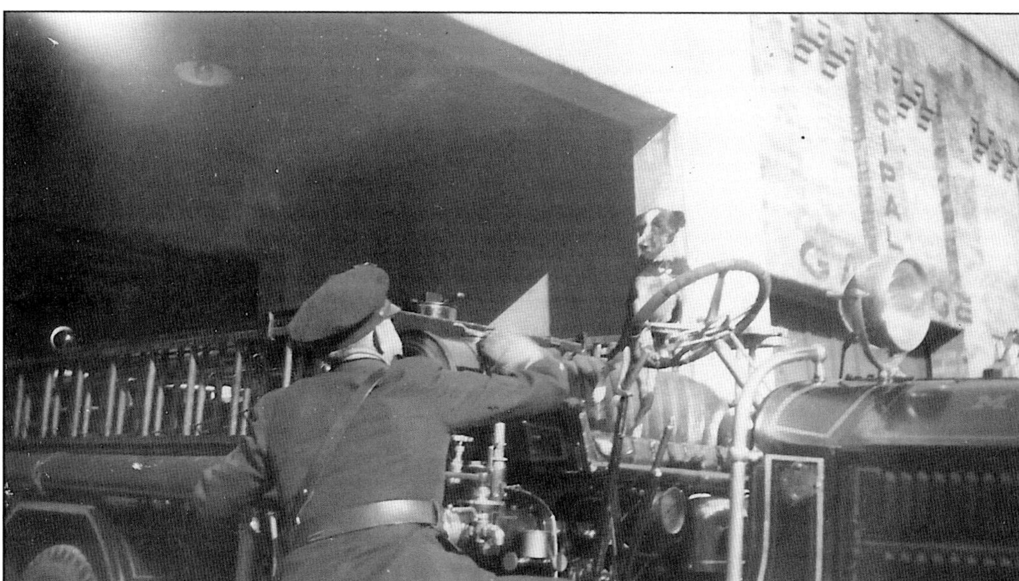

The emergency and rescue departments of Hopkins County and its cities have worked to serve the communities well. The fire truck in this photograph served at the East Center Street Fire Station. The vehicle can still be seen at the fire station and is housed in glass for easy viewing. (Collins Collection, HSHC.)

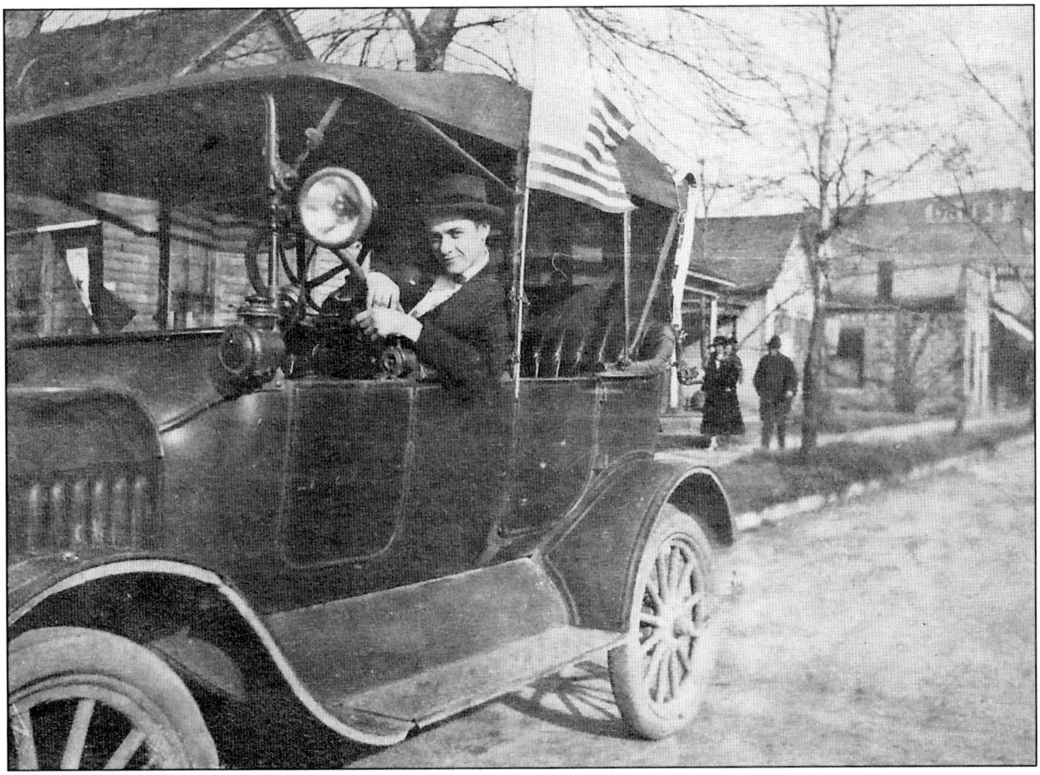

The special motor patrolman who answered calls to both the city and the county was Edgar Watson. Notice the spotlight near the window of the vehicle. He also has his hand on a hand-crank siren. The car is a Model T Ford. The policeman's uniform in the 1920s was a blue suit with brass buttons and a wide-brimmed hat. (HSHC.)

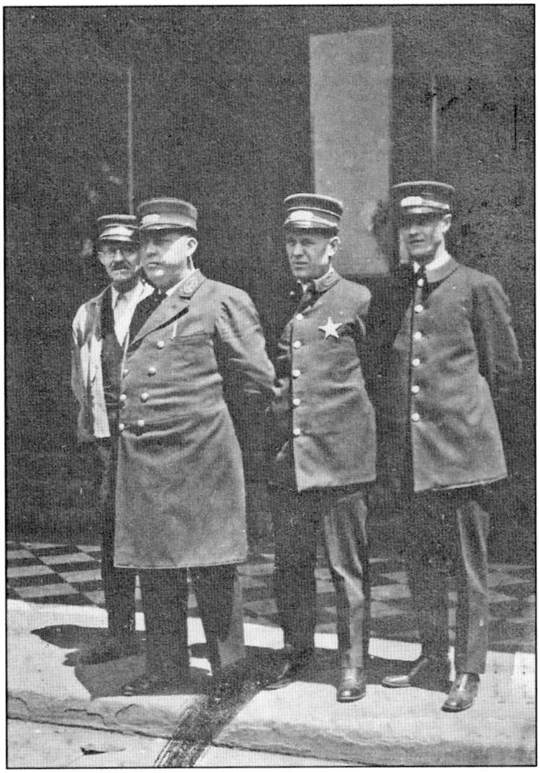

The Madisonville Police Department was proud to have, from left to right, Sam DeMoss (day patrolman), Chief John H. Ashby (called Uncle Johnny), Henry Dukes (first night patrolman), and Whitnell Jackson (second night patrolman). Chief Ashby was killed in the line of duty in 1929 while attempting to arrest the Cooksey brothers. While Ashby was handcuffing one of the brothers, the other one pulled a pistol and shot the chief in the back. (HSHC.)

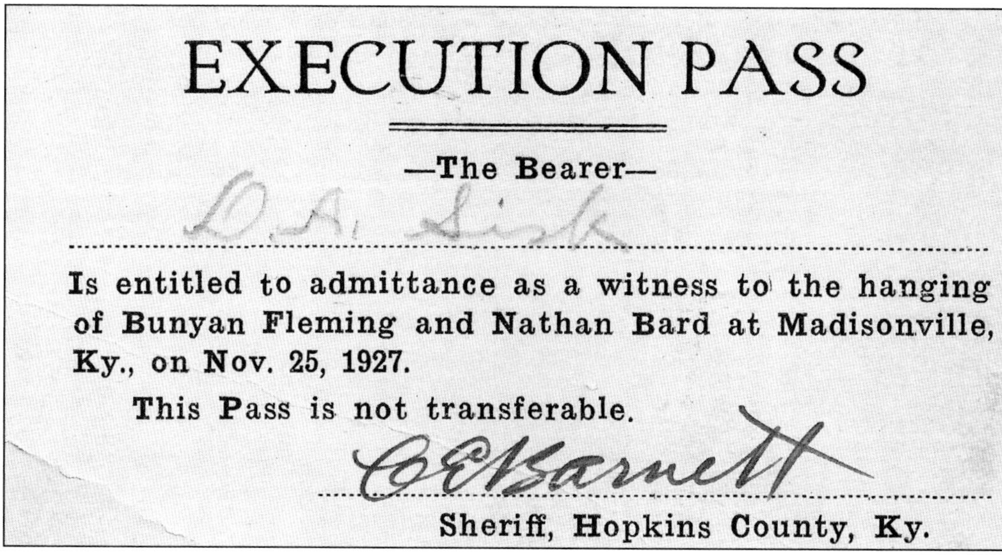

EXECUTION PASS

—The Bearer—

D. A. Sisk

Is entitled to admittance as a witness to the hanging of Bunyan Fleming and Nathan Bard at Madisonville, Ky., on Nov. 25, 1927.

This Pass is not transferable.

C. E. Barnett

Sheriff, Hopkins County, Ky.

The last hanging in Hopkins County was on November 25, 1927. It was the next-to-the-last hanging in Kentucky. Over 7,000 men, women, and children gathered on that Friday to see the hanging of Bunyan Fleming and Nathan Bard. Execution passes were issued by the sheriff to those permitted to be within the walls during the execution, although a throng of people watched from outside the gate. (HSHC.)

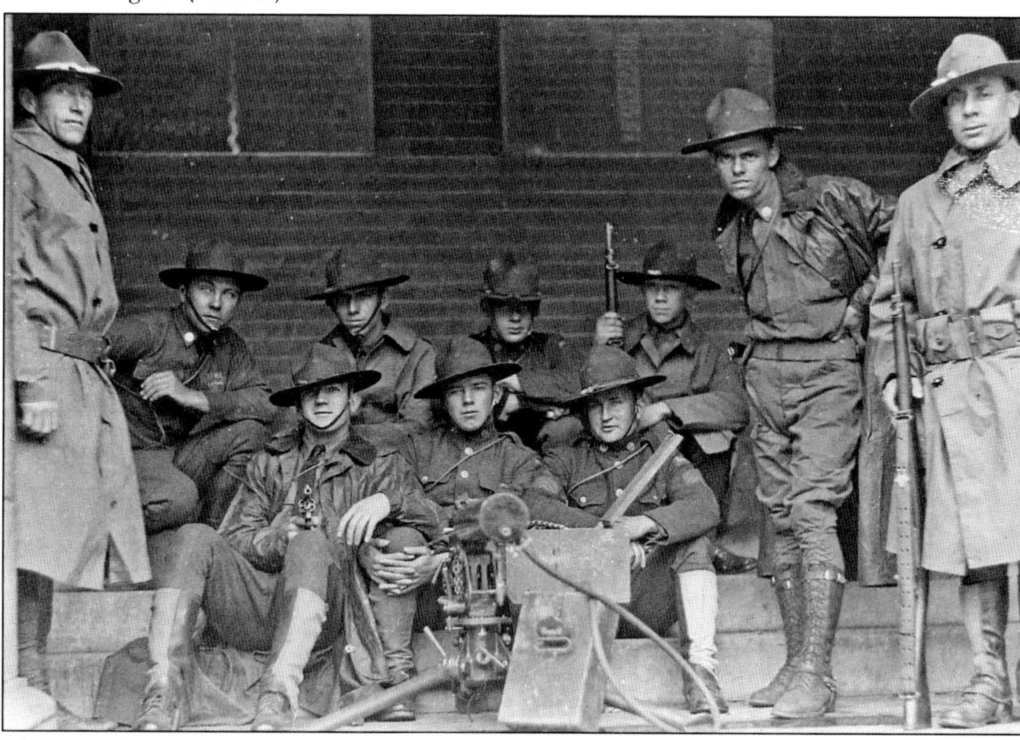

The men who were hanged went to trial in November 1926. The same year, the Kentucky Militia was changed to the Kentucky National Guard. The guard was activated for the first time to make sure that Fleming and Bard were not lynched on the way to their trial. The man to the left of the old machine gun has his revolver pointed at the cameraman. (HSHC.)

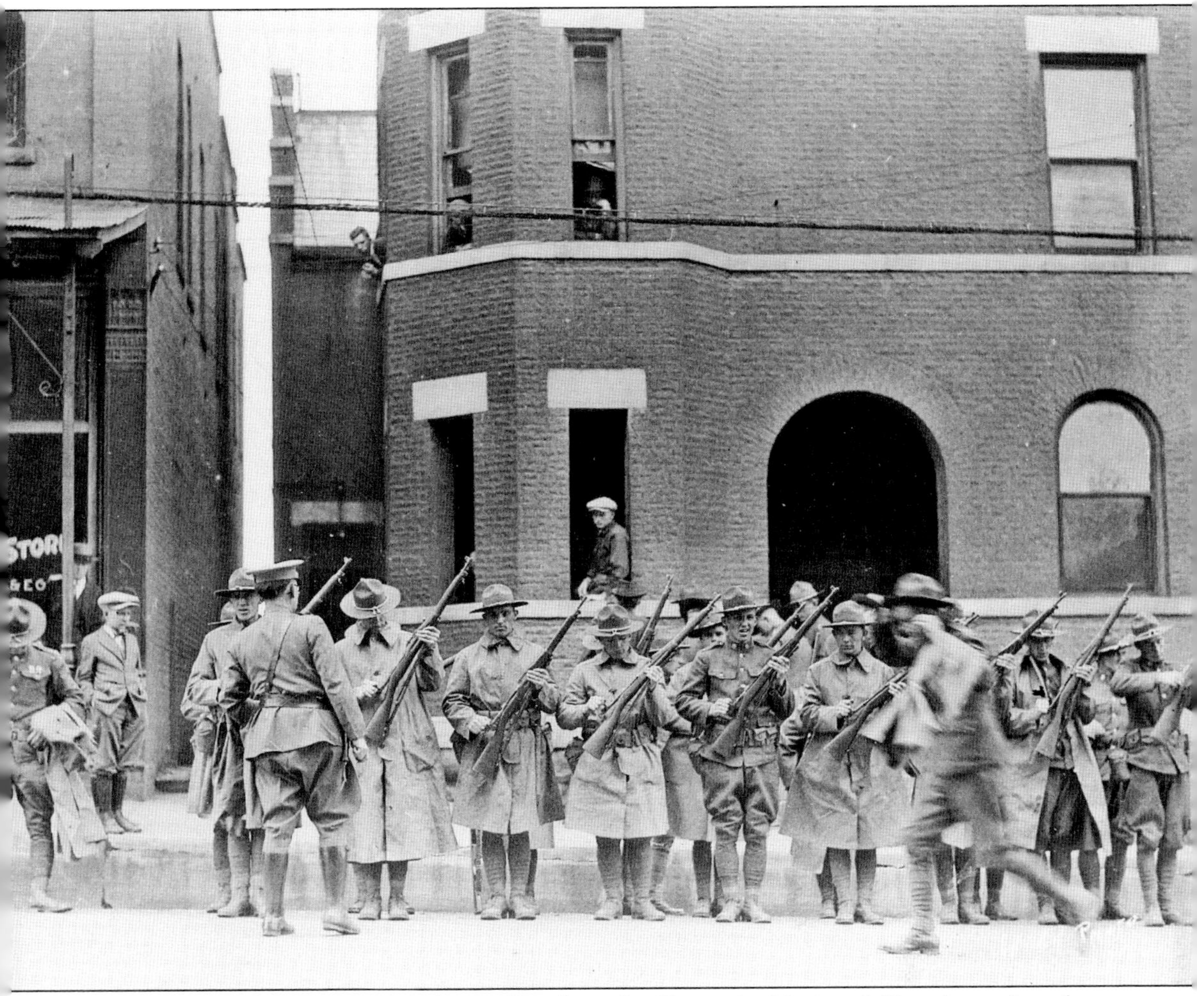

It was a day full of tension in Madisonville when the Kentucky National Guard stood ready to guard the two accused prisoners. The photographs of the event were taken by an amateur photographer, E. L. Henry. In this photograph, the guard stands in front of Hopkins County Jail preparing the weapons and checking equipment to make sure that the prisoners were not captured and lynched before a proper trial had been completed. The prisoners had been accused of raping a woman early in the winter, and emotions were high. Notice the men looking out the windows in the photograph. (HSHC.)

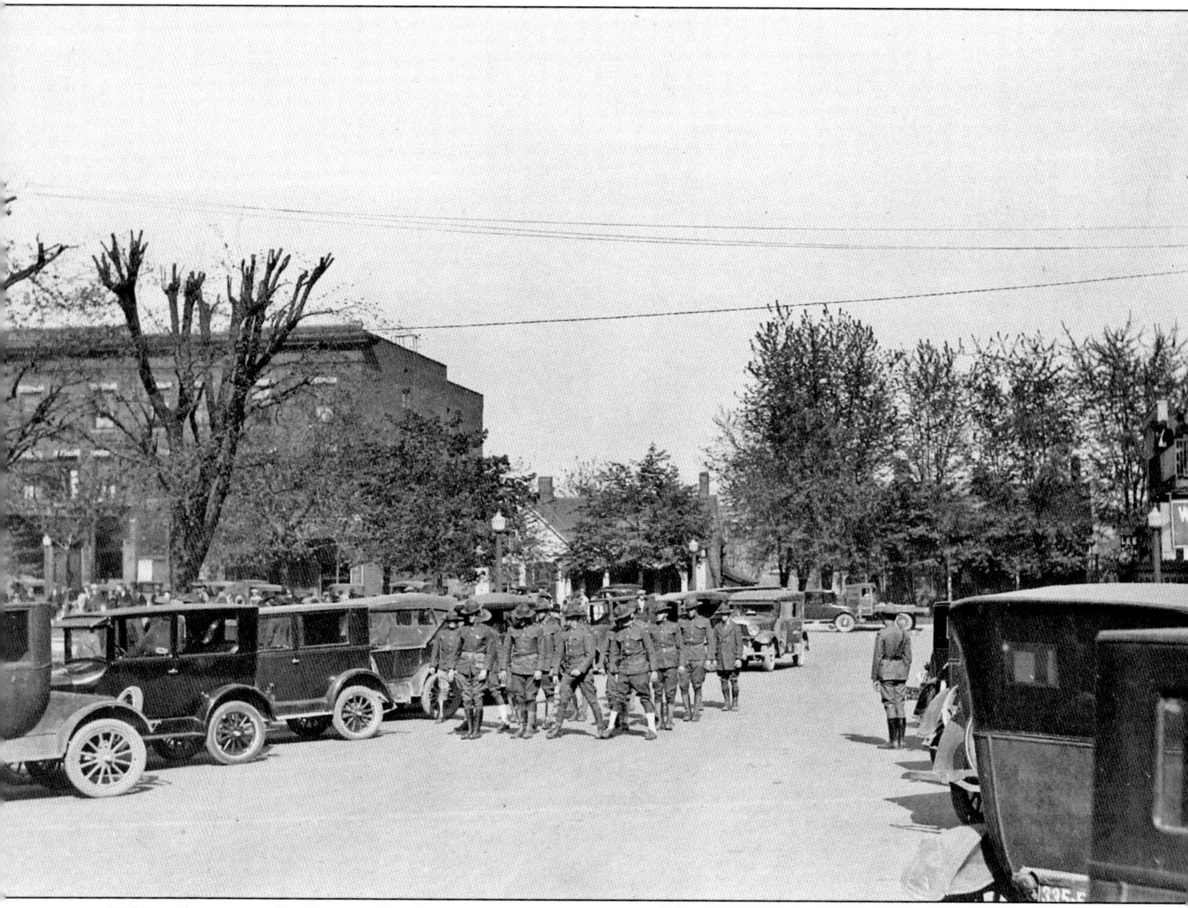

This photograph shows the local guard unit assembling on the court street for trial. The men were convicted of the crime. Afterwards, the guard escorted them to a train, and they were held in Eddyville State Penitentiary until the execution date. Most of the cars in the photograph are Ford automobiles. The buildings in the background on the east side of Union Street, from left to right, are Hotel Madison, the Basset home, and the home of the Plain sisters. The Bassett home is where Dr. Loman and Faull Trover had their first offices in Madisonville. The lot is vacant now between the clerk's office and the parking lot for city employees. (HSHC.)

Six

Black Coal and Rail

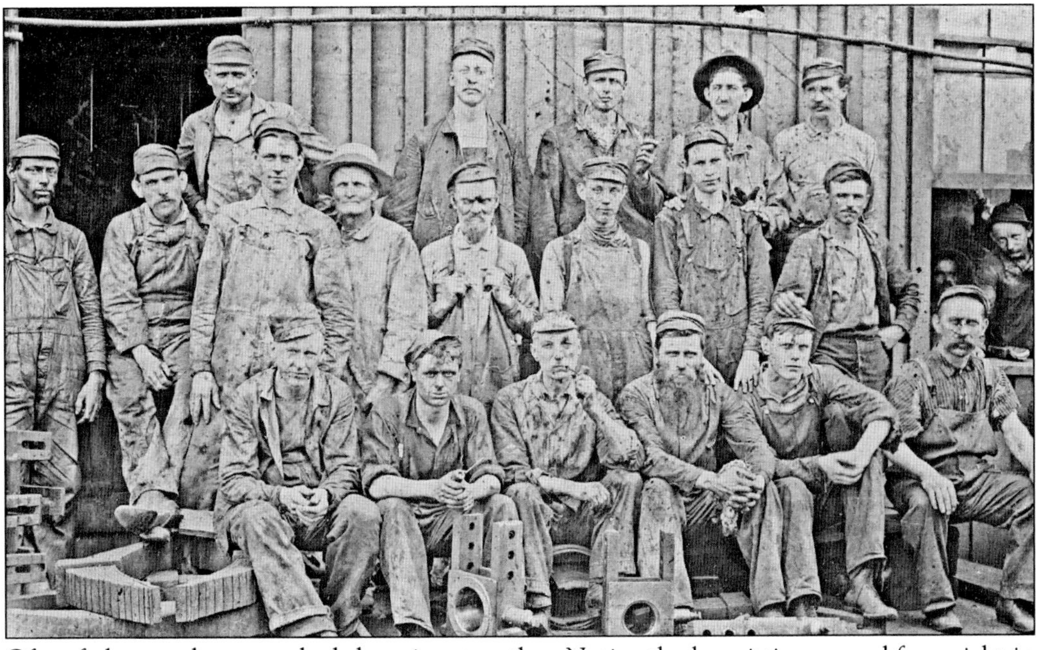

Often fathers and sons worked the mines together. Notice the boy sitting second from right in the first row of this photograph. The man behind him has his hand resting on the boy's head. By an act approved March 21, 1914, the Kentucky General Assembly repealed all previous acts relating to child labor and provided that no child under 14 could work in any business during school. (HSHC.)

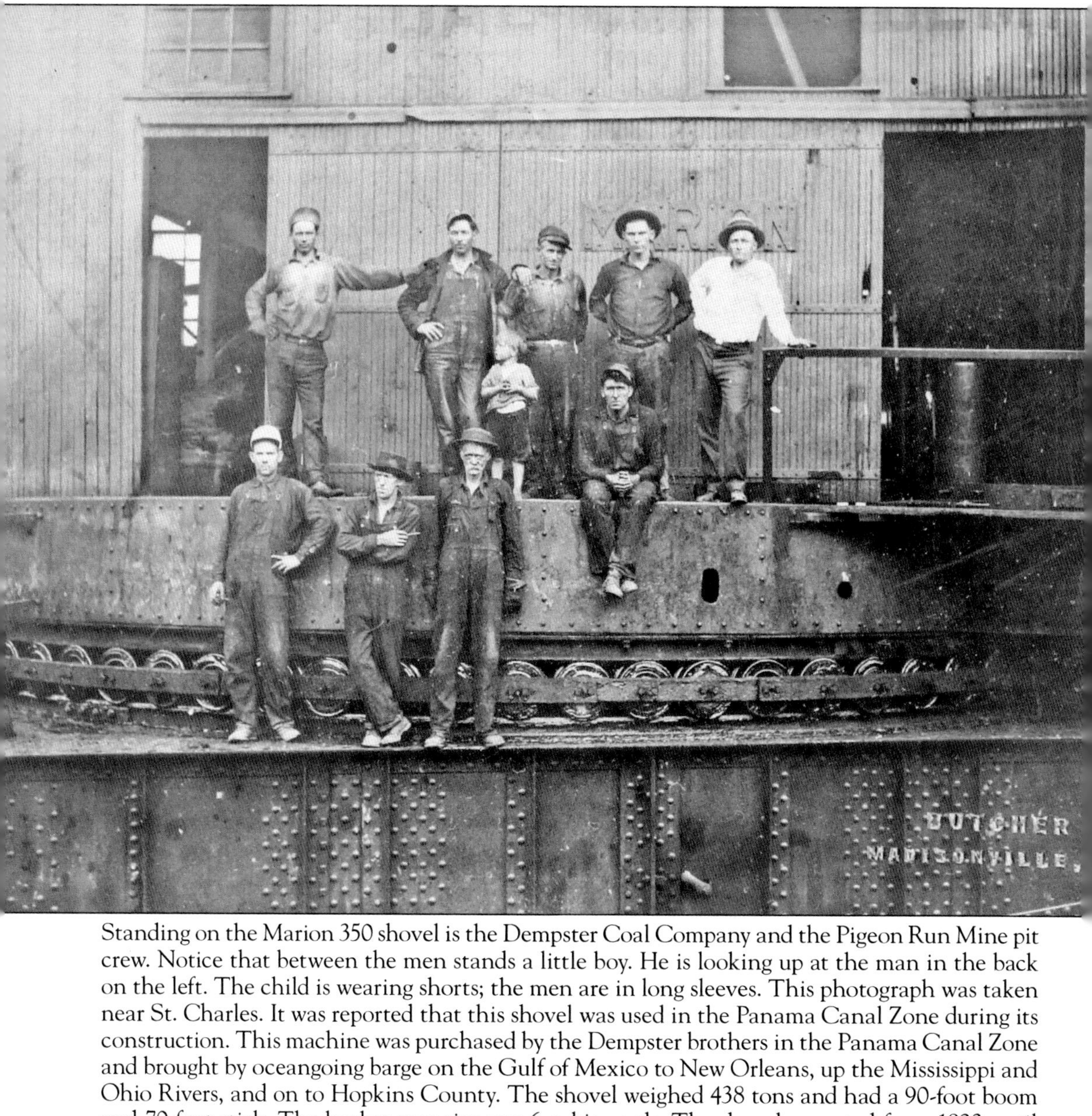

Standing on the Marion 350 shovel is the Dempster Coal Company and the Pigeon Run Mine pit crew. Notice that between the men stands a little boy. He is looking up at the man in the back on the left. The child is wearing shorts; the men are in long sleeves. This photograph was taken near St. Charles. It was reported that this shovel was used in the Panama Canal Zone during its construction. This machine was purchased by the Dempster brothers in the Panama Canal Zone and brought by oceangoing barge on the Gulf of Mexico to New Orleans, up the Mississippi and Ohio Rivers, and on to Hopkins County. The shovel weighed 438 tons and had a 90-foot boom and 70-foot stick. The bucket capacity was 6 cubic yards. The shovel operated from 1923 until the Depression hit around 1930. (J. Harold Utley.)

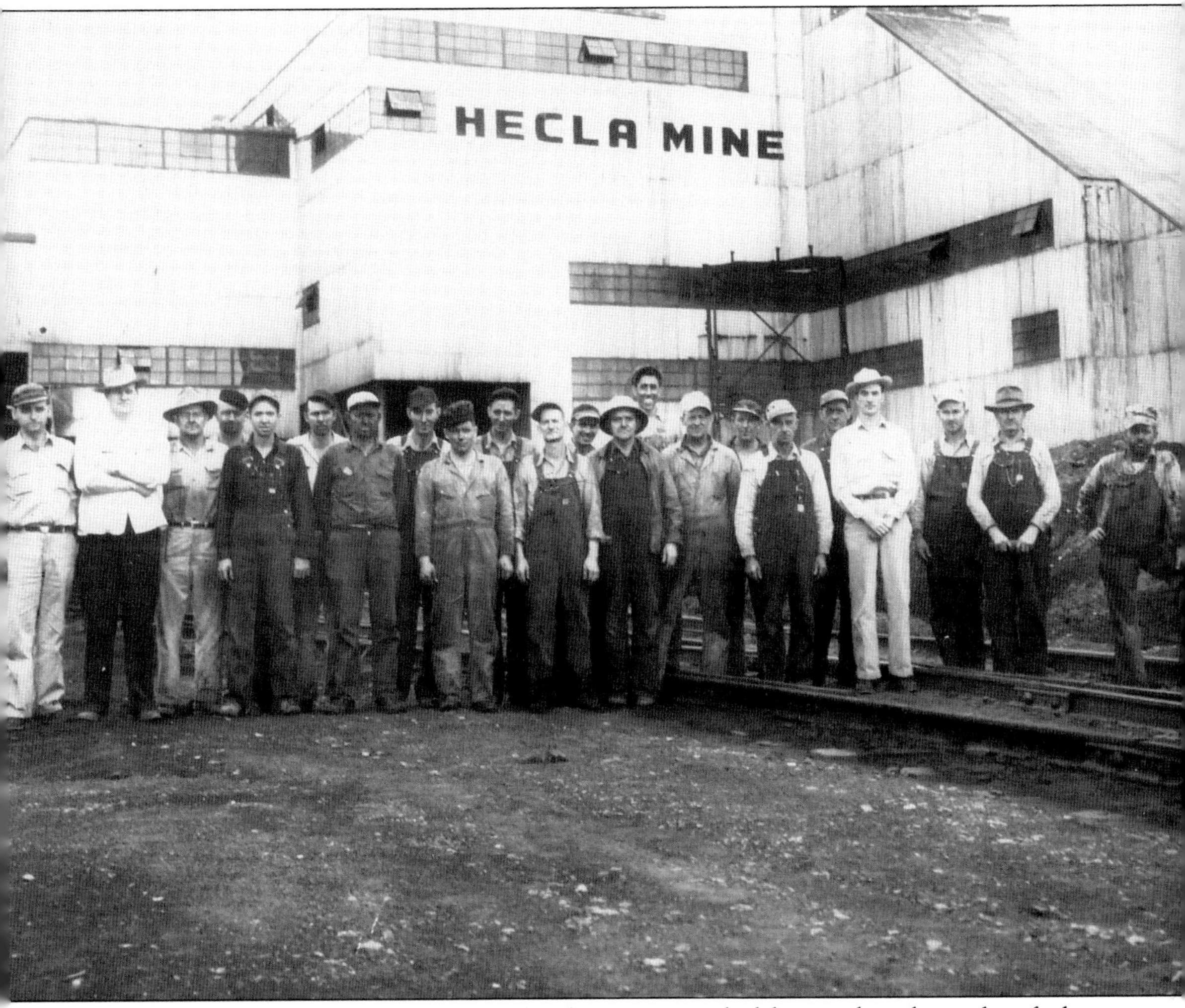

In this photograph of the Hecla Mine west of Earlington, several of the men have been identified. From left to right are (first row) Raymond Peyton, Russell Baggett Jr., Robert Brothers, two unidentified, M. T. Hicklin, Henry Todd, three unidentified, and Hugh "Bud" Cartwright; (second row) Marvin Newbold, unidentified, Henry Carter, J. T. Hamby, unidentified, J. D. Cartwright, three unidentified, Joe Martin, and Frank Key. The Hecla Mine of Badgett Mine Stripping Corporation was opened in 1944 on property of West Kentucky Coal Company. The coal was owned by the West Kentucky Coal Company and sold by the West Kentucky Coal Sales Agency. The mine operated for 10 years until the coal was all mined. After closing the mine, two draglines were walked over 16 miles across Hopkins County, loaded on a barge, and taken on water to the St. Lawrence Seaway Project. Rogers Badgett calculated that this method was cheaper than dismantling the machines, transporting them by truck, and reassembling at the site. (HSHC.)

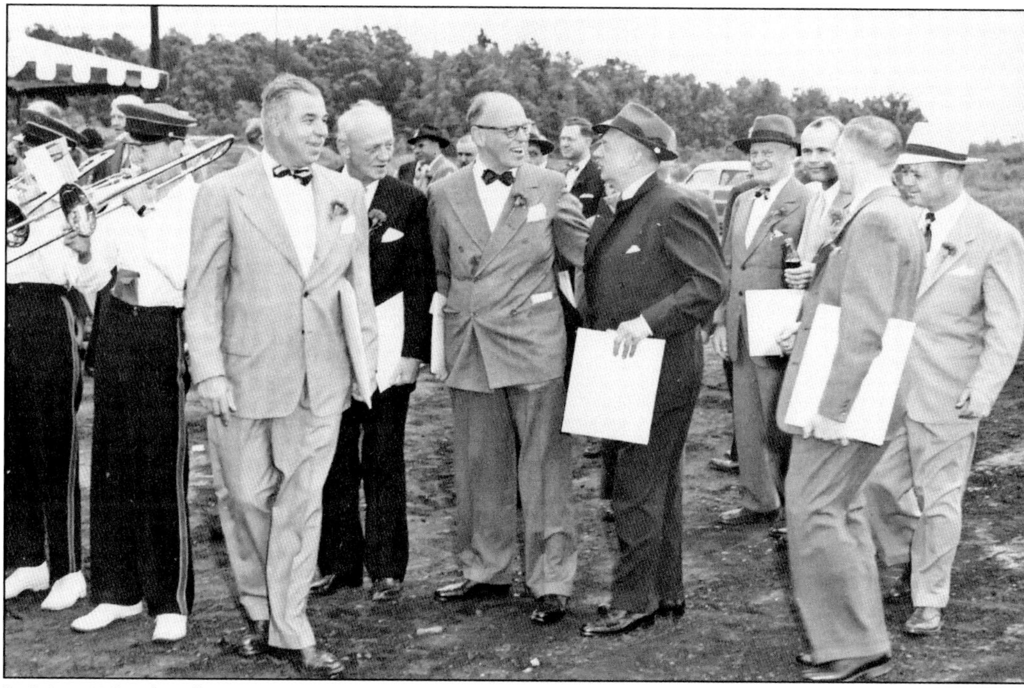

In May 1951, the Illinois Central Railroad held a celebration at the East Diamond Mine. The mine opened in 1946 and was owned by West Kentucky Coal Company. The original Diamond Mine was located in Mortons Gap. South Diamond was located southwest of Diamond Mine. North Diamond Mine was west of Earlington and Hecla. Interestingly, there was no West Diamond Mine. The lower photograph shows that, as a part of the celebration, the Madisonville High School marching band was invited. The band director, Dean Dowdy, is standing to the right of the band with his hand on his neck. Beside the railroad, company photographer George Land is taking photographs. (Both, HSHC.)

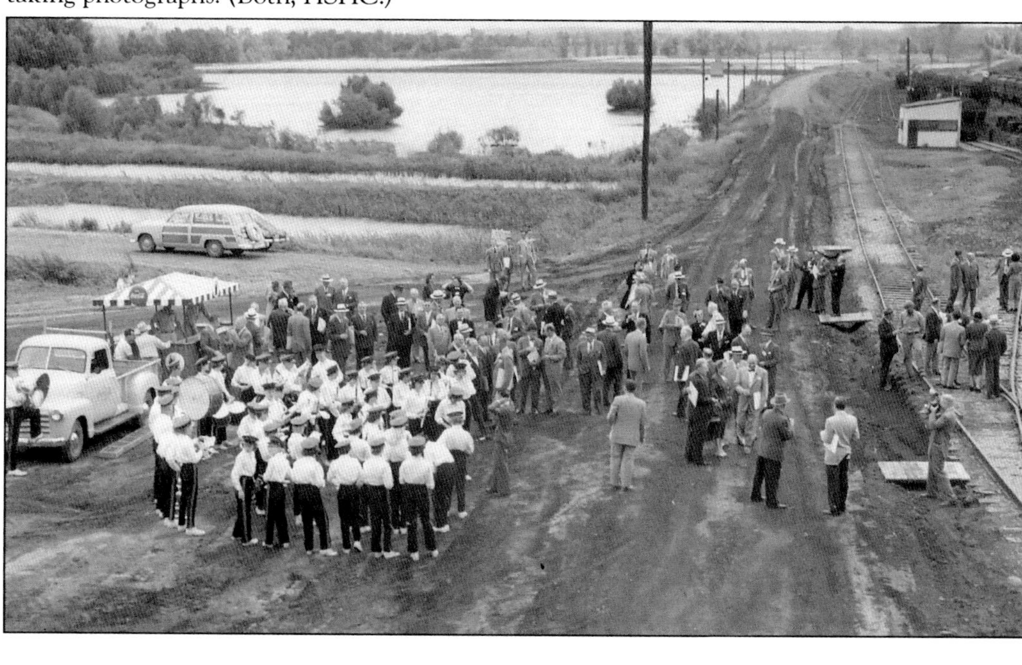

West Kentucky Coal Company was created in Union County in 1905. On May 1, 1924, the company purchased St. Bernard Mining Company in Earlington and moved its headquarters from Sturgis to Earlington. In 1946, the company bought the Inkerman Bailey house from L. E. Ruby, who lived there at the time. The company then moved its headquarters to Madisonville. In 1949, the company was sued under the Antitrust Act and forced to sell part of its assets by the federal government. The company sold off all of its holdings in western Webster and Union Counties. It retained the eastern Webster County and Hopkins County properties. The photograph to the right is Truman Smith, a supply truck driver. The below photograph is a man working underground in the Nisbet Mine using a Goodman Shortwall cutting machine. Nisbet Mine opened in 1913 and lasted until 1924. (Right, Ronnie Lewis; below, HSHC.)

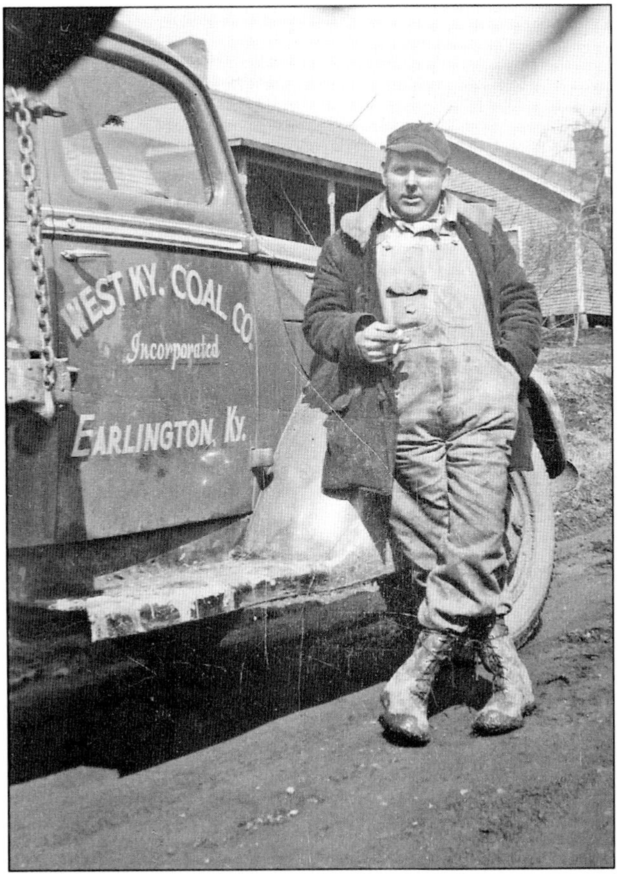

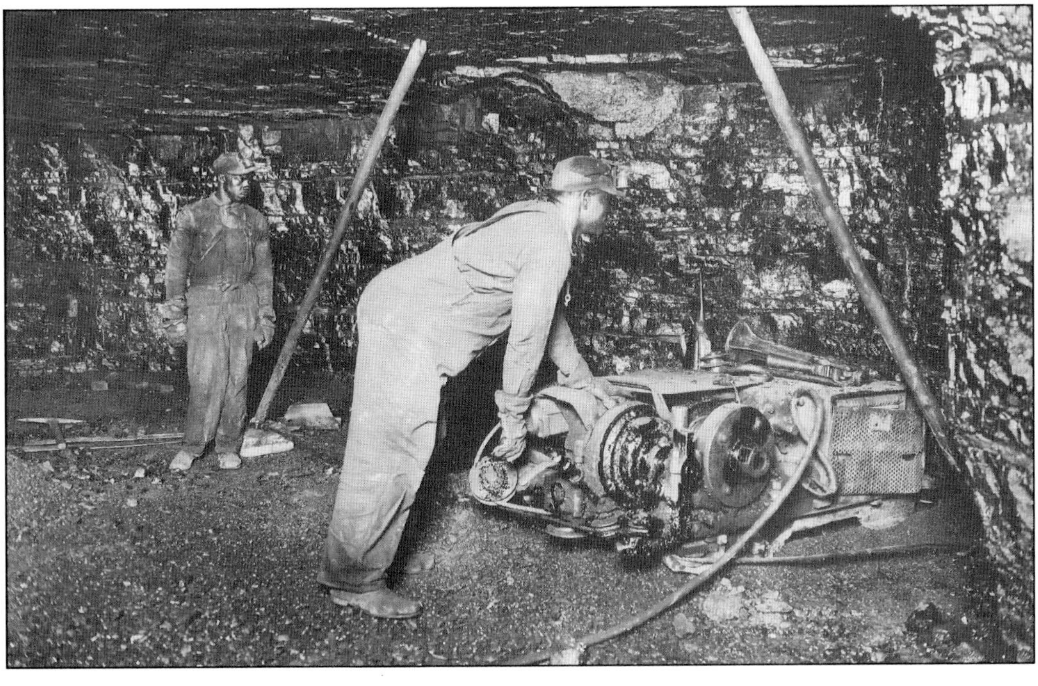

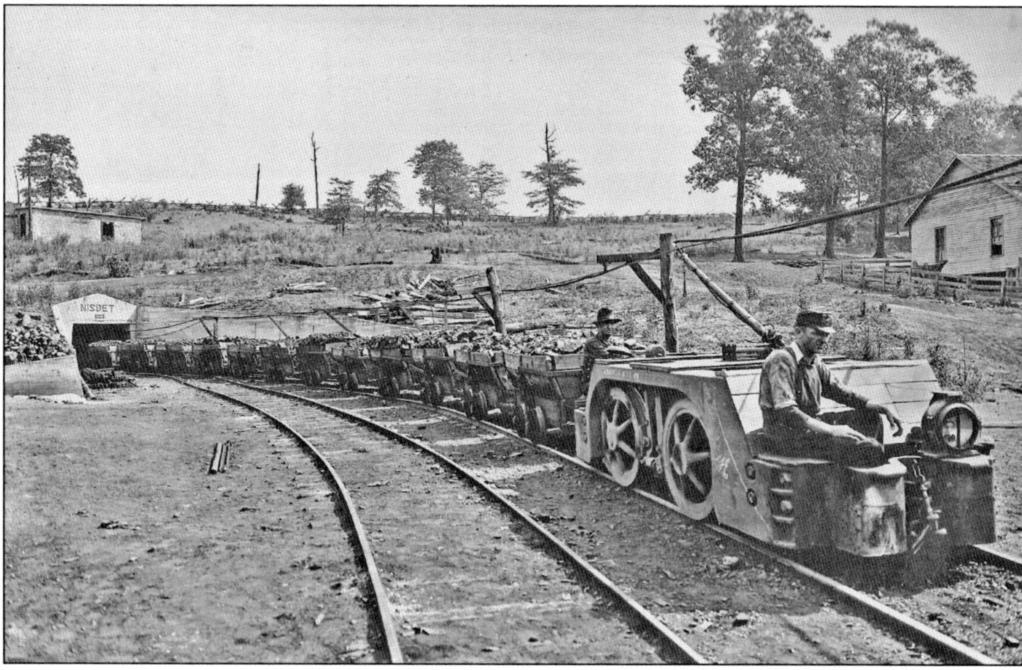

The Nisbet Mine mined the underground area of the Wesco Subdivision and the Country Club Golf Course. Motorists could see the locomotive pictured in the above photograph run across the ground outside and, when it got to "log town hill," go back underground, then come back out again next to the railroad in Earlington. The operator on the front is Elgie ("Tommy") Smith, (Spencer Brewer's grandfather); the man at the rear is Don Lamb. Below is another mining photograph of African American miners standing together. The round lunch buckets were typical miners' belongings. In the photograph, most of the men are wearing long-sleeve jackets. The man second from the end is the only one with short sleeves, and his pants have a large hole in them. (Both, HSHC.)

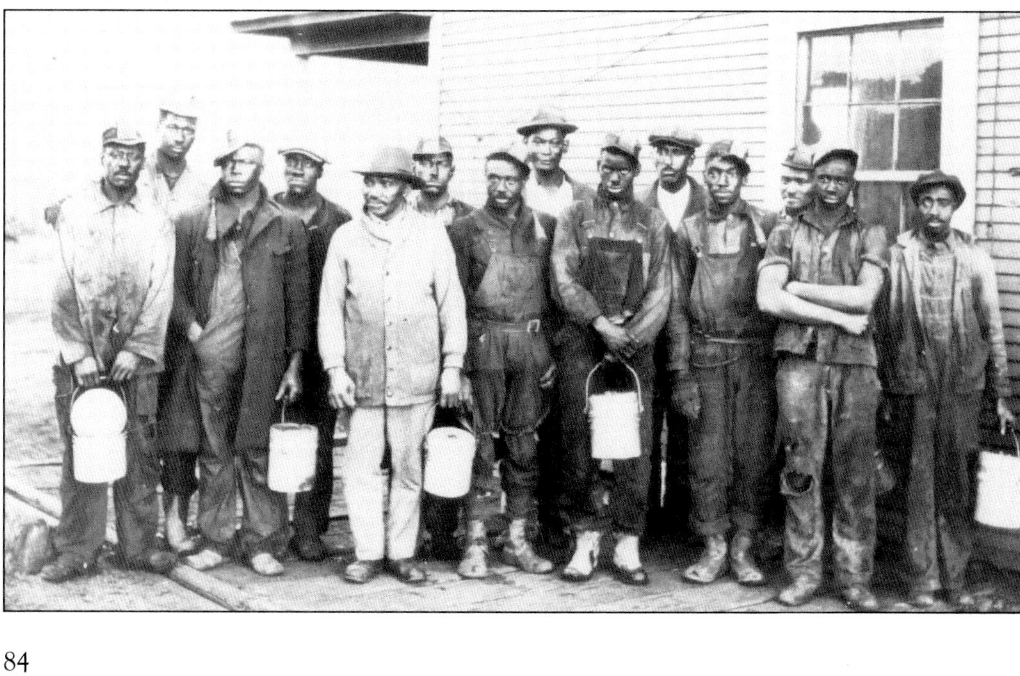

This photograph, taken by Falcon O. Fugate, shows of the Bucyrus 35 steam-powered loading shovel used to load coal into the dinky train. The track was laid from tipple to pit; there were no big trucks to haul the coal at the time, so they ran a train to the coal. The Bucyrus shovel loaded the coal to haul to the tipple. (J. Harold Utley.)

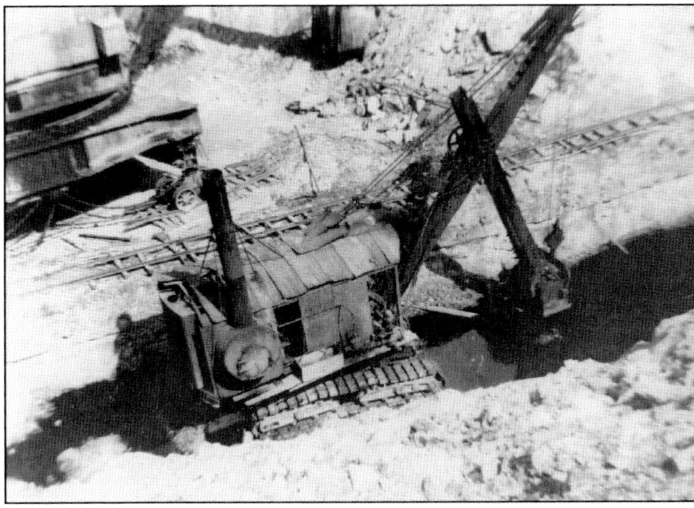

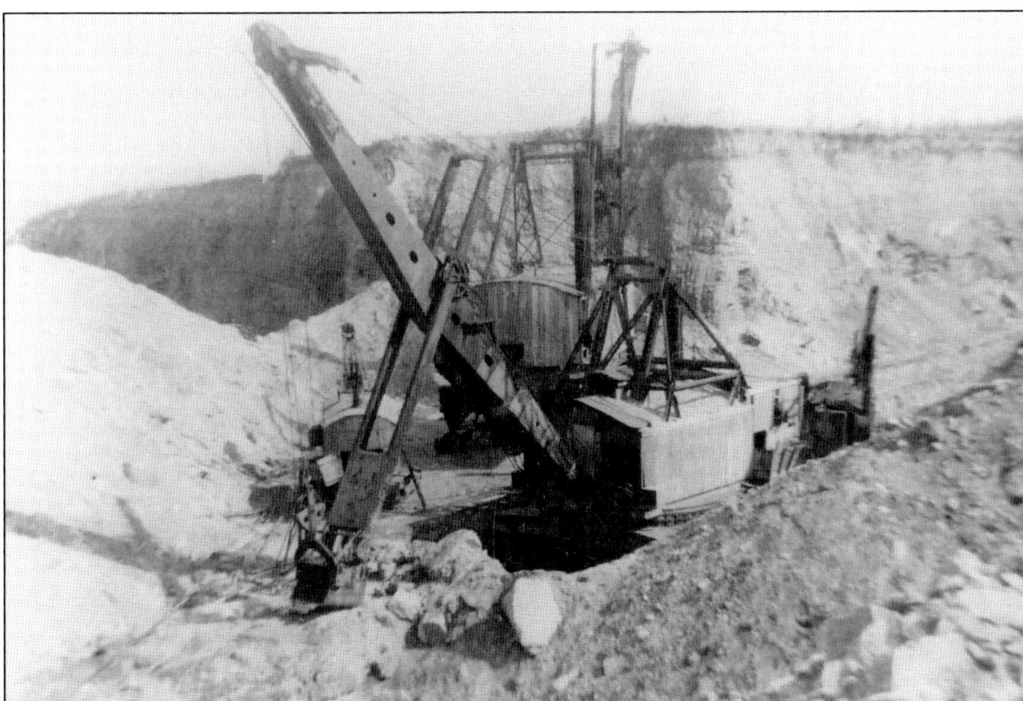

This is another photograph by Falcon O. Fugate taken about 1923 of the Bucyrus 225-B steam-powered, stripping shovel, used to remove overburden. Overburden is material over the coal seam. The material consists of dirt, clay, shale, sandstone, and limestone. Sterling Lanier, the owner of Norton Coal Company, wrote in the Nortonville Centennial booklet that $2 million worth of equipment was sold to the Japanese government for $20,000 and probably became part of bombs dropped on the United States later in World War II. (J. Harold Utley).

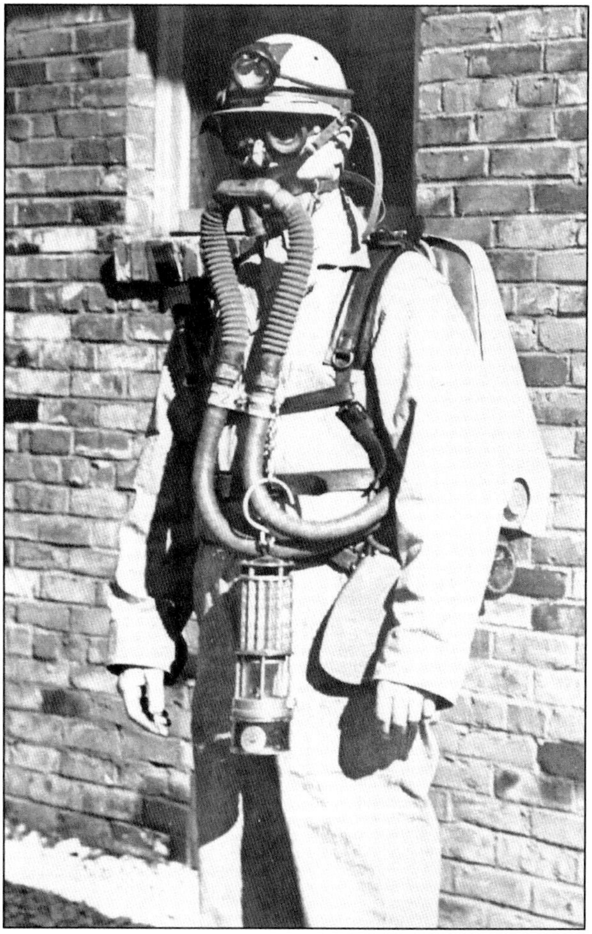

Mine rescue team members are trained and equipped to rescue miners in case of fire, explosion, or a cave-in. The teams are trained to protect themselves while exploring the mine to locate missing miners. They are trained to administer first aid while rescuing the trapped miners. The training of mine rescue and first aid teams began after the creation of the U.S. Bureau of Mines in 1910. Annual contests of teams have been held in Western Kentucky since 1936. These photographs show rescue team members in their rescue gear. (Both, HSHC.)

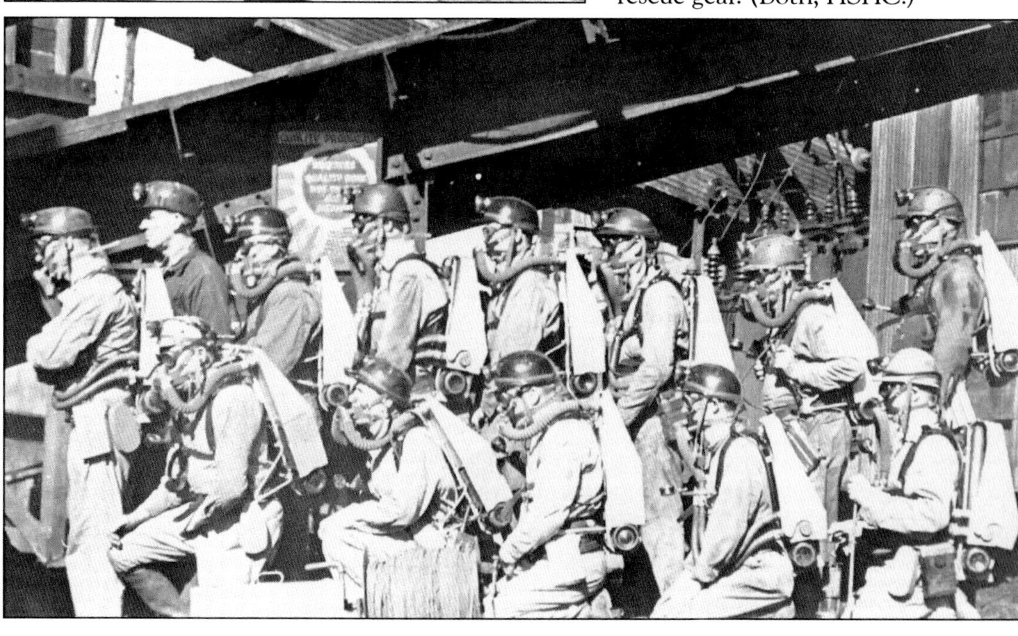

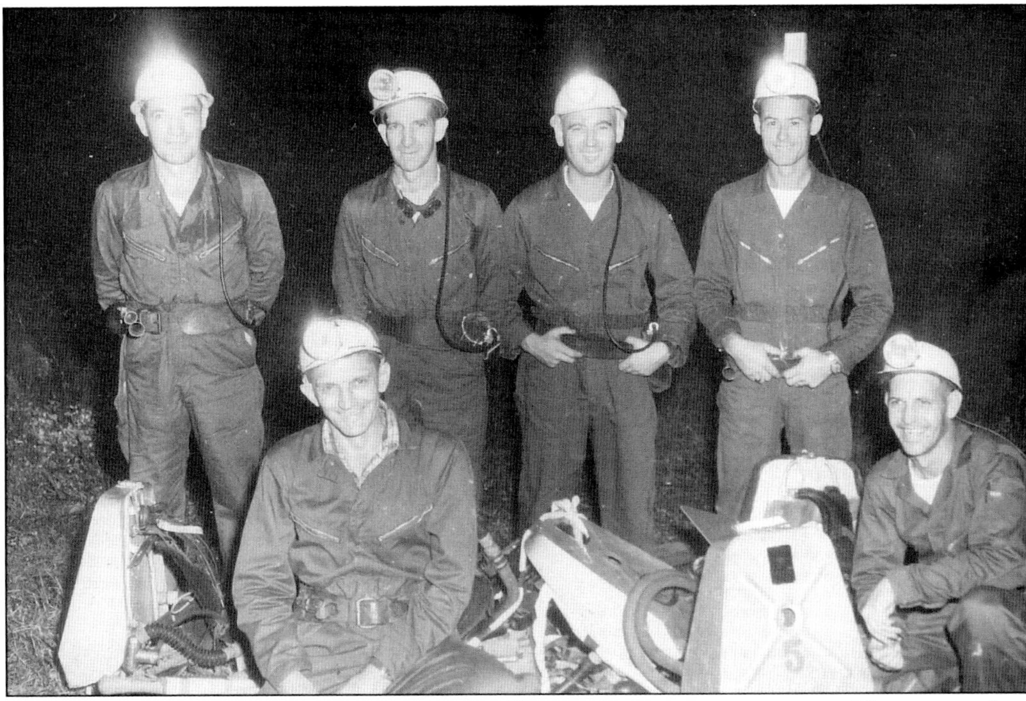

The 1962 Champion Mine Rescue Team proudly won the rescue competition. The team is from Pleasant View Mine, West Kentucky Coal Company. The contest gives the teams experience in rescue and demonstrates the skills they have learned. The third man from left in the back row is Bobby Clark; the next man to the right is James "Bud" Reynolds. (HSHC.)

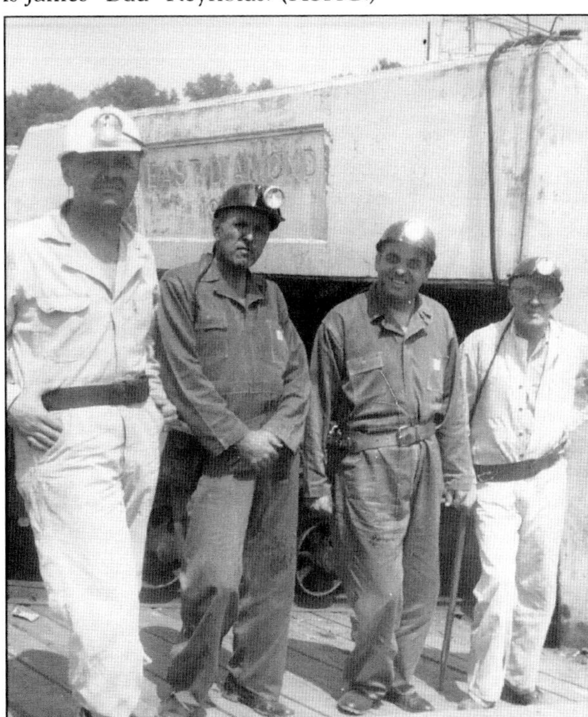

In August 1960, a representative from the Department of Revenue from Frankfort, Kentucky, visited the East Diamond Mine. This photograph was taken at the mine, located 2 miles east of Madisonville. From left to right are Bob Welch (director of purchasing), Mark Eastin Jr. (president), William Scent (Department of Revenue), and Moss Patterson (general manager). (Mark Eastin Collection, HSHC.)

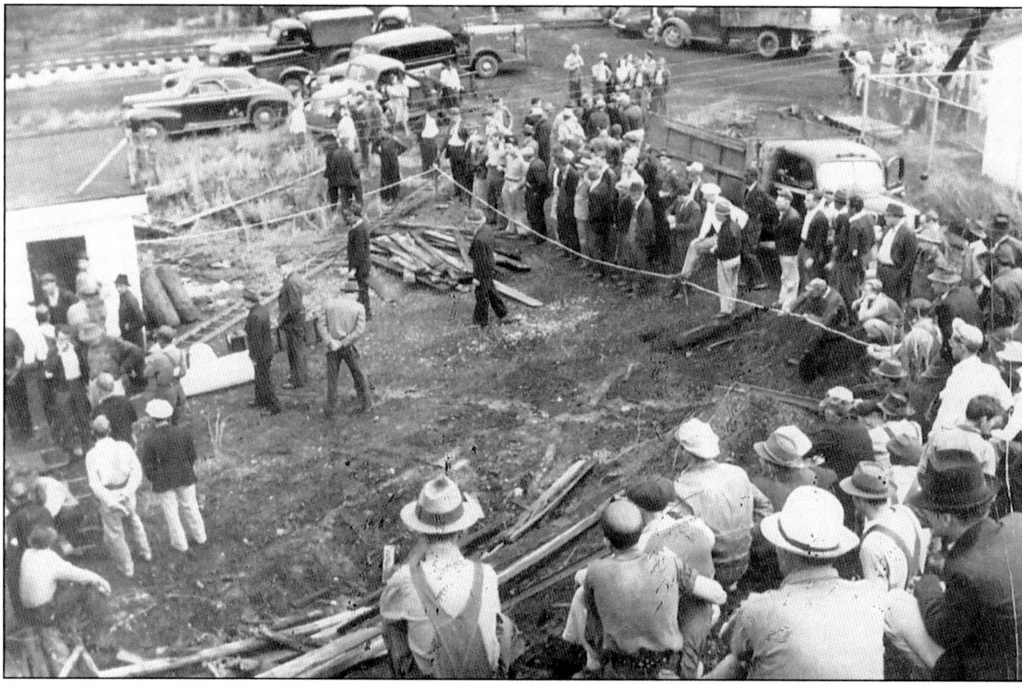

An explosion at the Daniel Boone Mine, owned by the Sterling Coal Company, occurred on October 27, 1941. This distraught crowd gathered at the mine after the report of the explosion. There were men who escaped through the intake air course, but 15 men were killed in the disaster. (James M. Hicks.)

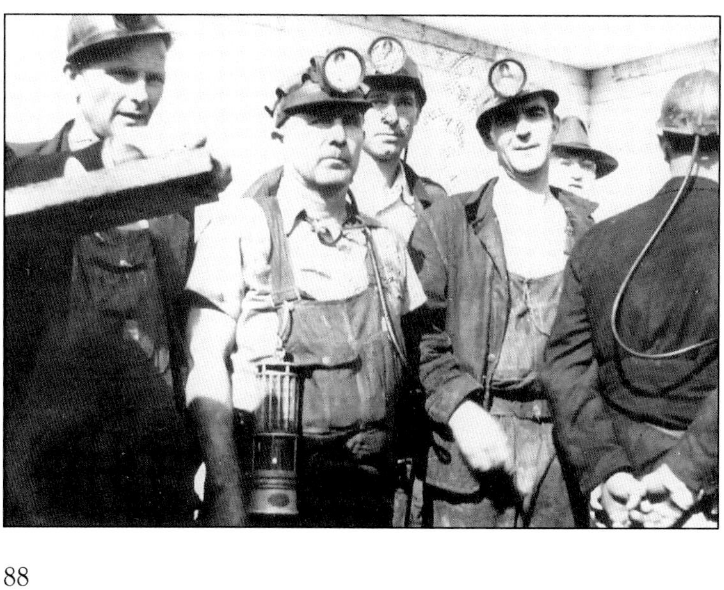

Members of the first rescue team attempting to recover the victims' bodies were captured in this somber photograph. Rescue team members from left to right are Felix Cook, Willie Welch, Lawrence Shelton, James Ashby, A. H. Kelly, and McKinley Hicks. A. H. Kelly later became a Madisonville postmaster. (James M. Hicks.)

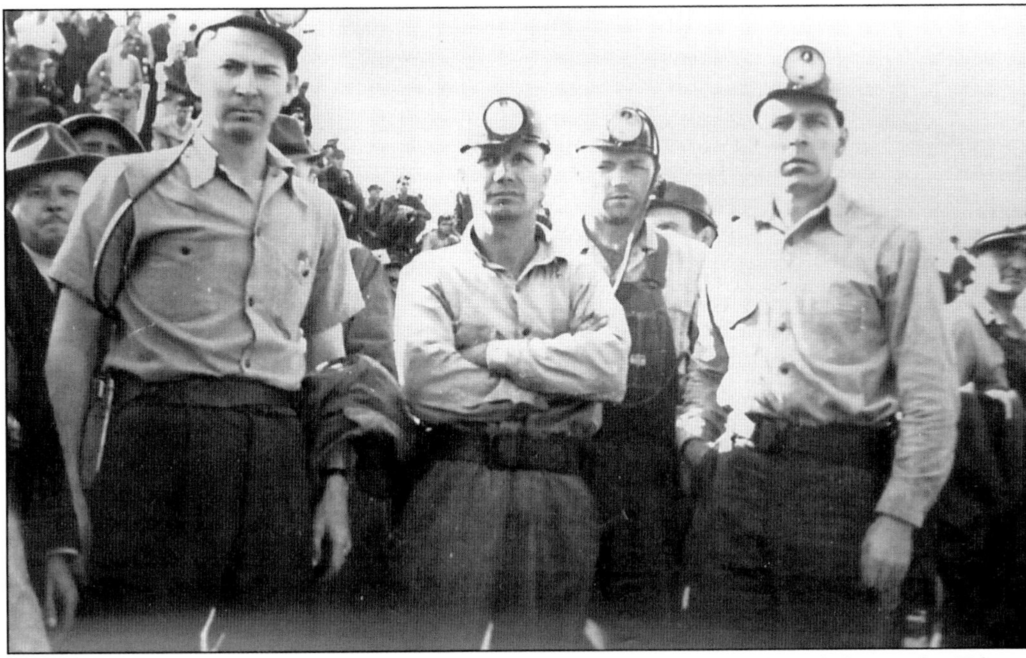

A second rescue team worked to recover bodies. The team included, from left to right, Edward Ford, George Stinnett, Leonard Bateman, and Willie Todd. There were three miners at the bottom of the airshaft building steps. The men could not escape until the fire department attached three ladders together in order to reach the bottom of the shaft. (James M. Hicks.)

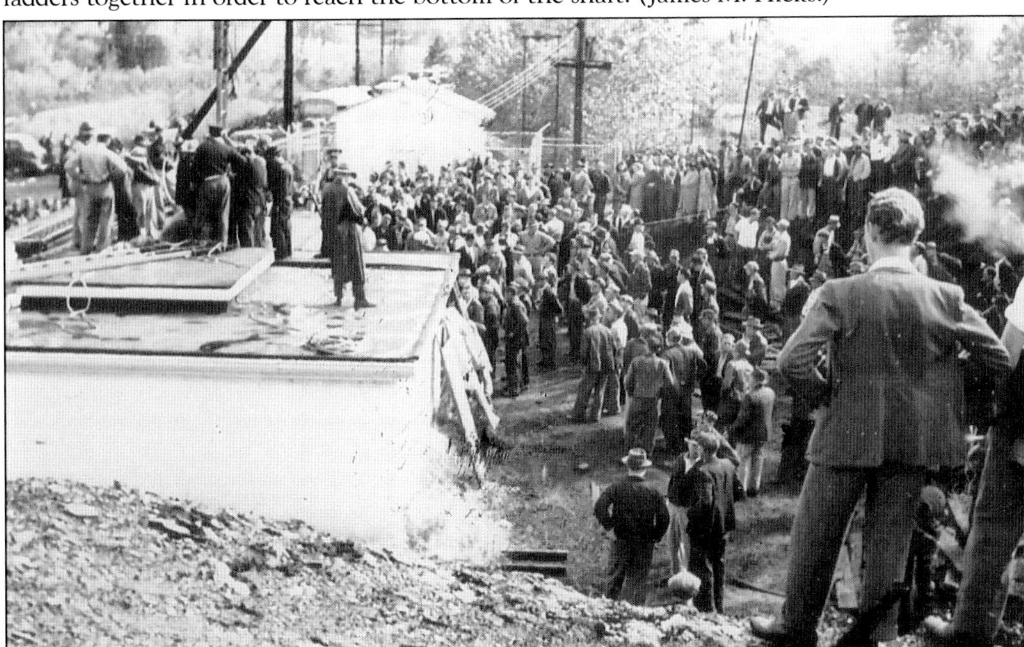

The crowd continues to gather outside of the Daniel Boone explosion site. The explosion occurred from ignition of methane by an open flame. Two ladders can be seen in the photograph. The platform to the left where the men are gathered has a ladder standing with ropes hanging from it, and one ladder is on the ground. (James M. Hicks.)

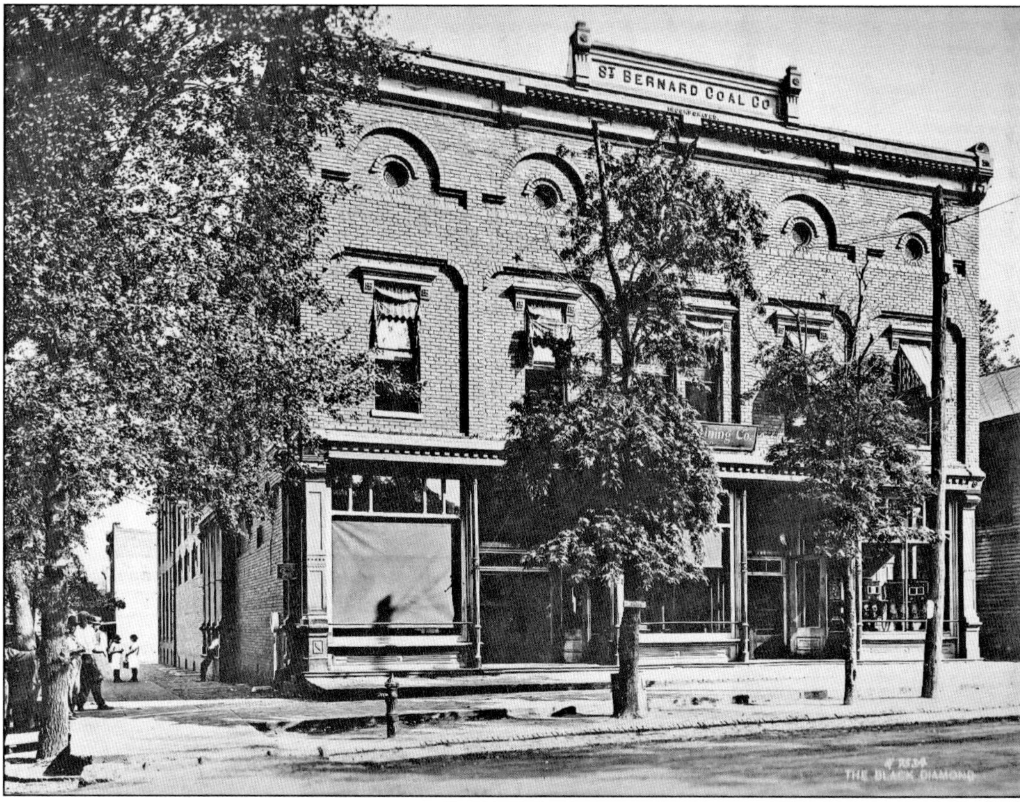

The St. Bernard Coal Company home office and store in Earlington, shown here, started in 1870. John Bond Atkinson declared the company would never be unionized. When it became apparent that it would have to deal with the union, the name was changed to St. Bernard Mining Company in 1901. Therefore, St. Bernard Coal Company was never unionized. (HSHC.)

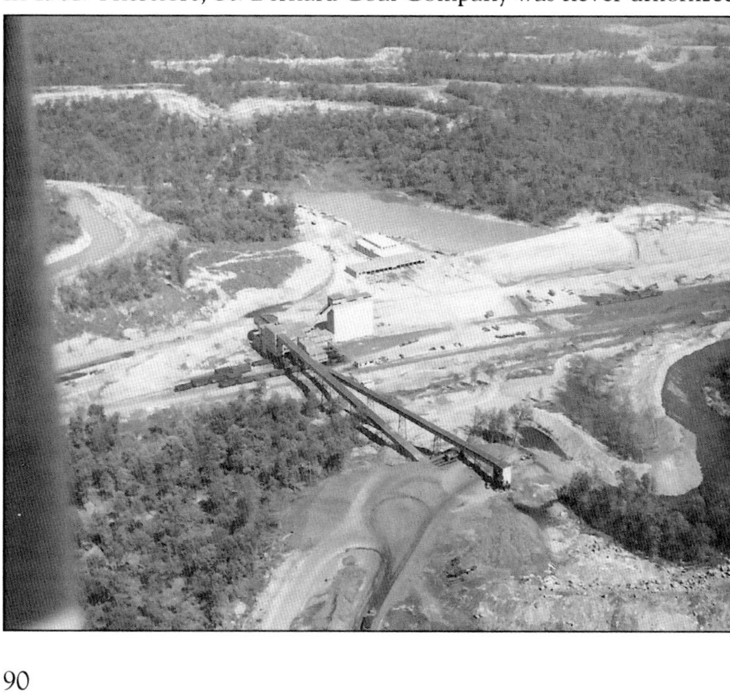

Homestead Coal Company, a subsidiary of Sentry Royalty Company, opened in 1946. The mine mined coal owned by the West Kentucky Coal Company. The coal produced was sold by the West Kentucky Coal Sales agency. Sentry Royalty merged with Peabody Coal Company in 1955 and continued in operation until 1959. When the mine closed, the equipment was moved to White City. (HSHC.)

A winter wonderland view of the Pleasant View Mine of West Kentucky Coal reveals a beautiful inconvenience. The tank ruptured, the water froze as quickly as it came out. The water tank held water used for the coal washing preparation plant, the bathhouse, and the surface bathroom. The height of the tower was needed for the pressure for the bathhouse. (HSHC.)

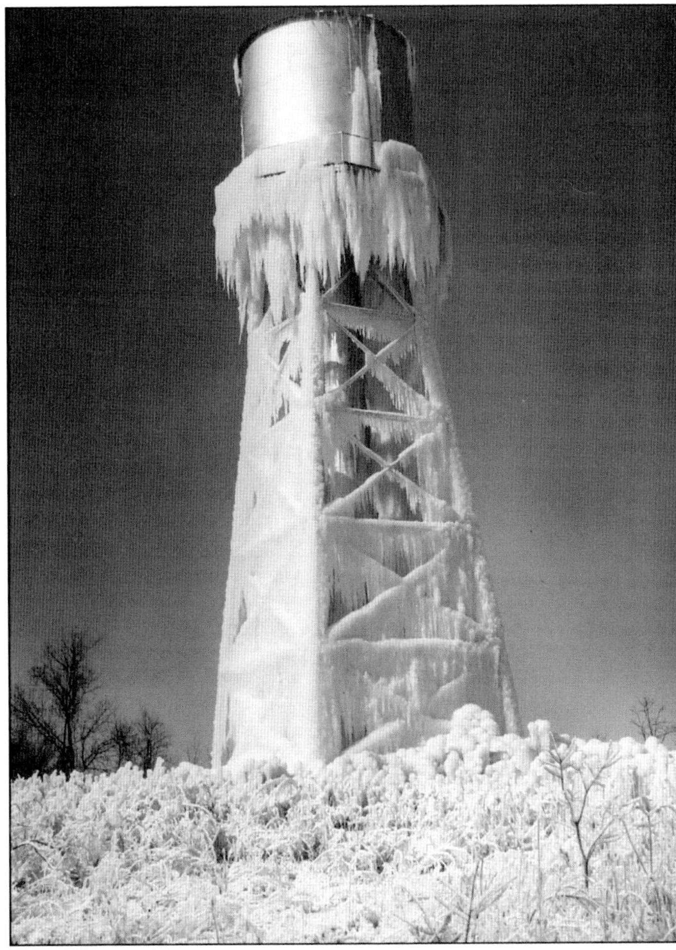

When the union attempted to organize the Dawson Daylight Coal Company in 1933, violence broke out, and an upset picketer fired shots through the windshield of the 1929 Ford roadster in the photograph when non-union workers tried to get to the mine to work. The car has a Caldwell County license plate on it. (HSHC.)

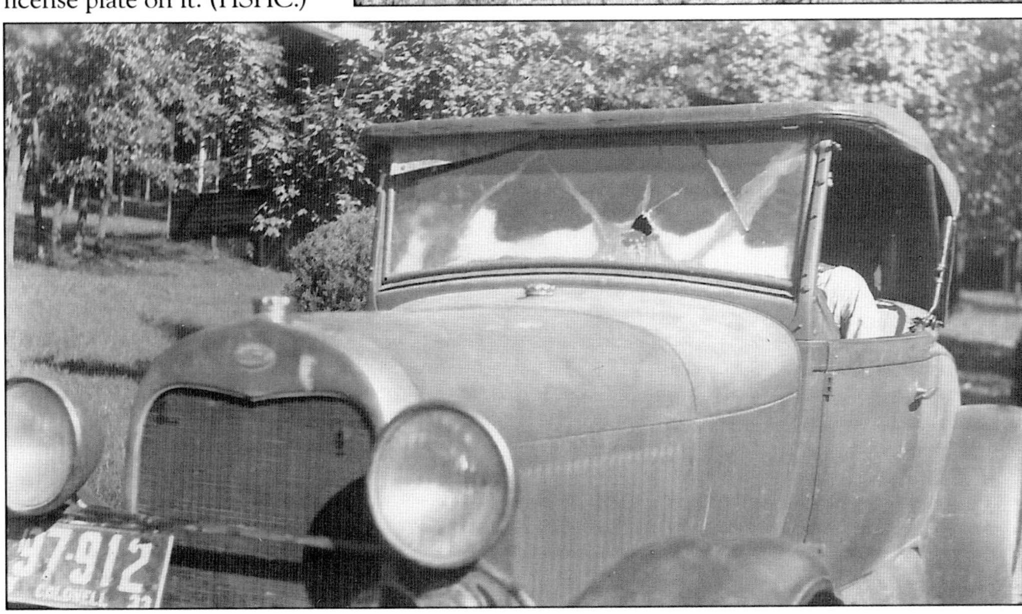

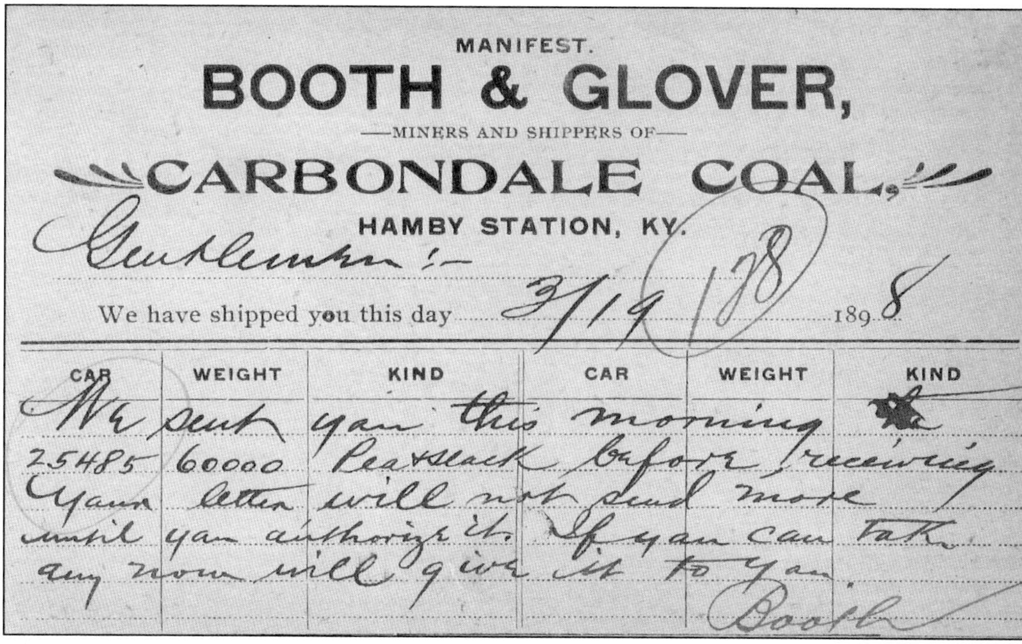

MANIFEST.

BOOTH & GLOVER,

—MINERS AND SHIPPERS OF—

CARBONDALE COAL,

HAMBY STATION, KY.

Gentlemen:—

We have shipped you this day 3/19/98 1898

CAR	WEIGHT	KIND	CAR	WEIGHT	KIND

We sent you this morning
25485 60000 Pea & slack before receiving
your letter will not send more
until you authorize it. If you can take
any now will give it to you.
Booth

This is a copy of the shipping ticket for a railroad carload of coal shipped by Booth and Glover from the Carbondale (Ilsley) area. The ticket shows 60,000 pounds (30 tons) of coal being shipped. Apparently Booth and Glover was a coal sales agency that had sold the coal for a mine operating at Carbondale. Hamby Station was located on the Illinois Central line that ran from Elizabethtown to Paducah. On back of the Booth and Glover ticket is the notation that "30 tons is all you can get in a railroad car." (WPM.)

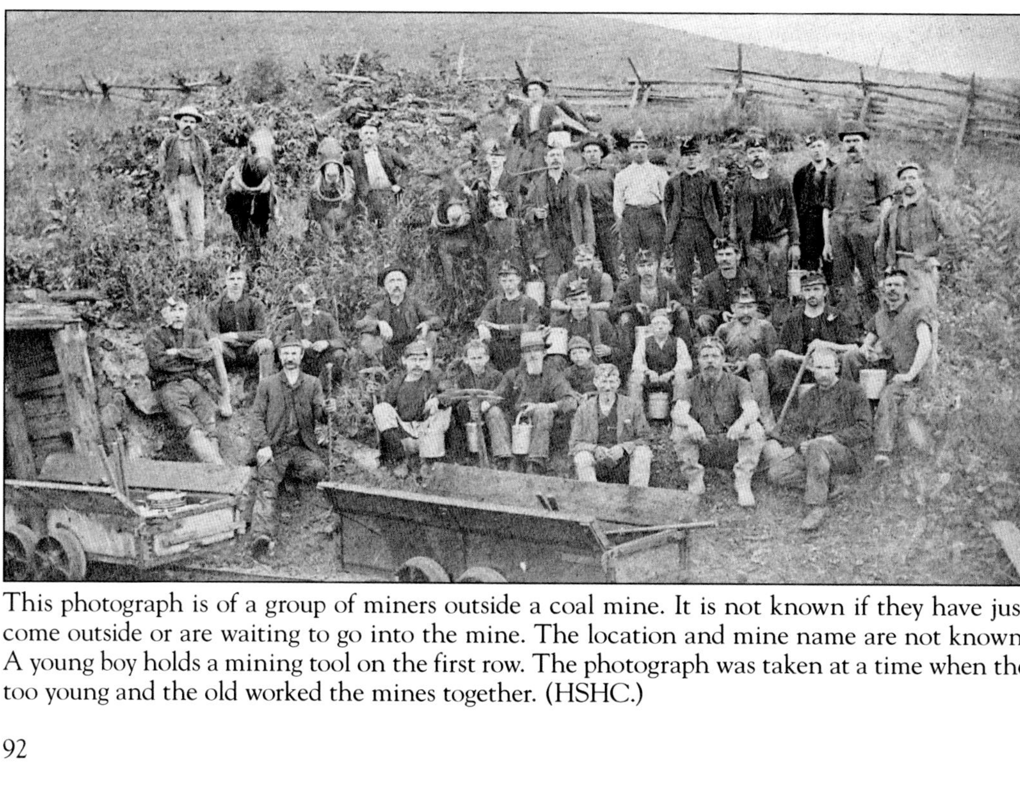

This photograph is of a group of miners outside a coal mine. It is not known if they have just come outside or are waiting to go into the mine. The location and mine name are not known. A young boy holds a mining tool on the first row. The photograph was taken at a time when the too young and the old worked the mines together. (HSHC.)

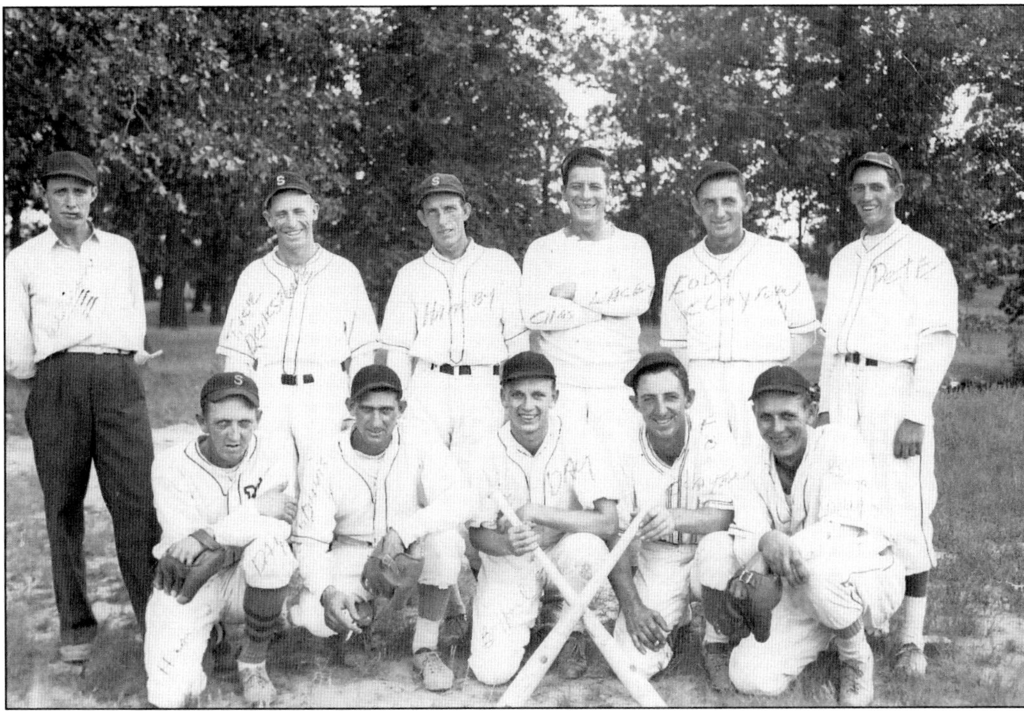

The coal companies each had their own baseball teams. Shown here is the Sentry baseball team made up of coal miners. Floyd Allison was the manager. From left to right are (first row) Homer Day, ? Davis, Bufford Day, F. Clayor, and Burt Day; (second row) Wilson, T. Dearstone, ? Hamby, Charles Lacy, Cody Clayton, and Pete ?. (Roy Day.)

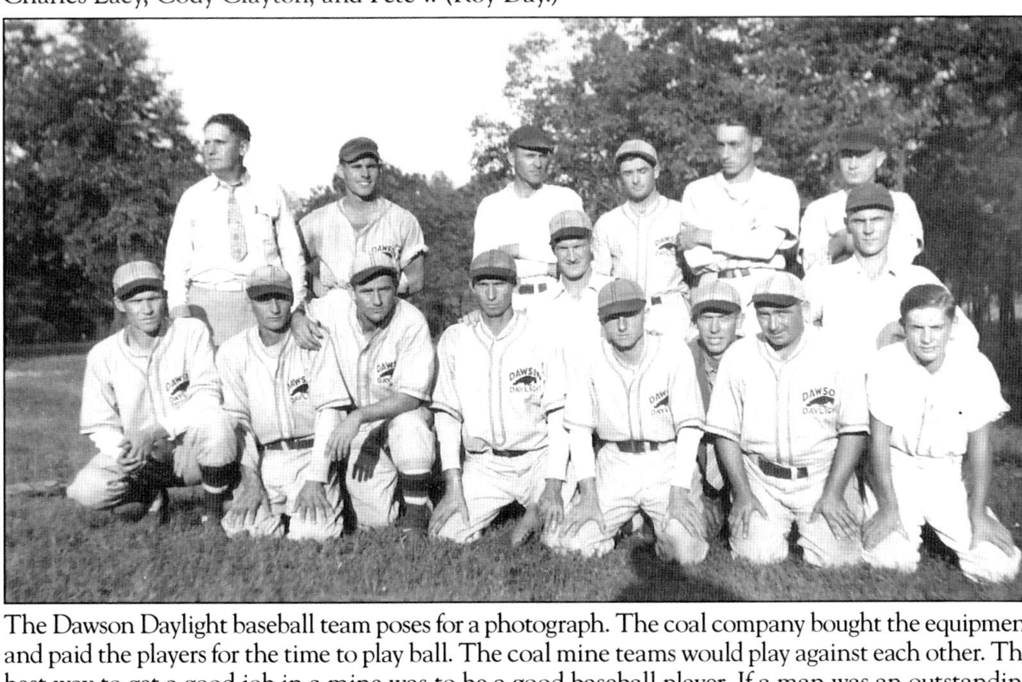

The Dawson Daylight baseball team poses for a photograph. The coal company bought the equipment and paid the players for the time to play ball. The coal mine teams would play against each other. The best way to get a good job in a mine was to be a good baseball player. If a man was an outstanding baseball player, he could get any coal mine job he wanted in the 1920s–1940s. (HSHC.)

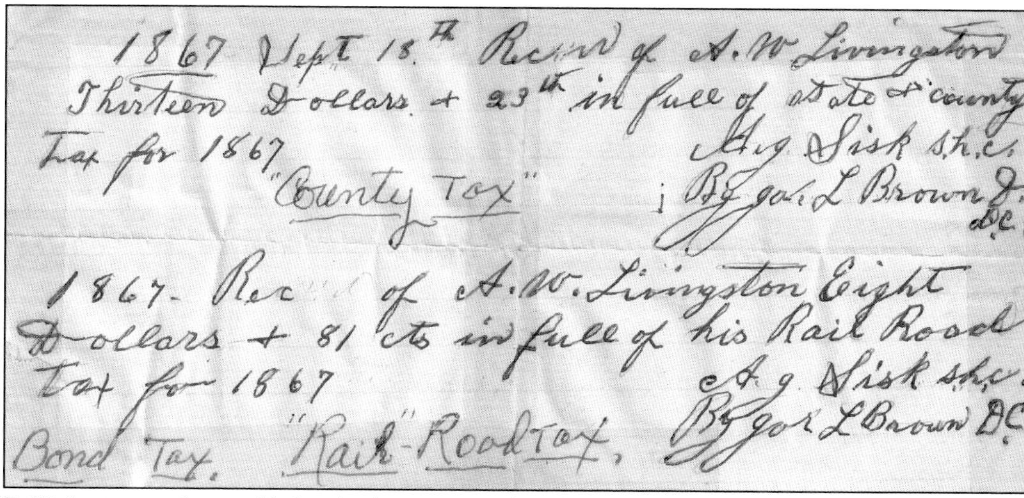

1867 Sept 18th Rec'd of A. W. Livingston
Thirteen Dollars + 23cts in full of state & county
Tax for 1867 A. G. Sisk sh.c.
"County Tax" By Jos L Brown D.C.

1867- Rec'd of A. W. Livingston Eight
Dollars + 81 cts in full of his Rail Road
Tax for 1867 A. G. Sisk sh.c.
Bond Tax. "Rail"-Road Tax. By Jos L Brown DC

F. W. Livingston's grandfather had to pay a railroad tax in 1867. This photograph is a copy of the receipt given to Arthur Wilson Livingston when he paid his county and railroad taxes. The railroad was not built into Hanson until 1869, so taxes were being paid two years before they ever saw the railroad. (F. W. Livingston.)

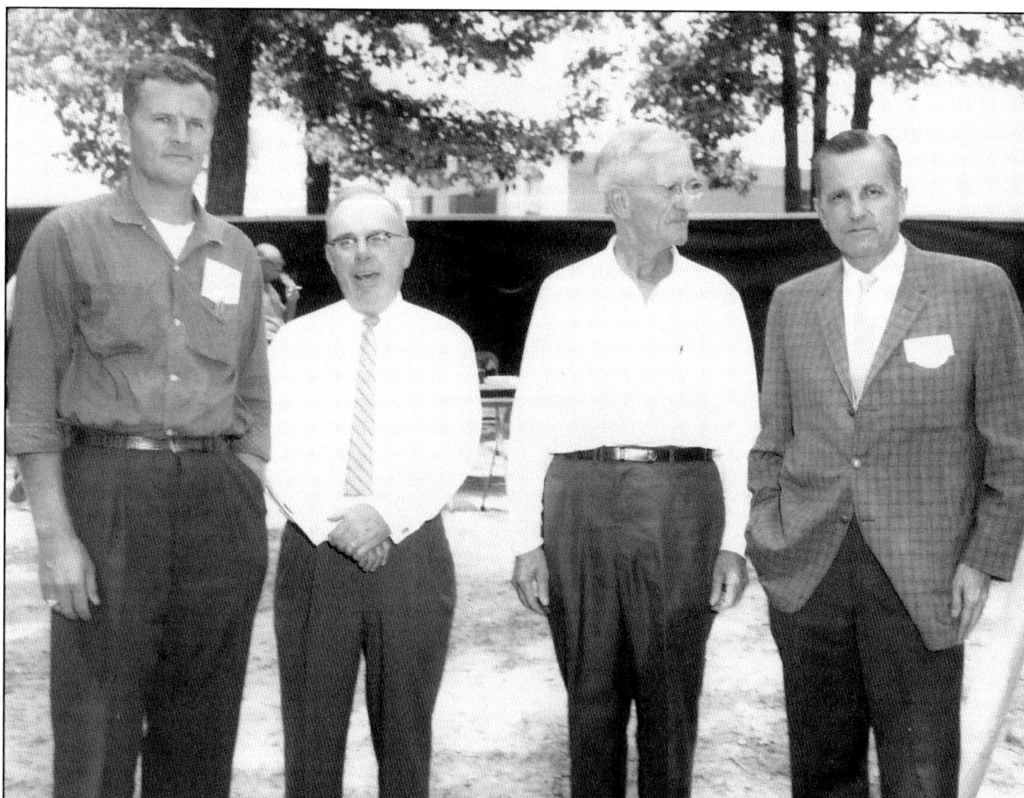

The railroads and coal companies depended on each other for business. The Illinois Central Railroad company picnic was held annually from 1946 to the 1960s for mine operators and employees. This 1960 photograph was taken at a picnic. From left to right are Russell "Rusty" Badgett Jr., Marshall Hicks, Russell "Cap" Badgett Sr., and Mark Eastin. (Mark Eastin Collection, HSHC.)

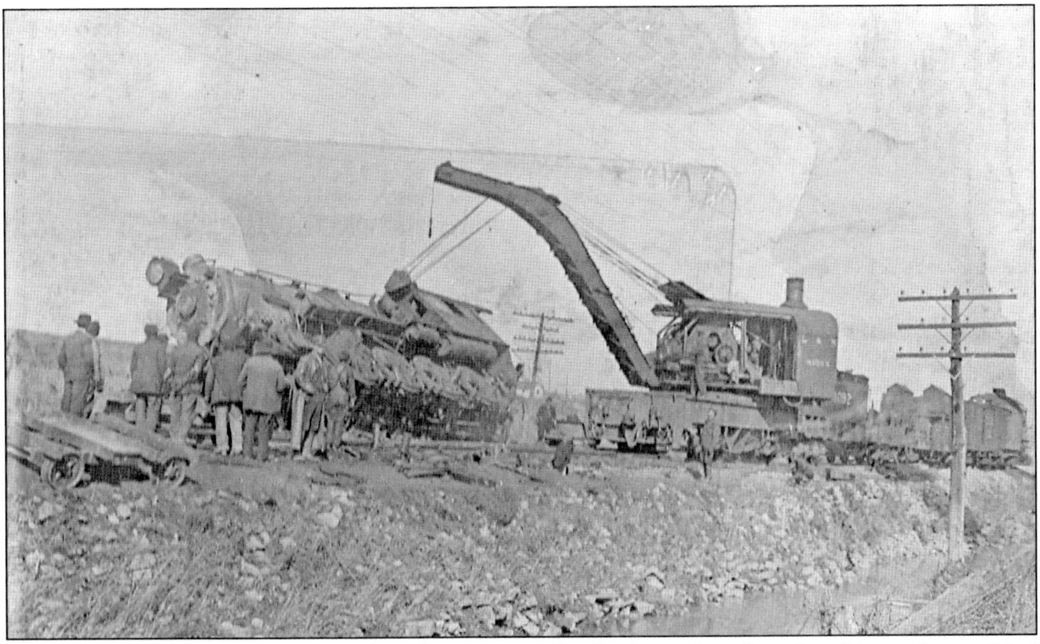

In the early 20th century, the railroad's access to the high grades of coal in Kentucky enabled the Louisville and Nashville Railroad Company (L&N) to make the nation's longest non-stop trip, about 500 miles from Louisville to Montgomery, Alabama, without refueling. These two old undated photographs show the L&N Railroad Company equipment used to build and repair the railroads. Above, a crane is being used to re-rail an overturned locomotive. There was a train wreck on the main line between Madisonville and Henderson. Below, an engine is used to pull the work train to the needed location. (Both, HSHC.)

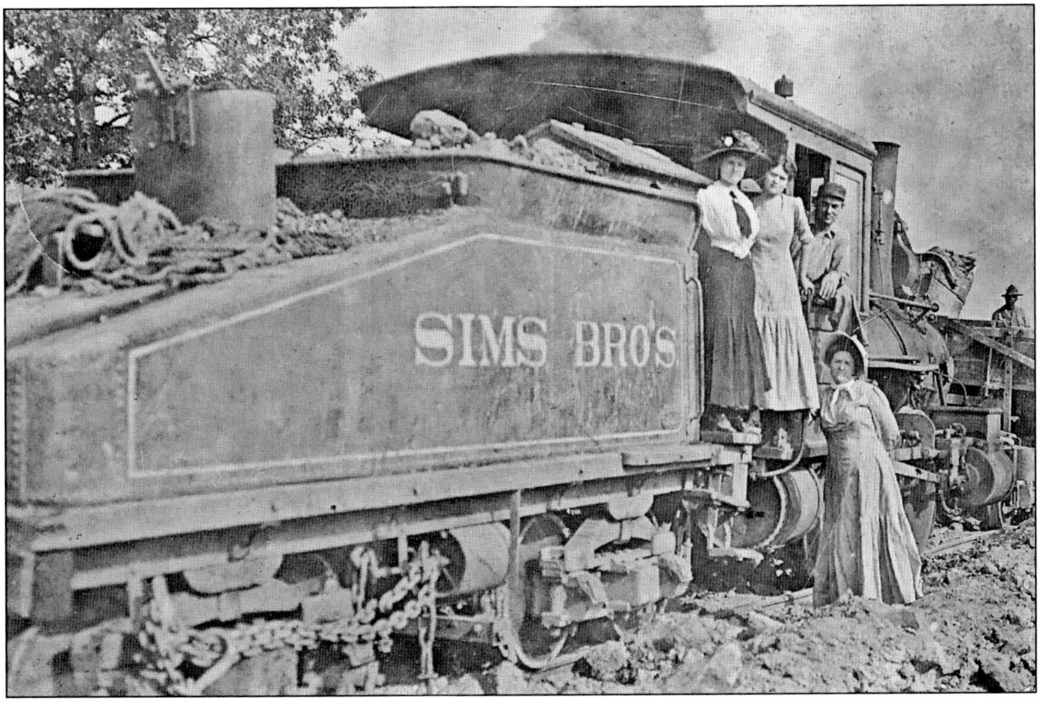

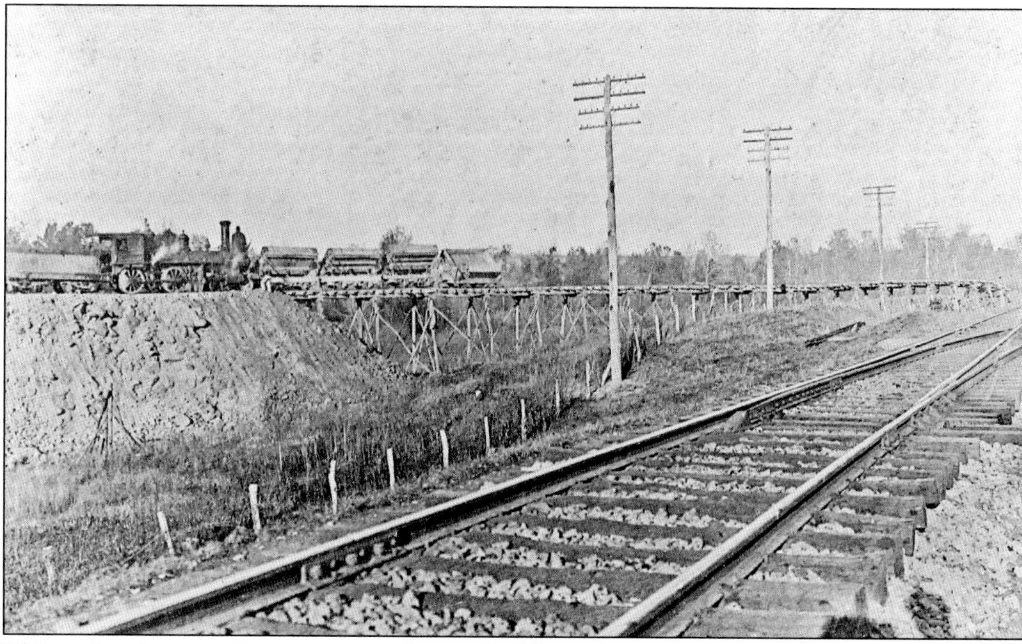

This undated postcard captures a work train building a new spur line adjacent to the main line. Note in the photograph that a wood structure supports the rails that the train runs on to dump the loaded cars. This is a very primitive way to build up a fill area of a railroad. (HSHC.)

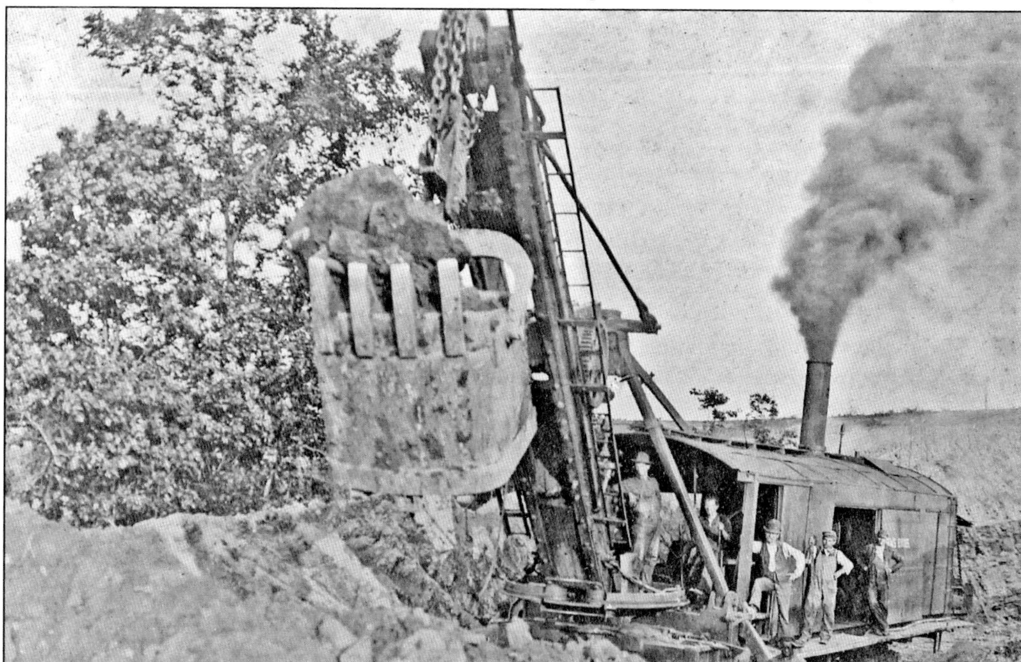

The ratio of the size of the men to their machine reveals the magnificent size of this railroad steam-powered shovel, used to excavate through a hill. The material was loaded on the work train and moved to a fill area. This type of shovel was later used as a strip mine excavator. The boom of the shovel would swing (rotate) 90 degrees right or left. (HSHC.)

Seven

CHARACTER OF A PEOPLE

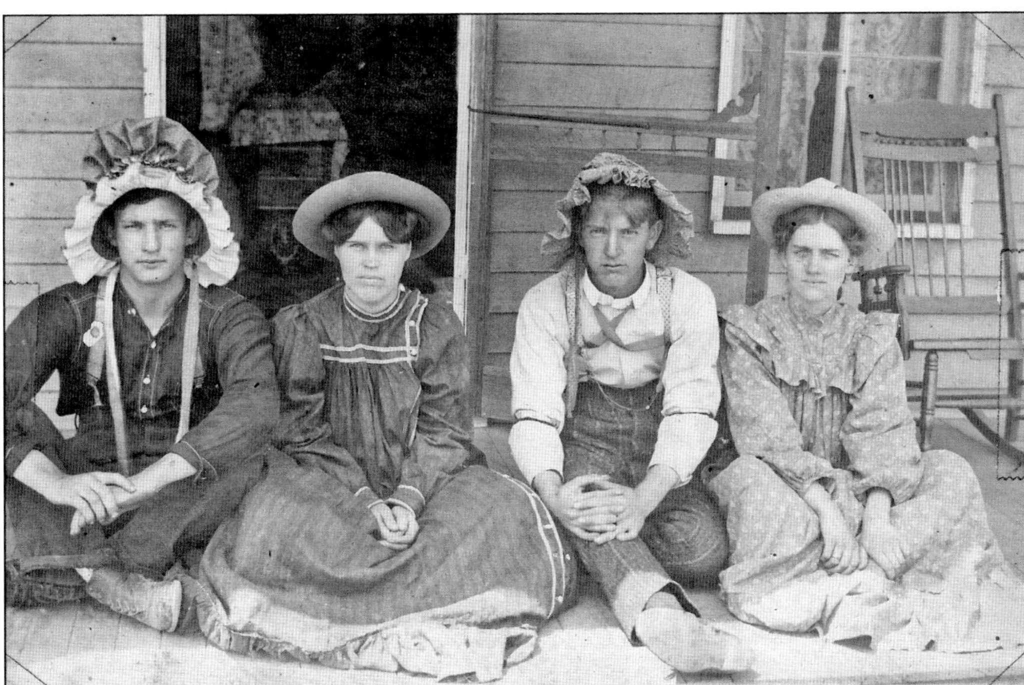

An amusing photograph of friends around 1900 portrays some of the fun-loving people of the communities; from left to right, John "Stull" Clark, Nora Maddox, Earnest Kinsella, and Lizzie Shanks sit on a porch in the Mortons Gap area. Stull and Earnest switched hats with the girls and sat like it was a normal thing to do. (Gail Warren.)

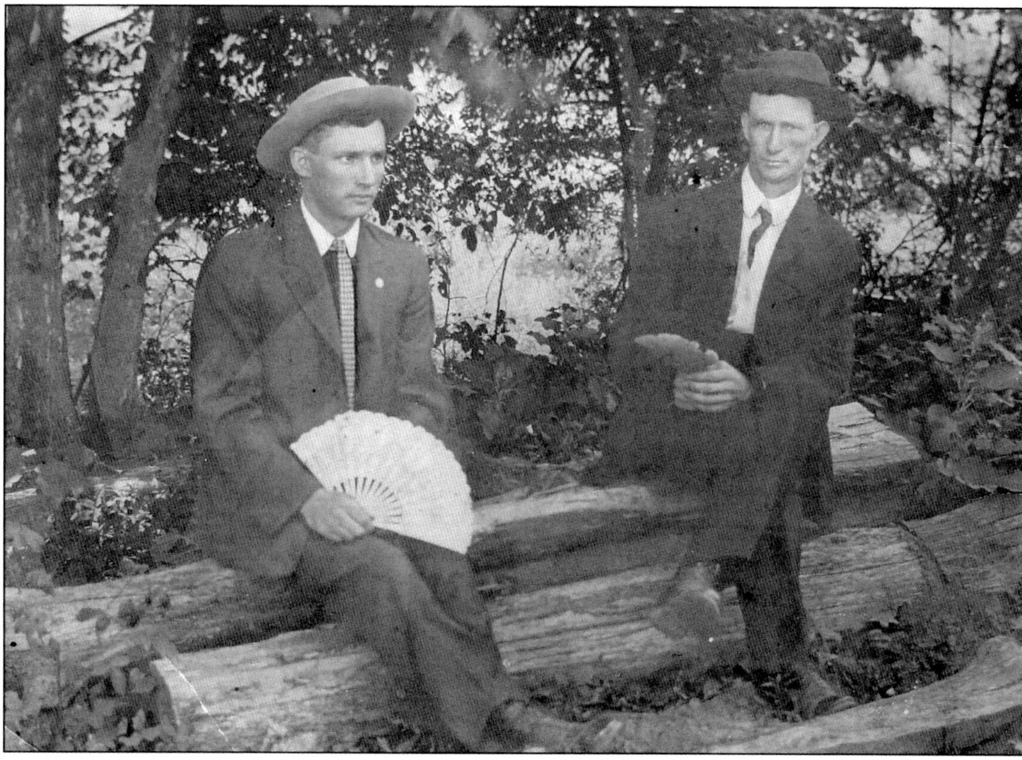

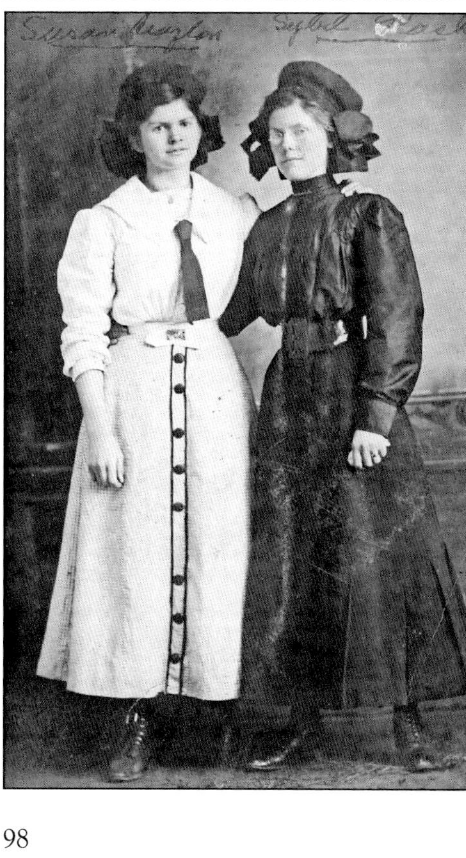

John "Stull" Clark was born in Hopkins County in 1884 and was the son of Joshua Green Clark, a police judge from Mortons Gap. Stull is sitting to the left of his best friend, Les Earl, on this log in 1907. The men pose on the trunk with fancy fans. After Stull married, he named his daughter, Fannie Earl Clark, after his best friend. (Gail Warren.)

Susan Crafton (left) and Sybil Rash (right) were known as the "Moss Hill Beauties." The women pose together in an undated photograph. Moss Hill is located southeast of Mortons Gap. There are three hills in the area. The names are Moss Hill, North Hill, and South Hill. (Helen Brown.)

Jane Hardwick was about 15 when this photograph was taken during the Great Depression. On the day this photograph was taken, her father would not let her go to the show. She recalls that accessories were not easy to come by, but a boy gave her the green scarf and hat she is wearing in this picture. (Jane Hardwick Rogers.)

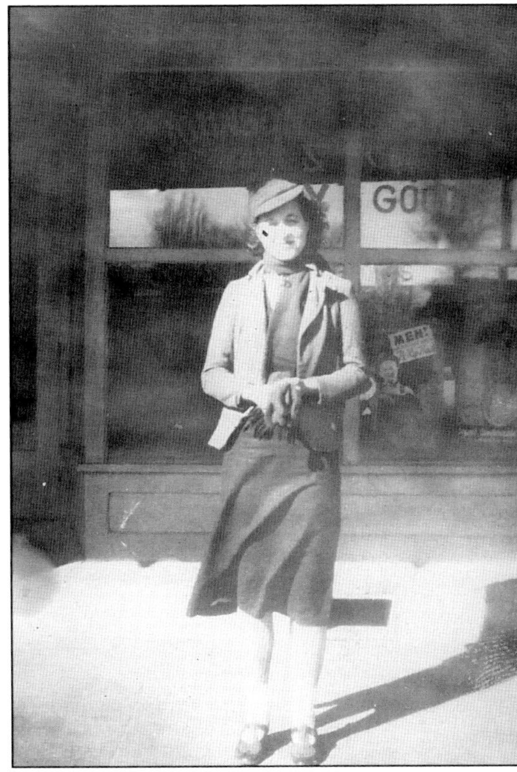

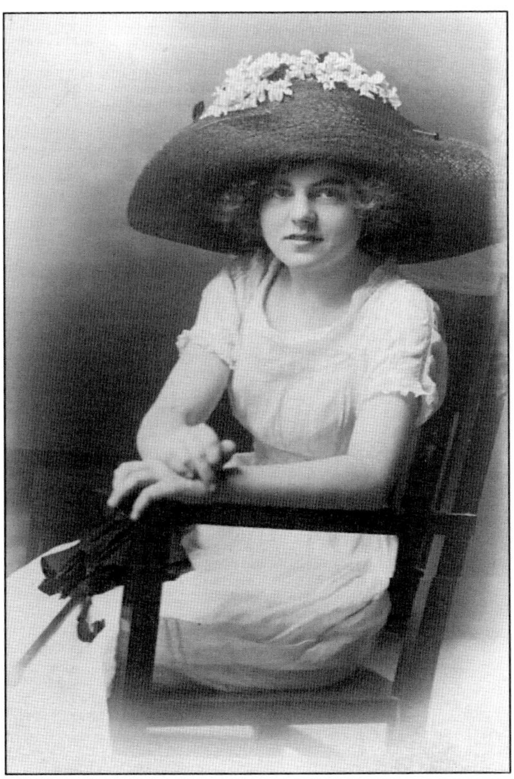

Margaret Igleheart is sitting in this undated photograph wearing what was considered to be a beautiful hat. Notice the long hatpin holding up the brim of the large headwear. Hat pins could be very long, so in 1908, the United States limited the length of a hatpin because of the concern of the pins being used as weapons. (Helen Brown.)

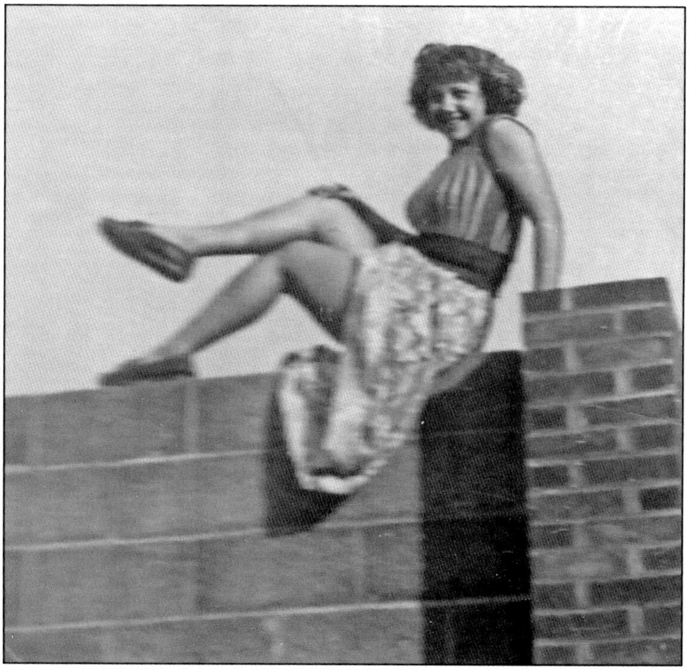

The Nortonville School is now the home of Nortonville City Hall. However, in this photograph, it is likely it was the place where Loretta Long took up a friend on a dare. She climbed to the top of the school, and this photograph was taken of the spirited young woman. (Piccola Hunt.)

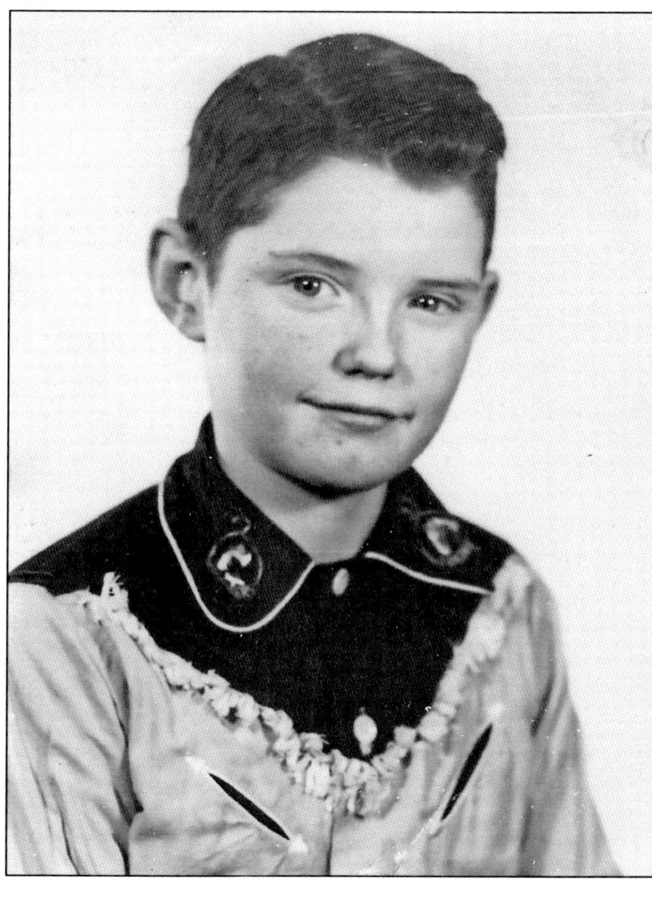

Young Tilford Neatherly poses for a photograph in his cowboy shirt. Tilford still lives in White Plains and owns the home his great-grandfather lived in when Jesse James spent the night there after robbing a bank in Russellville. His great-grandfather's home was built before the Civil War. (WPM.)

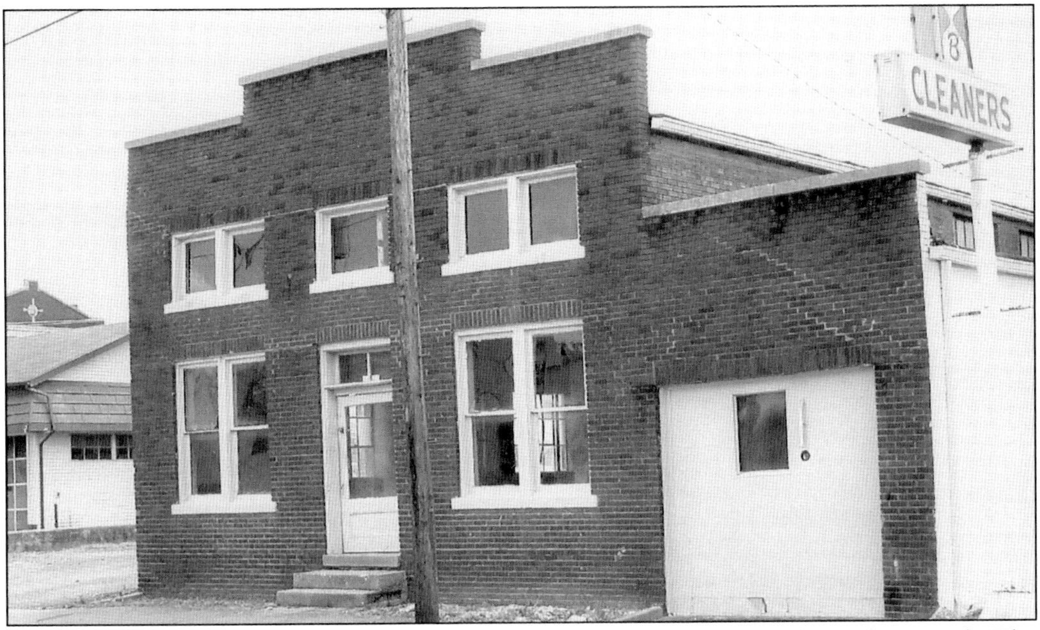

The original Coca-Cola Plant building in Madisonville is shown in the above photograph. The building is scheduled to be demolished to make way for the new Hopkins County Judicial Center. One of Coca-Cola's slogans was, "Things go better with Coke!" That seems to be a true statement when looking at the photograph below of lifetime friends Bob Wilkins and Roger Shelton (right). The cute little five-year-old boys sit on the steps of the plant on East Center Street in Madisonville in 1937. (Both, Roger Shelton.)

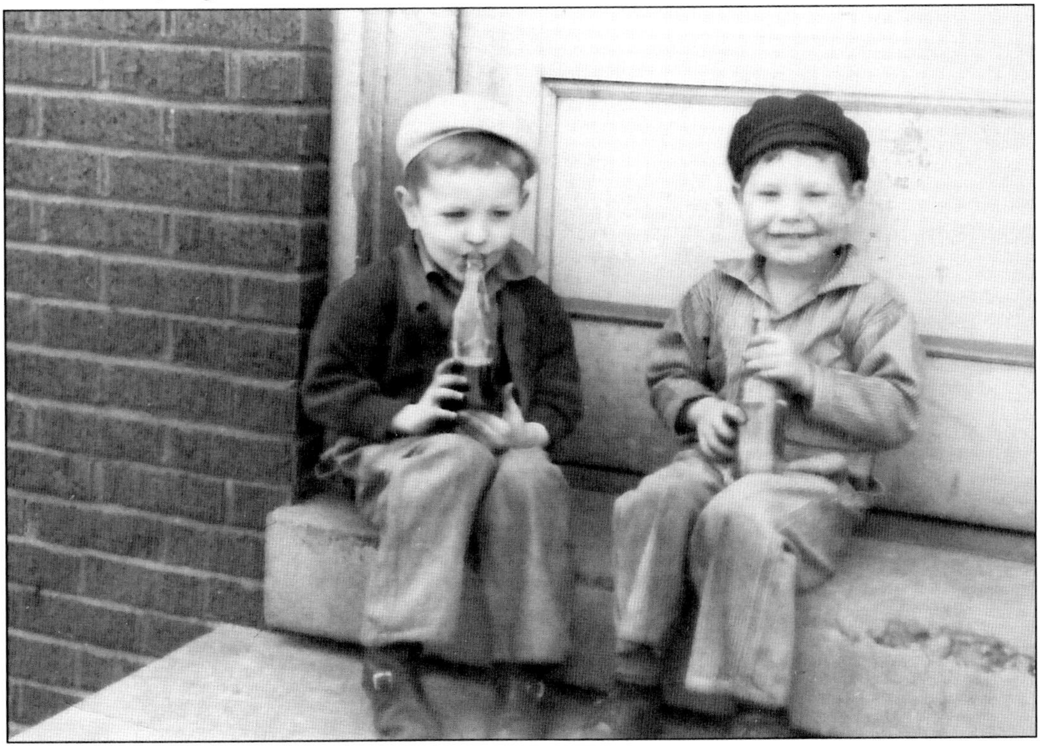

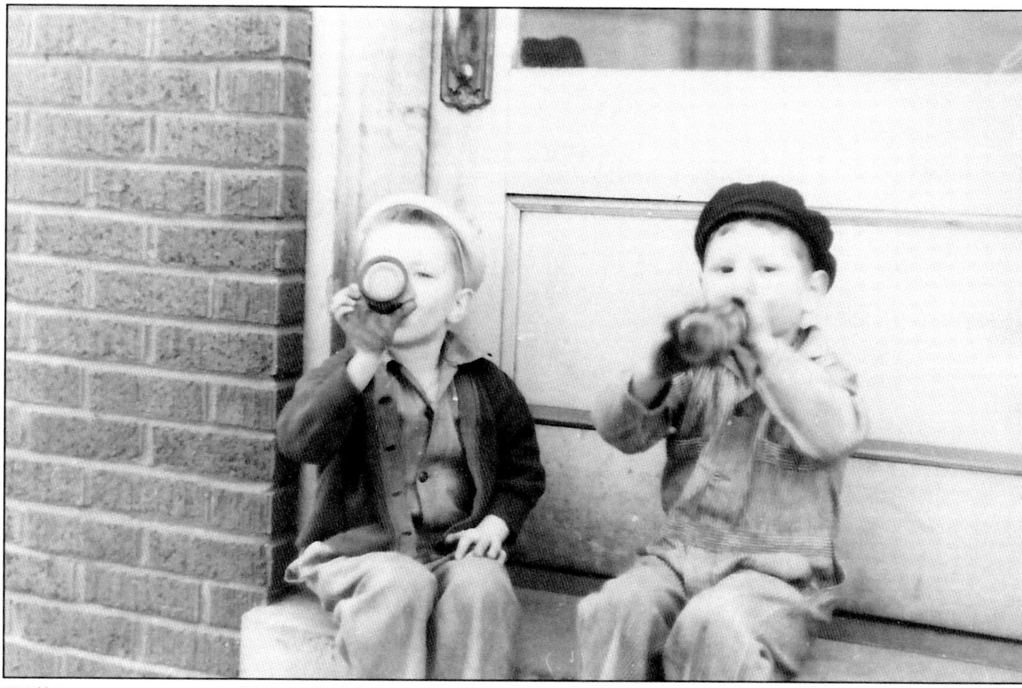

Wilkins turns up an old bottle of Coca-Cola while Shelton quenches his thirst with an orange flavor. Roger recalls that his father, who worked at the plant, sometimes allowed the boys to observe the bottles after the filling process. The boys were instructed to remove a bottle if it was under- or overfilled. He also reported that there may have been some bottles that came off the line but fit into neither category. (Roger Shelton.)

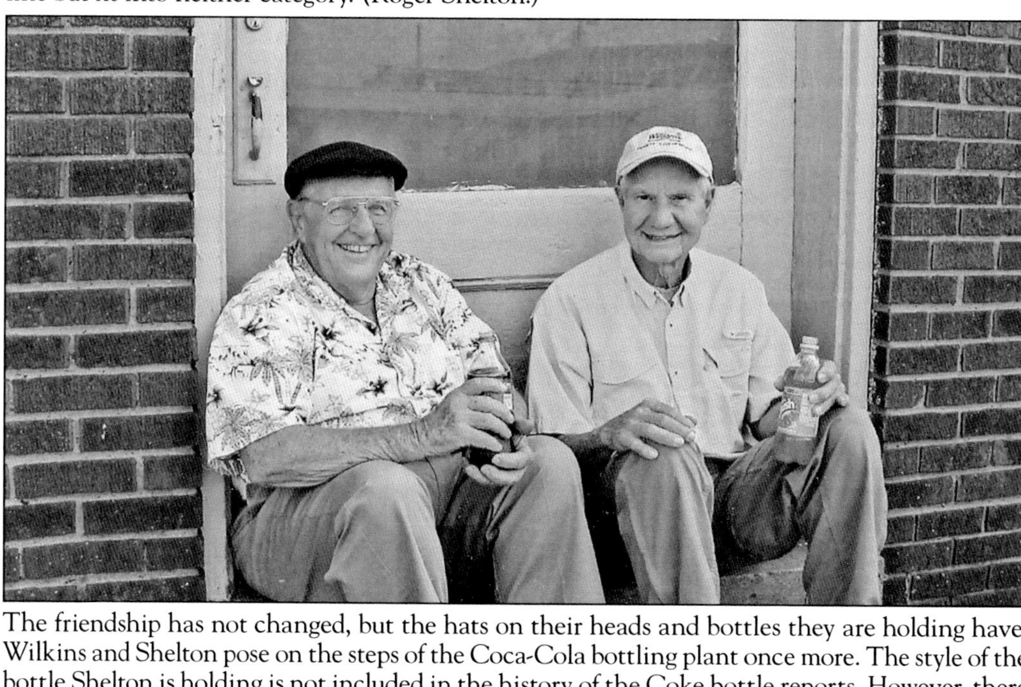

The friendship has not changed, but the hats on their heads and bottles they are holding have. Wilkins and Shelton pose on the steps of the Coca-Cola bottling plant once more. The style of the bottle Shelton is holding is not included in the history of the Coke bottle reports. However, there is a bottle just like it on display at the Historical Society of Hopkins County. (Roger Shelton.)

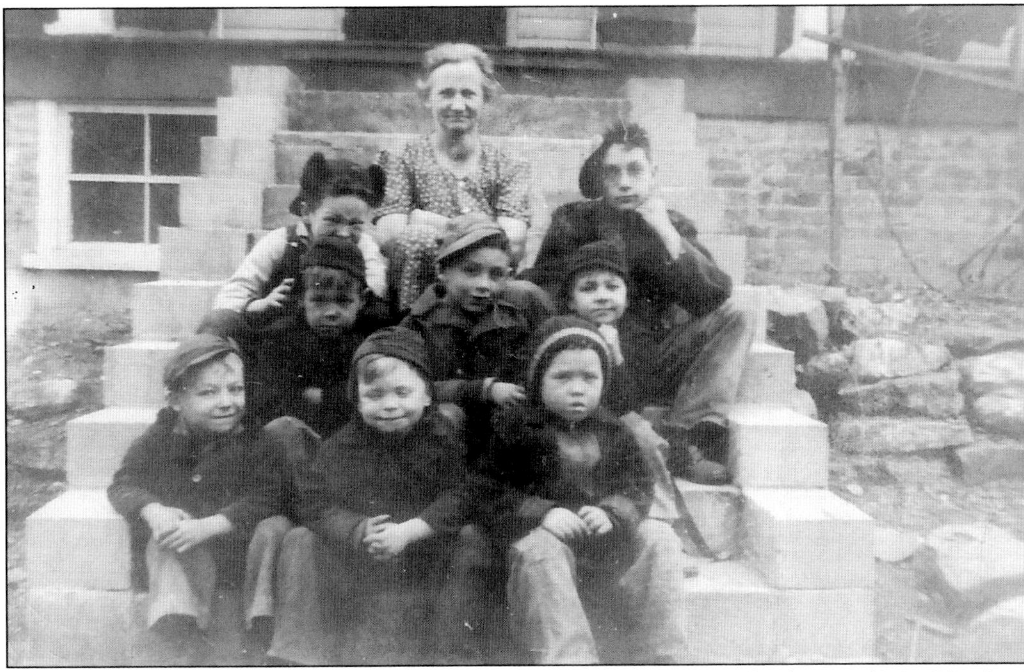

Mae Hartline and all of her grandsons, in about 1950, sit on the steps of Robert and Mae Hartline's home in Barnsley. From left to right are (first row) Doug Hartline, Jerry Hartline, and Roger Warren; (second row) David Hartline, Dallas Huddleston, Daniel Hartline (David's twin); (third row) Huston Hartline (notice he is biting David's hat), Mae Hartline, and Billy Joe Huddleston. (Gail Warren.)

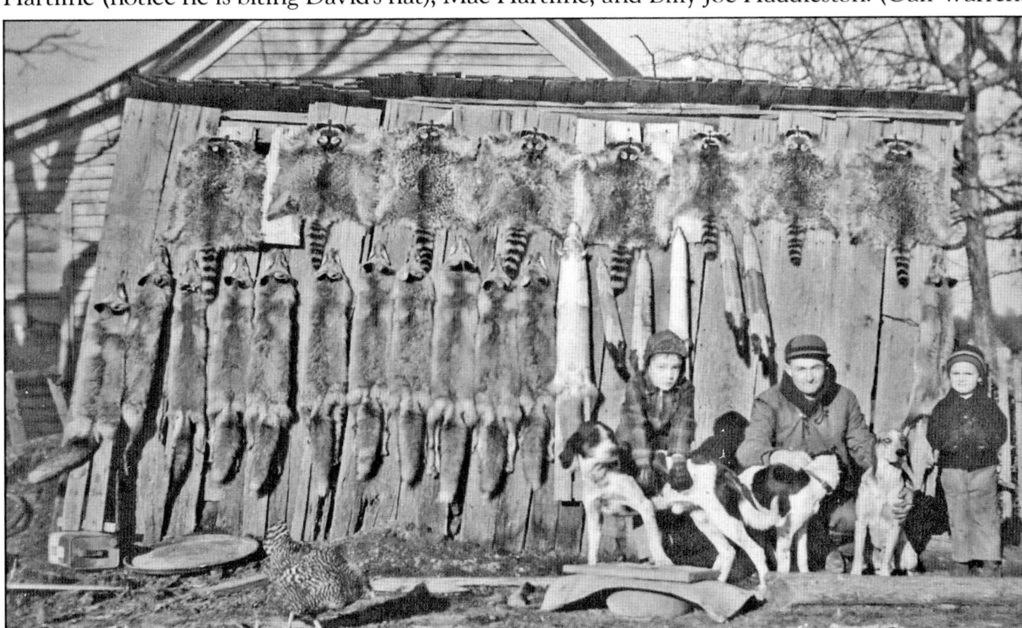

David Herbert Roger Osborn squats between his two sons, Charles David Osborn (left) and Roger Winston Osborn, in this photograph taken at the old Bell place at Pratt Bottoms in the late 1940s. One of the dogs had just bitten the father right before the photograph because Roger bit the dog's tail. (Jan Dixon.)

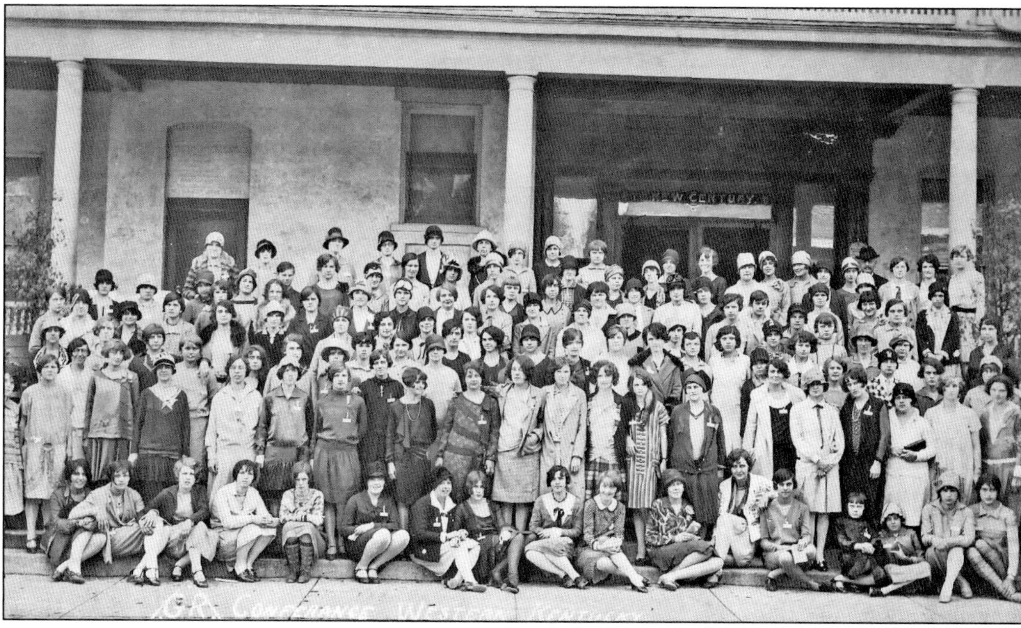

Dawson Springs at one time had more than 40 hotels and boardinghouses. Thousands of visitors came to taste and bathe in the mineral waters and participate in social activities. This group photograph was taken on October 29, 1927, in front of the New Century Hotel. (One man stands in the back; the rest are women.) The 150-room grand hotel was built in 1902 and was called "Queen of Western Kentucky Hotels." (HSHC.)

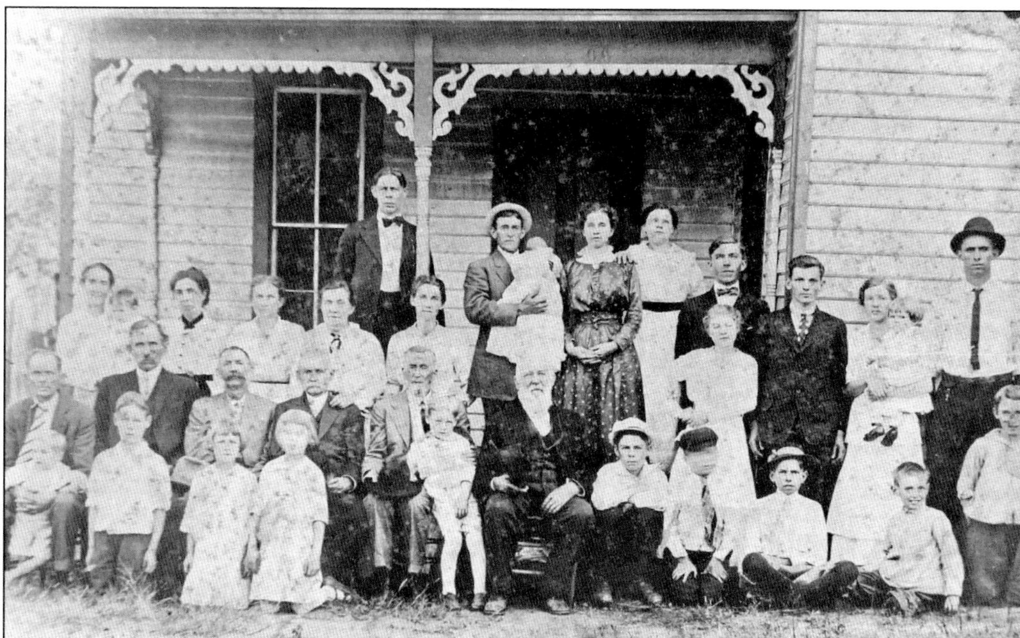

This family photograph is believed to have been taken in the Grapevine area of Hopkins County about 1916. Grandpa John Ray Rash sits to the middle right between his family members. The photograph has been of particular interest to many because of the image that was said to have been a ghost to the far left. (Gail Warren.)

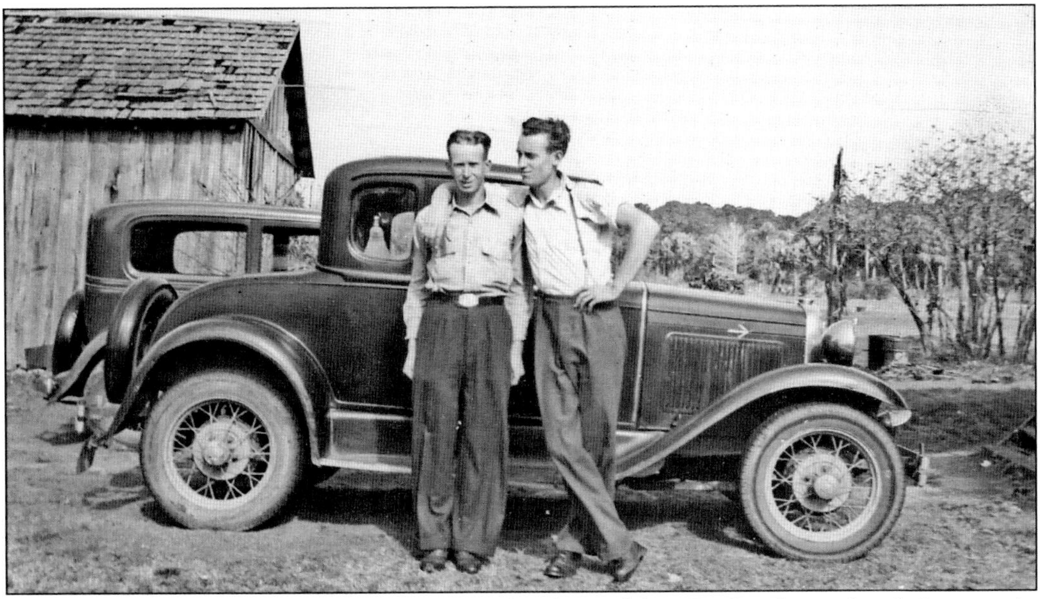

Aubrey Beeny (left) and Roelan Ledbetter stand in front of their Ford in this undated photograph. The young men were photographed while visiting family members. The boys traveled to Florida in their automobile. This was quite an adventure, as U.S. 41 had been built but not paved, only graveled. (HSHC.)

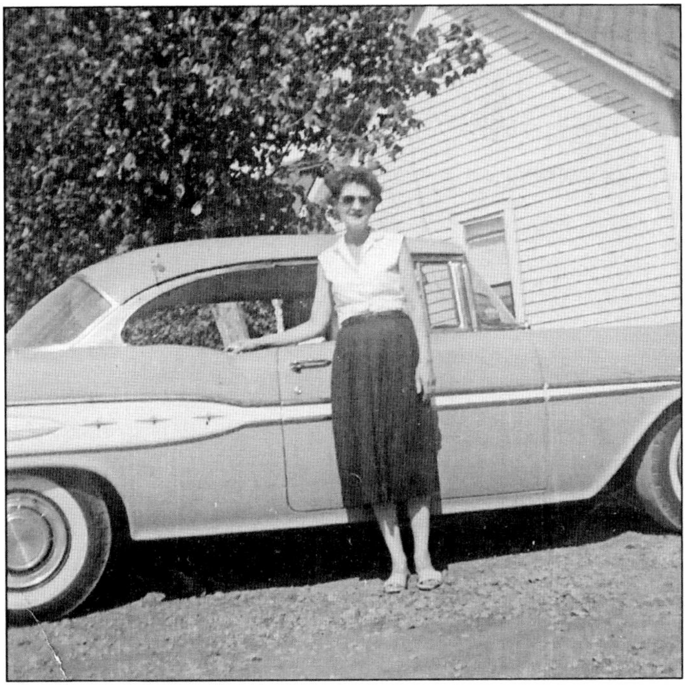

Louis Crick Steins is shown in this undated photograph posing beside her 1957 Pontiac Bonneville at her sister Pearlie Pyles Carlton's home on High Street in Nortonville. Pearlie was well loved in the community. She was born on September 22, 1900, and lived to be 105 years old. (Mildred Stanley.)

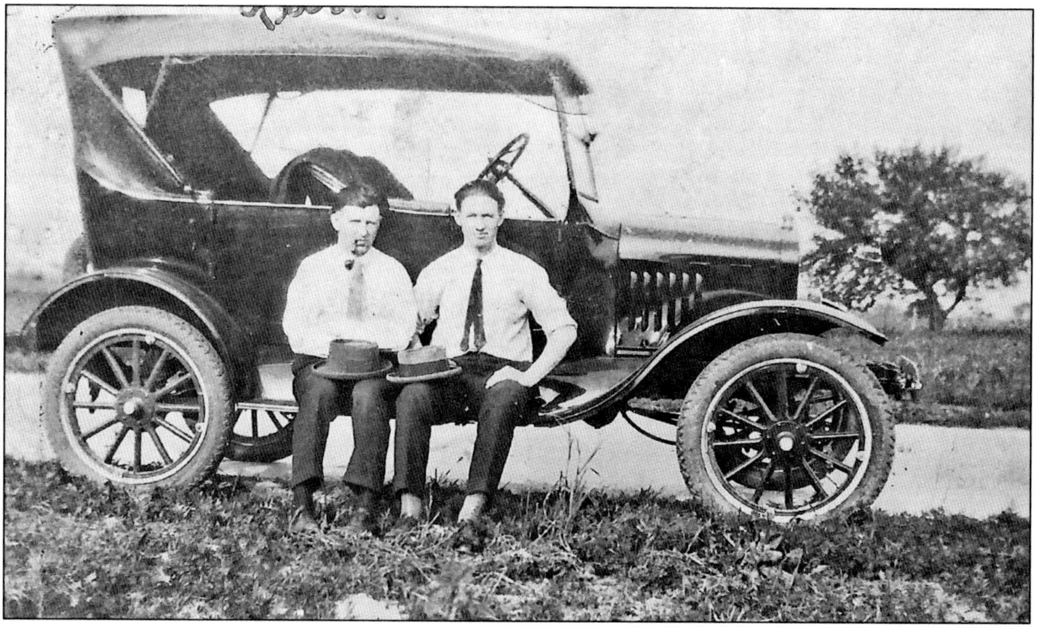

In the early 1920s, this photograph was taken of brothers Luther Stearsman (left) and Wavery ("Wavy") Stearsman. Luther left Mortons Gap around 1912 at the age of 14 and was only heard from two times in 50 years, once when he was 19 and once when he was tracked down by a brother and this photograph taken. Luther finally moved back to Kentucky in the early 1980s. (Gail Warren.)

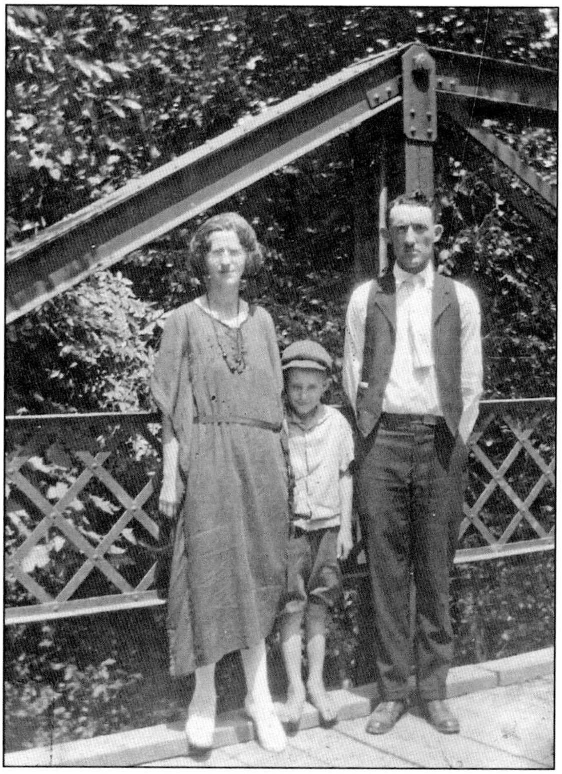

Dora Jennings "Vester" Young Farmer and her husband, Ruby Farmer, stand with their son James William "Jadie" Farmer in 1920 on the bridge that separates Hopkins and Christian Counties. The road is Highway 813 or Apex–White Plains Road. The location is the west fork of Pond River. Dora is believed to be pregnant in this photograph. (Gail Warren.)

This sweet photograph of three children was taken in 1908 on a boat on the Green River at Ashbyburg. The girl in the checkered dress is identified as Almsa McCain. Ashbyburg is 3 miles down the river from Jewel City. Notice the dark stockings the children are wearing. (Robert and Audrey McCain Collection, HSHC.)

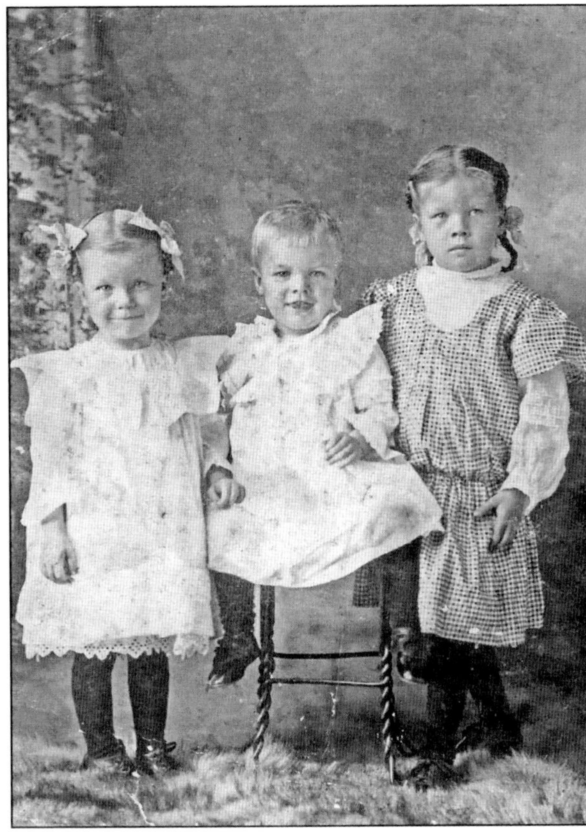

A Boy Scout troop from Hopkins County traveled to Mammoth Cave in the late 1940s. The Boy Scouts of America work to instill values such as honesty, good citizenship, and outdoor skills through a variety of activities such as camping, aquatics, and hiking. Roger Shelton is identified as the boy in the second row in the white shirt. (Roger Shelton.)

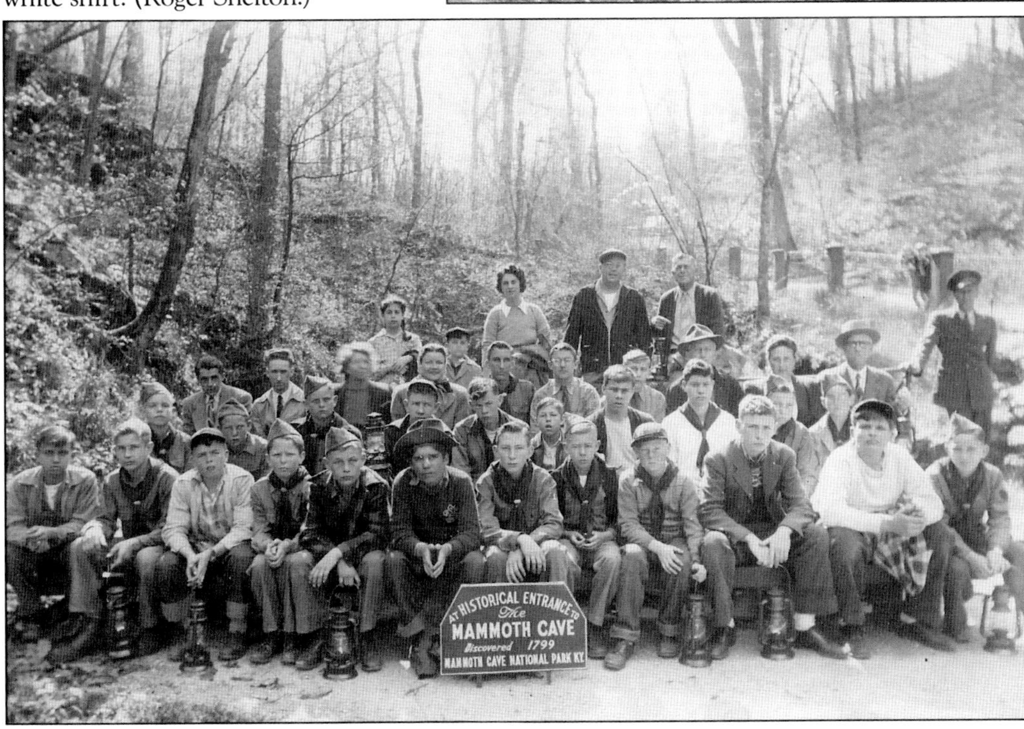

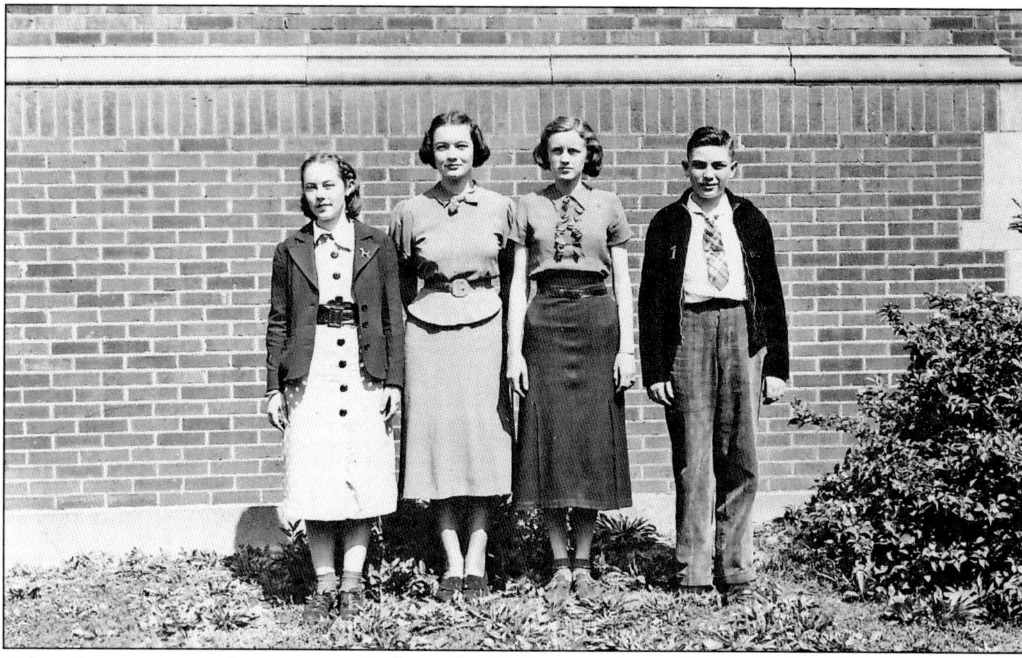

A handsome group of young people from the Earlington area poses in this undated photograph. The exact location is also unidentified. Standing from left to right are A. Baca, S. Baca, June Laffoon (who worked in Frankfort as secretary for at least seven Kentucky governors), and Bill Cuniff (former mayor of Earlington). (HSHC.)

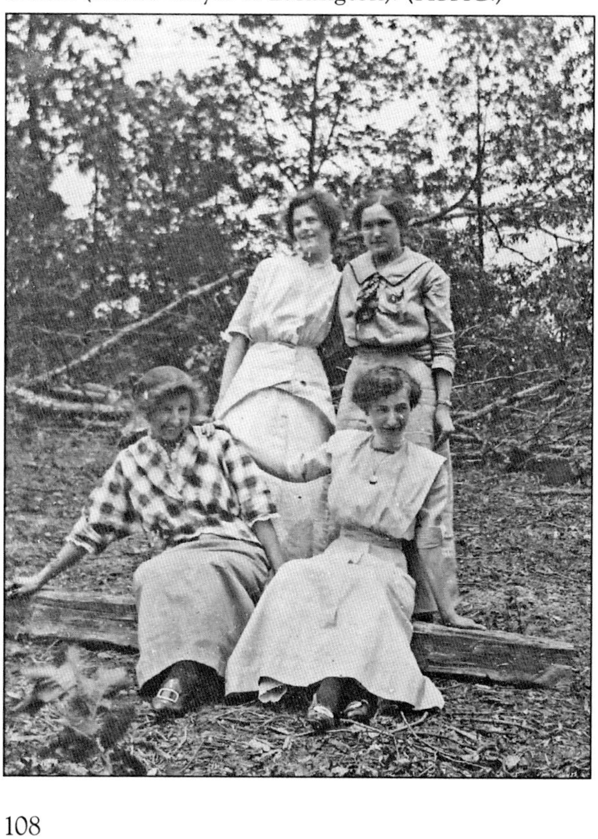

It appears that these four young women are having a good time near a wooded area in this undated photograph. From left to right are (seated on the log) Ninnon Whitfield and Elv Taliaferro; (standing behind the women) Nell Fugate and Lora Allen. Judging from the photograph, the popular hairstyle would have been to wear the hair up in the back. (Helen Brown.)

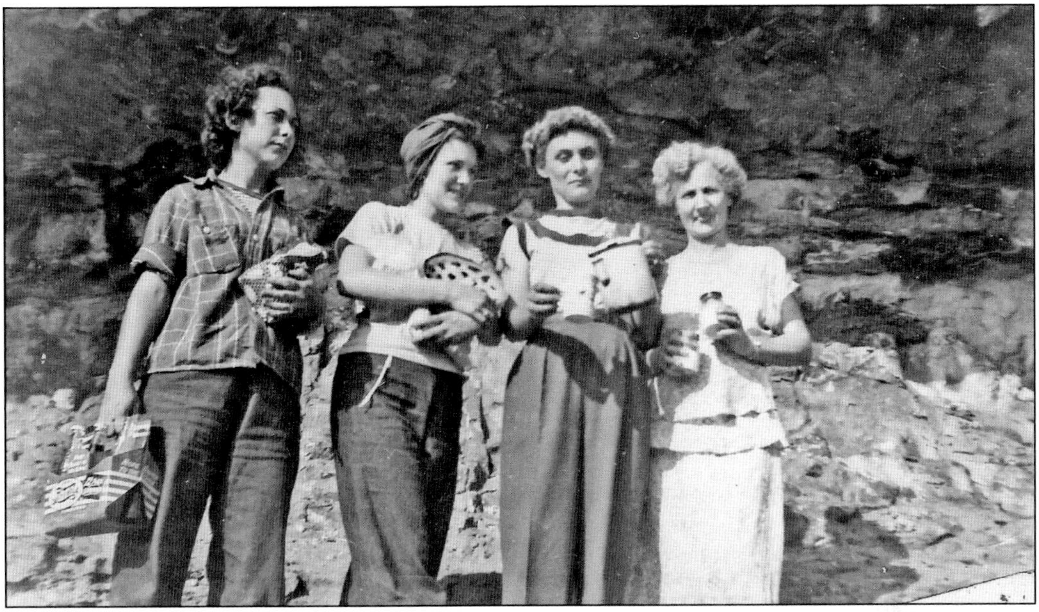

In 1953, the entire Hartline clan of Barnsley (approximately 20 family members) left Hopkins County to travel to Alabama. This photograph was taken along the roadside where the family pulled over for the night. They cooked their supper there and slept in the back of the trucks. Pictured from left to right with food are Martha Helen Smith, Nell Gibson, Geneva Huddleston, and their mother, Mae Hartline. (Gail Warren.)

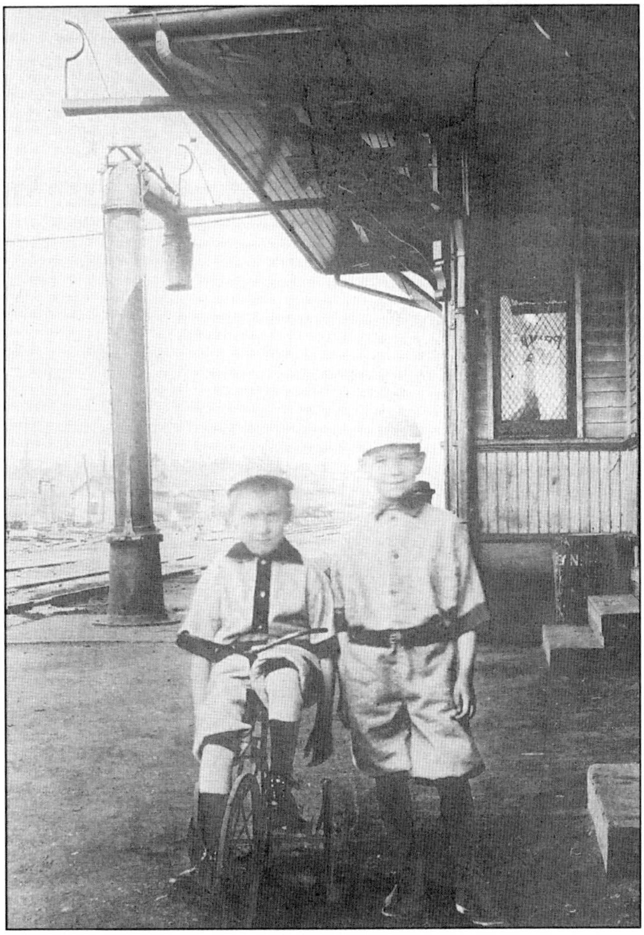

Two young boys pose outside of the Louisville and Nashville Railroad passenger depot in Earlington in the 1920s. The standpipe in the upper left was used by the railroad to put water in the tenders of their steam trains. One of the unidentified boys is riding an old tricycle. (HSHC.)

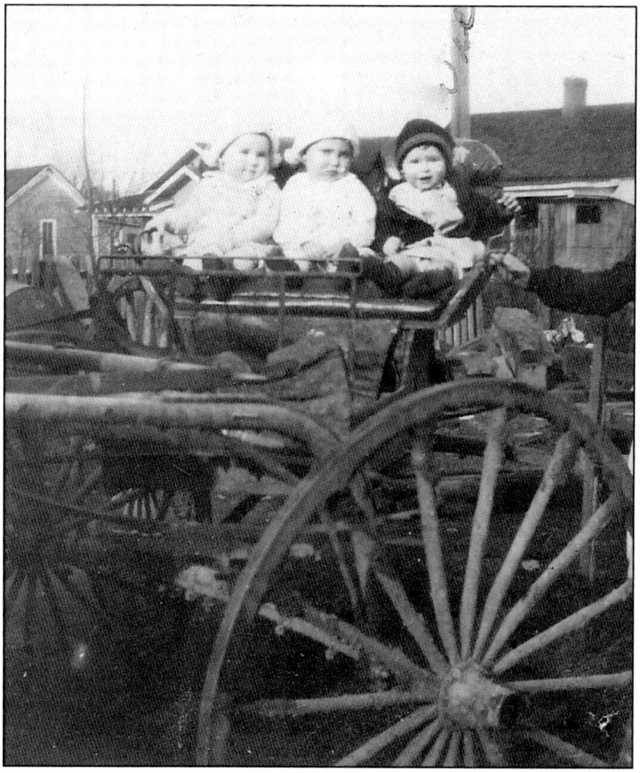

Three little cousins await a ride in an old buggy about 1927 in the photograph to the left. Only one of the babies looks happy to be sitting in the contraption. The photograph may have been taken in Nortonville or Mortons Gap. From left to right are Jeff Lamar Ruddell, Proctor Earl Farmer, and Willis W. Rash. The photograph below is an interesting image of an older Willis W. Rash holding a squirrel that his grandfather John "Stull" Clark had killed. The photograph was taken about 1930. It is Stull Clark's gun leaning against the tree. Willis Clark was born April 29, 1927, and is the son of John and Fannie Rash of Mortons Gap. (Both, Gail Warren.)

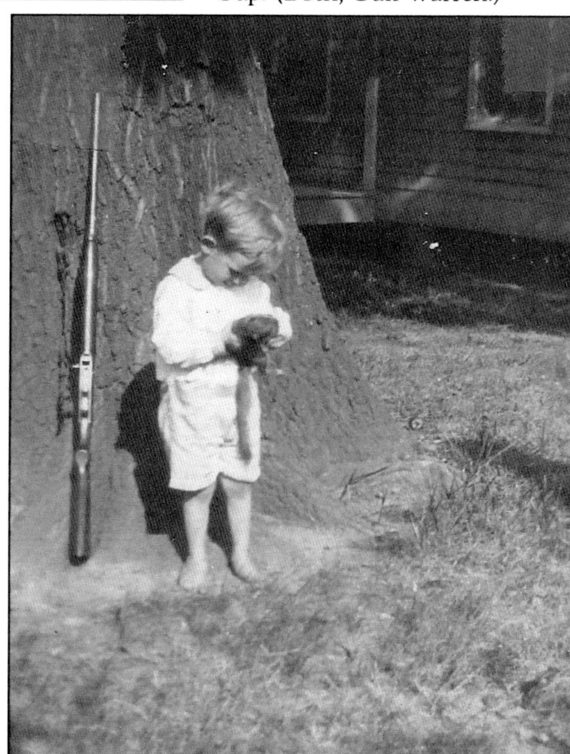

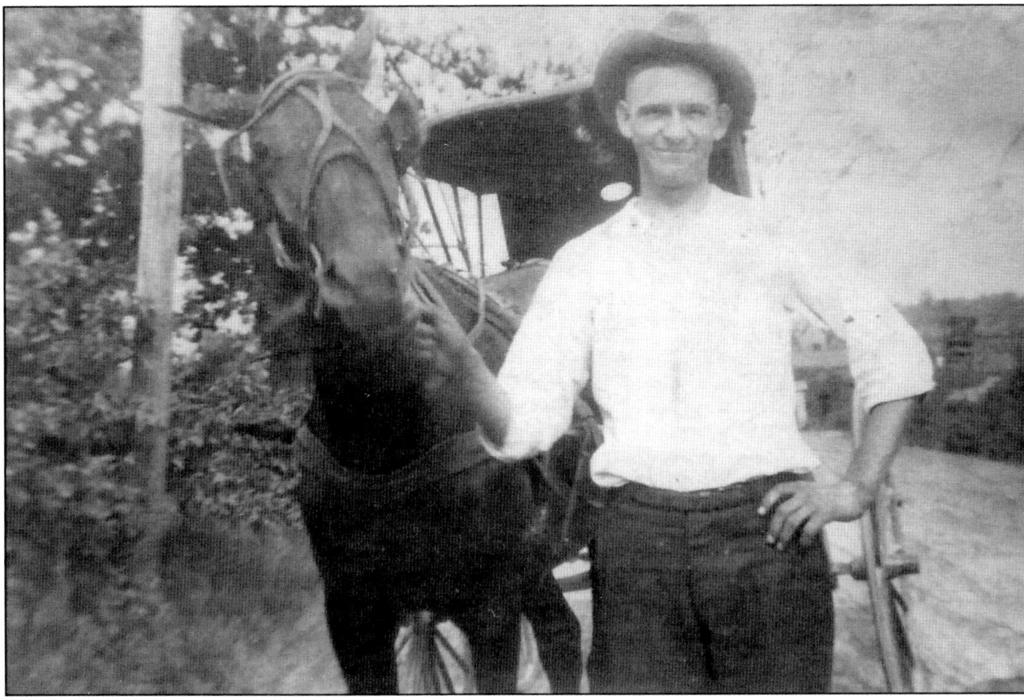

Jesse Lewis Dixon worked the George Beeny farm in Manitou for several years. Jesse is pictured leading his horse and buggy. He delivered the first load of milk with his horse and buggy to U. C. Milk Company when it opened. Lewis's grandfather Alexander Dixon fought in the Civil War on the Confederate side and is buried in the Clayton family cemetery in Shakerag. (Jan Dixon.)

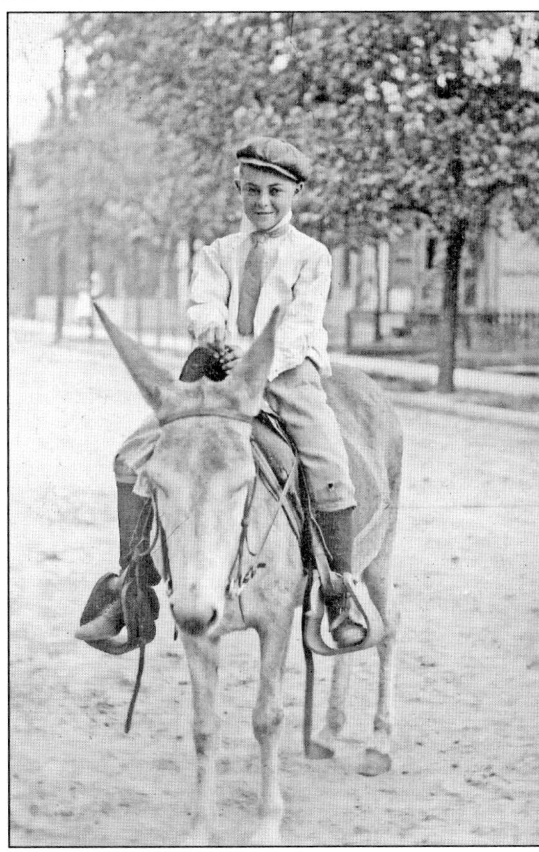

The little boy in this photograph is believed to be J. B. Moore. His mother was Lizzy Mae Morton Moore. J. B. was a pharmacist who owned a drugstore on West Center Street in Madisonville. He lived in what is now the Hammock Moore Bed and Breakfast. J. B.'s wife, Kiel, was the daughter of Dr. W. M. Hammock, and the couple inherited the home from the doctor. (J. B. Moore Collection, HSHC.)

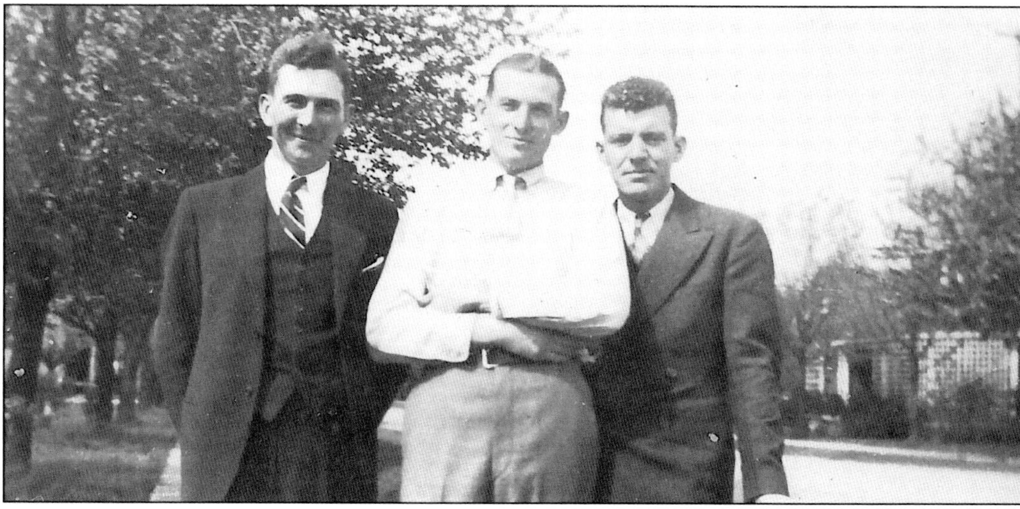

This undated photograph is believed to have been taken in White Plains. The three smartly dressed men, from left to right, are Urley Lee Gillam, Aubrey Oglesby, and Buel Oglesby. Buel Oglesby is the father of Ruth Anne Oglesby. She became an owner of the Nortonville restaurant Dixie Pan. (Jane Hardwick Rogers.)

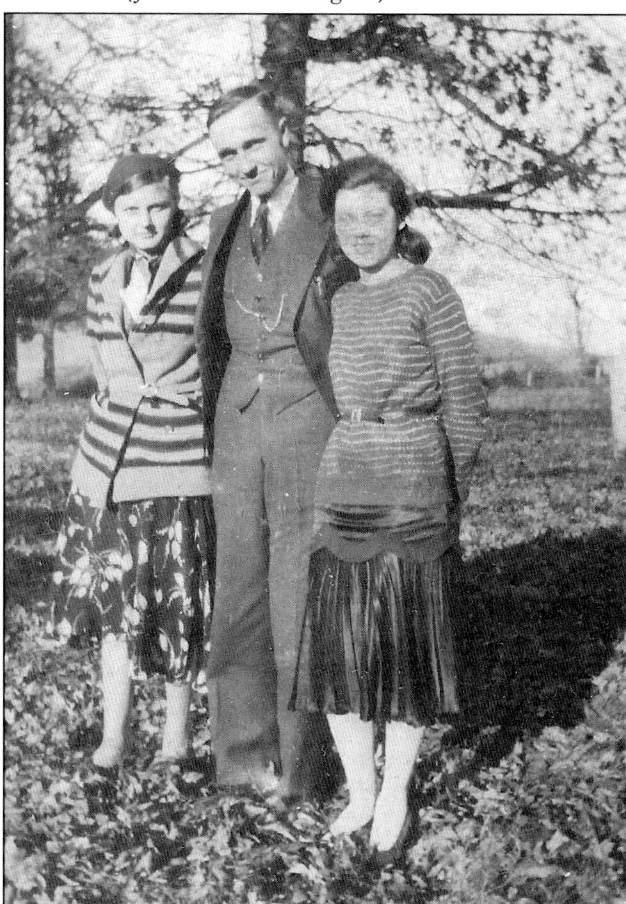

The handsome Harold Ledbetter stands between two women on a Sunday afternoon outing in an undated photograph. The women are identified as Ledbetter's girlfriend at the time, Mildred Johnson (left), and her cousin, Blanch Polley (right). Harold and Mildred did not marry. This photograph came from Harold Ledbetter's personal photograph collection. (HSHC.)

Mildred Utley was a tall woman, as shown in this photograph. She is leaning back on an old wire fence. Mildred later married Everett Johnson. This photograph also came from Harold Ledbetter's personal photograph collection. Notice the type of post the fence wire is wrapped on and the number of wires used for the fence. (HSHC.)

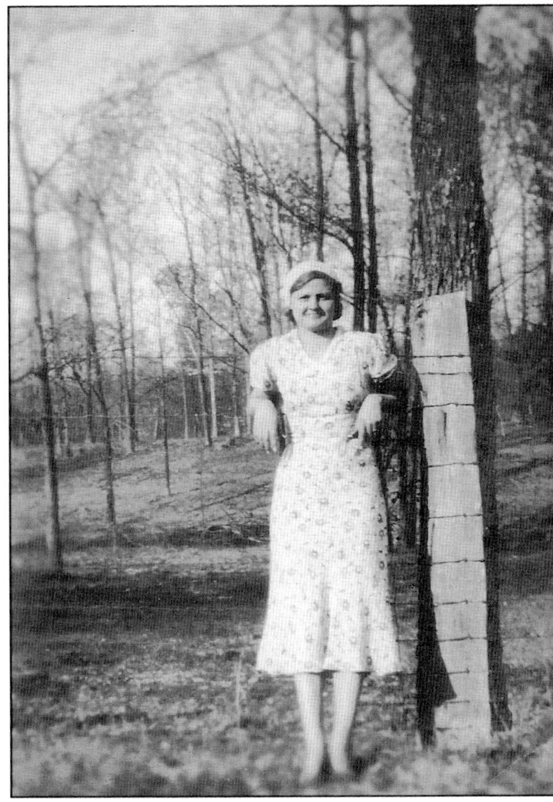

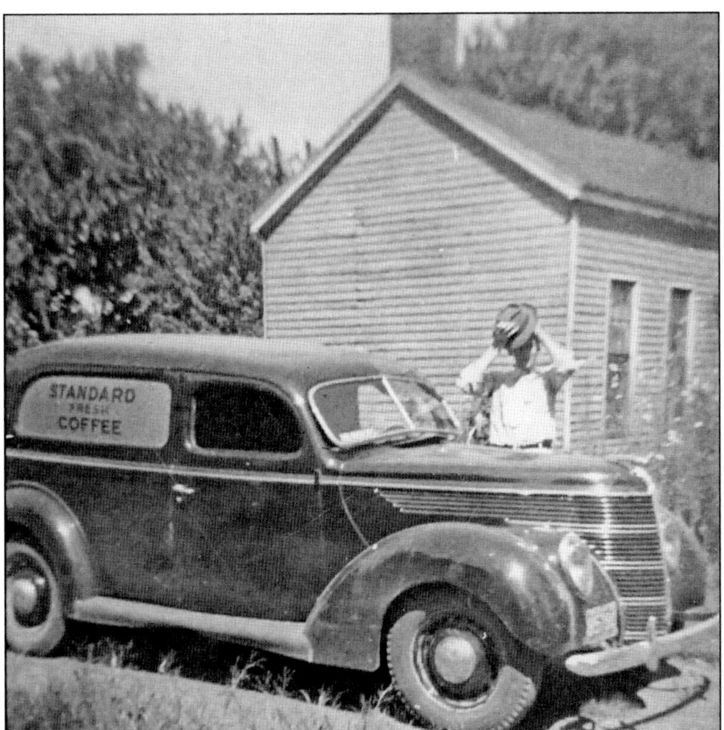

Standard Coffee was based out of New Orleans. Cecil Lewis was born in 1916 and worked for the coffee company. He used ingenuity to increase his sales and earn bonuses for higher profits. Cecil is standing beside his company vehicle in this undated photograph. The advertisement on the side of the newer Standard Coffee cars was, "Rain or Shine, Always on Time." One promotion that Standard Coffee ran was "Buy 1 or 2 pounds of coffee and get 5 pounds of sugar for Free!" (Ronnie Lewis.)

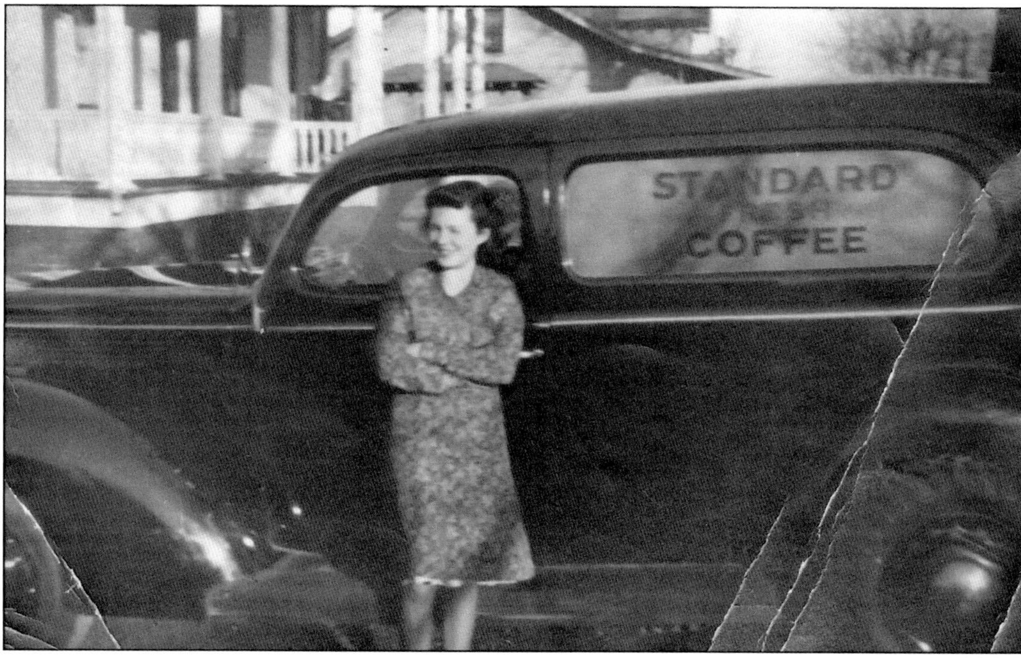

Cecil Lewis purchased a used car and turned it into a second company car that his wife, Sadie, drove. With his wife working with him, he doubled his route and set record sales. It is no wonder that no other salesman could keep up with his sales. The lovely Sadie Lewis is standing here with her car she drove for her husband's work with the Standard Coffee Company. (Ronnie Lewis.)

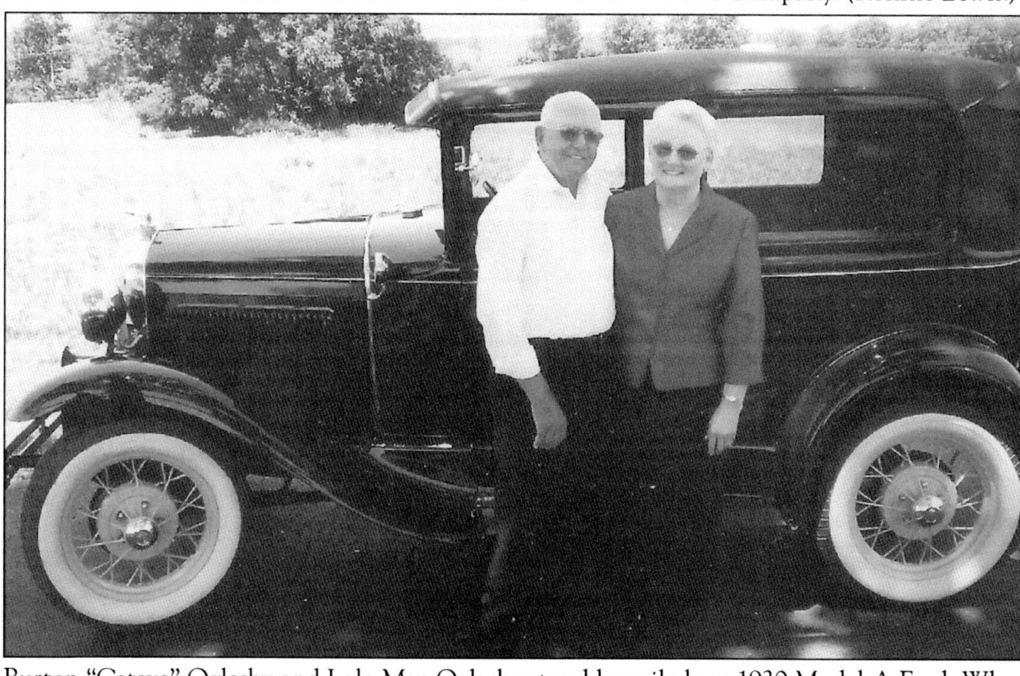

Burton "Cateye" Oglesby and Lola Mae Oglesby stand happily by a 1930 Model A Ford. When they courted, "Cateye" had a Ford just like this one. In 1946, he paid $175 for his vehicle but wrecked it. His wife purchased another one for him in 2008 for his 79th birthday. His mother's maiden name was Hanks. She was related to Abraham Lincoln's mother. (WPM.)

Eight

Faith and Education

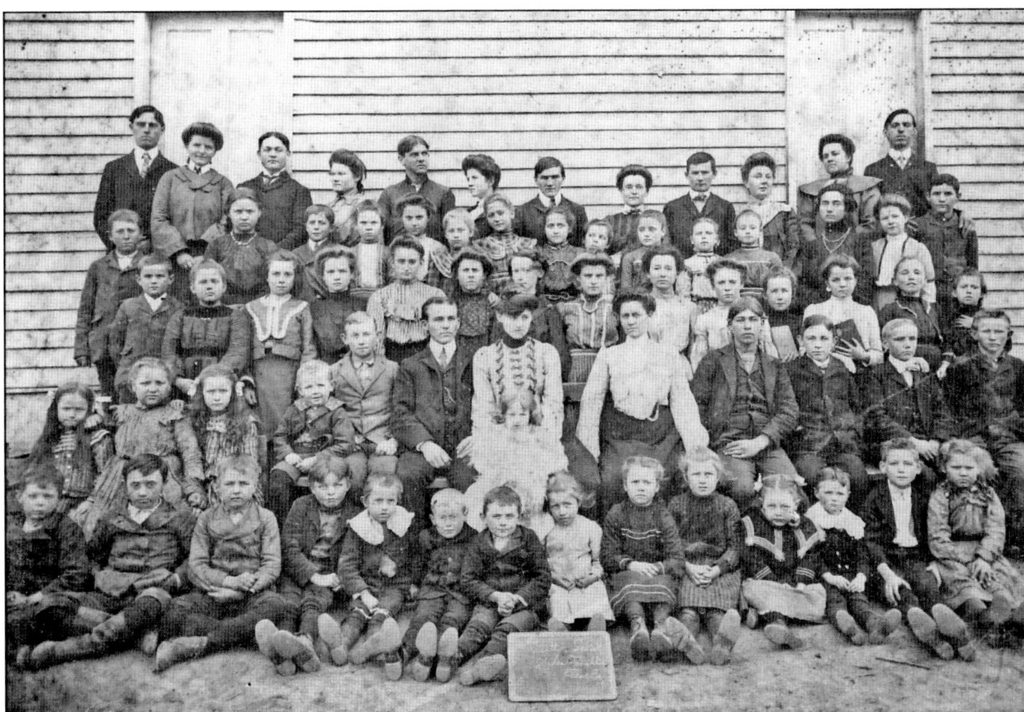

Dalton School educated all ages until 1962. West Hopkins was formed by merging the high school students of Charleston, Dalton, and Nebo Schools. Then, in 1996, Dalton closed its doors for good as the three schools consolidated again when the new West Hopkins High School was constructed. Shown in this photograph is the old Dalton School. The teacher has been identified as Silas Franklin. (Anne K. Morgan.)

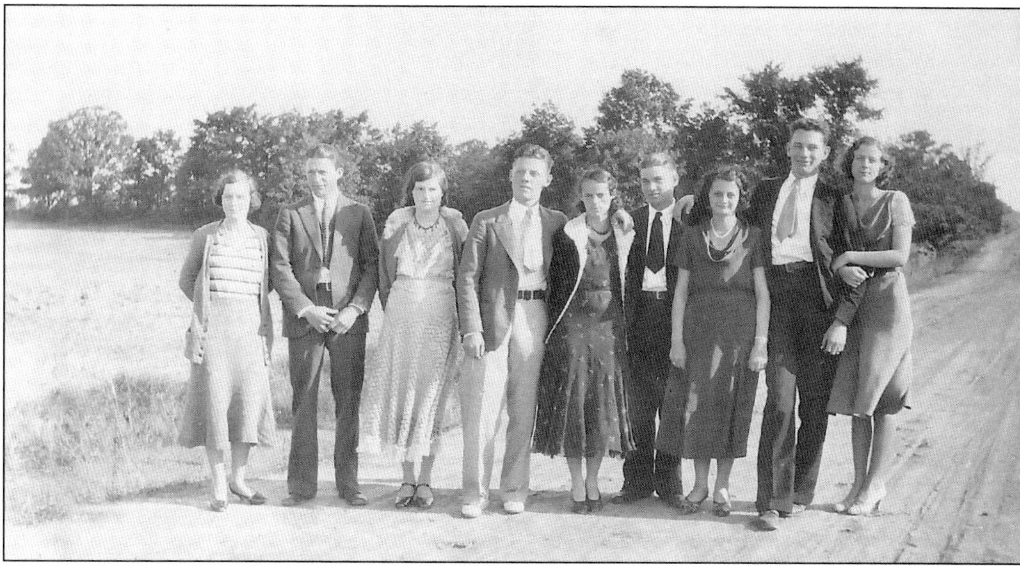

After the White Plains school burned, it was rebuilt, and students began classes in 1931. The first graduating class of the new White Plains High School is pictured above. The 1932 graduates are as follows, from left to right: Agnes Lile, Raymond Dillingham, Nola Dillender, Forrest Herring, Eunice Dobyns, Elmer Outlaw, Cordia Tyoson, Raymond Hight, and Marie Carty. The photograph below is the first graduating class of 1932 reunion. Alumni, students, and guests are, from left to right, as follows: Josephine Williams Ashmore, Forrest Herring, Eunice Dobyns Barnard, Nola Dillender Jordon, Marie Carty Ray, Catherine Blackford McDuffee (French teacher), Raymond Hight, Corrine Wells Jowers, Elmer Outlaw, and Etoile Whitfield Moore. (Both, WPM.)

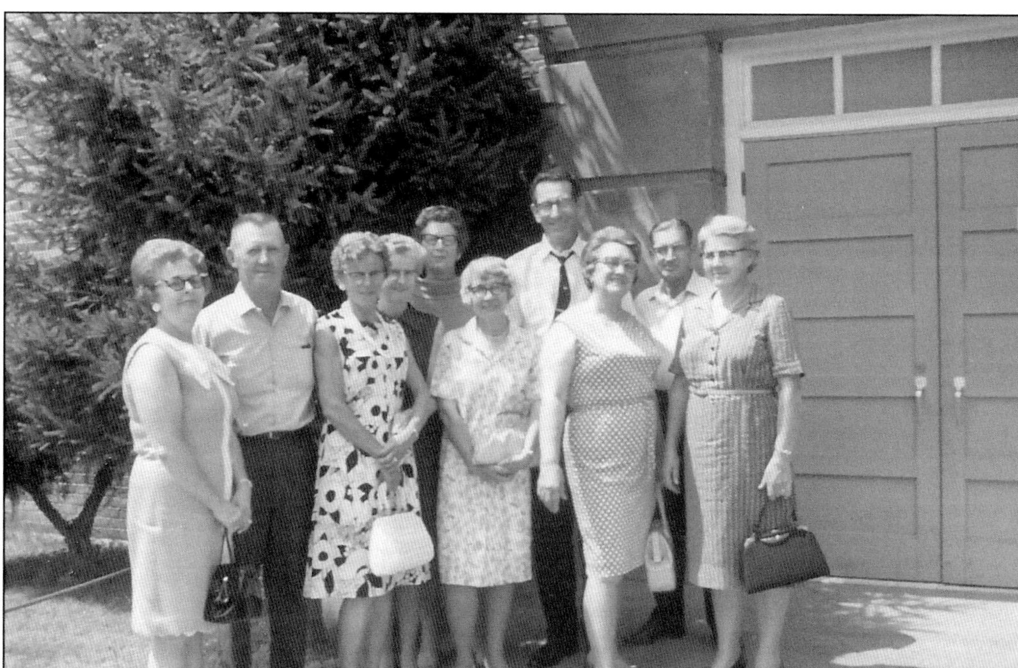

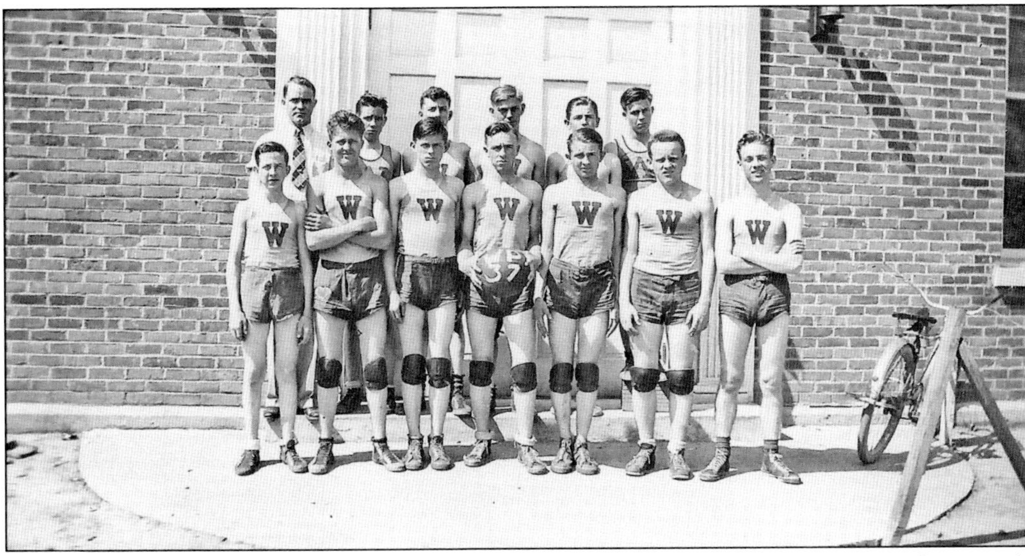

The White Plains basketball team of 1937 posed in front of the school for a team photograph. Notice the kneepads, sock length, and the old bicycle to the right. The back of the photograph has the following printed: "Tate, Tarp, J. W. Goron, Harold, Gaylers, Charlie S, Elisha James, C. S. J. P. Benny, and Junior." (Jane Hardwick Rogers.)

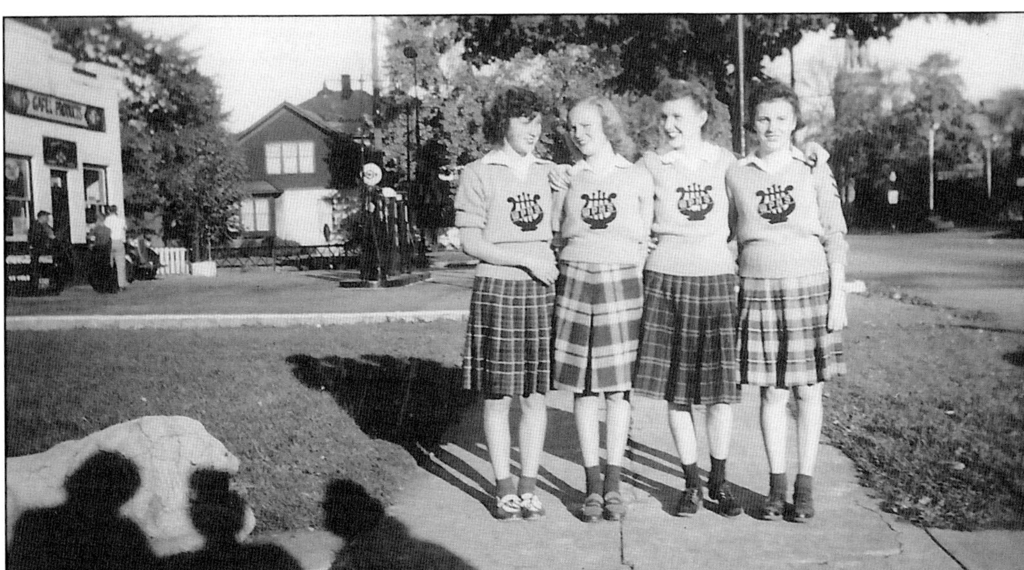

Members of the White Plains High School Band stand here for a photograph around 1949. The girls from left to right are Barbara Iglehart, Dolores Ray, Robbye Iglehart, and Marian Sue Ray. The location of the photograph is unknown, but a gas station to the left is advertising D-X products. (WPM.)

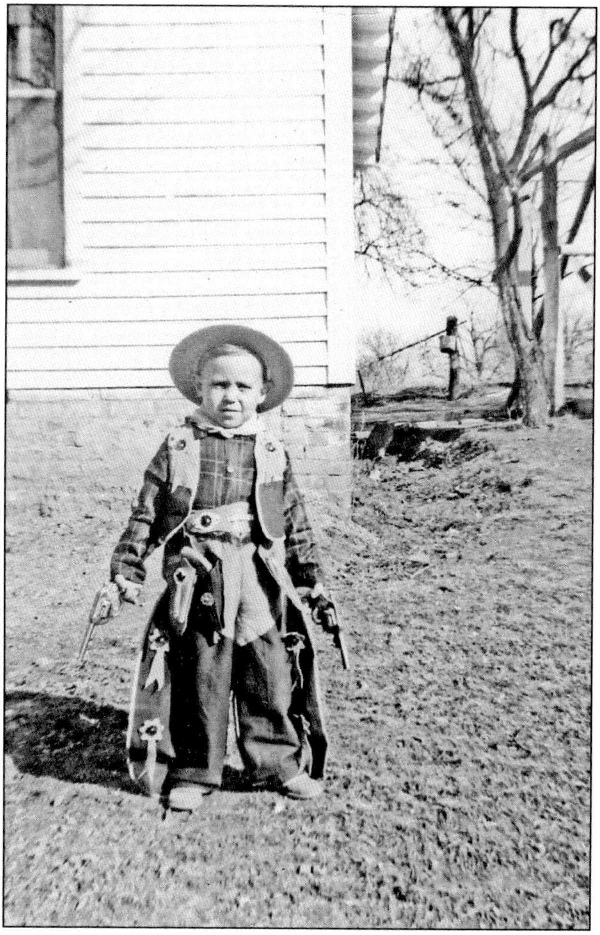

Cowboy Roger Dale Warren is the son of Charles and Margie (Hartline) Warren. The photograph was taken in Barnsley about 1950. Dr. Roger Warren is now a professor of mathematics at Madisonville Community College within the Kentucky Community and Technical College System in Madisonville and resides in White Plains. He is an avid golfer and popular tournament competitor. (Gail Warren.)

The Moss Hill School Group students are as follows, from left to right: (first row) Juanita Fox Suthard, Helen Allen Brown, Betty Harris, Nell Tyson Lee, Martha Moore, Mary Jewell Foster, and Fairy Shelton Ross; (second row) Mary Moore Powell, Mary A. Moore Larmouth, Virginia Sisk, Lula A. Fowler Boyd, Helen McDonald Fugate, Martha Fowler Moore, Edith Fugate Bone, and Martha Fox Starks. (Helen Brown.)

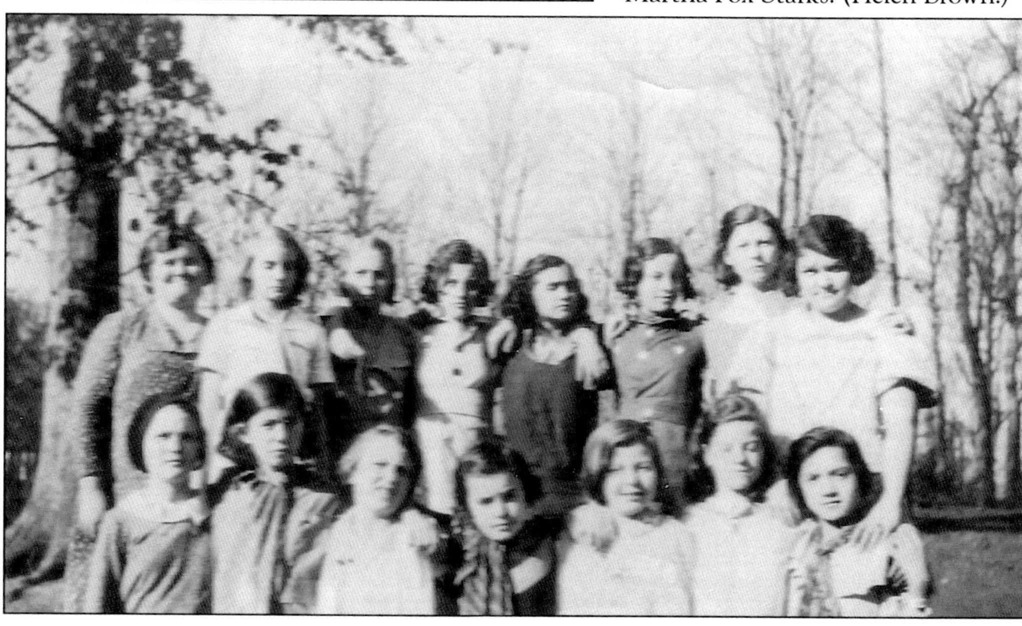

White Plains High School students stand together in 1930 before the new school was built in White Plains. It is interesting that the teacher's mouth is open, one student is getting his nose flicked, and the kneeling children are laughing. From left to right are (first row) Kermit Lovelace, Hall Oates, Elmer Outlaw, and Mylber Clark; (second row) teacher Bailey Winstead, Edward Atkinson, Durrwood Johnson, Harlan Neatherly, Forrest Herring, and Raymond Hight. (WPM.)

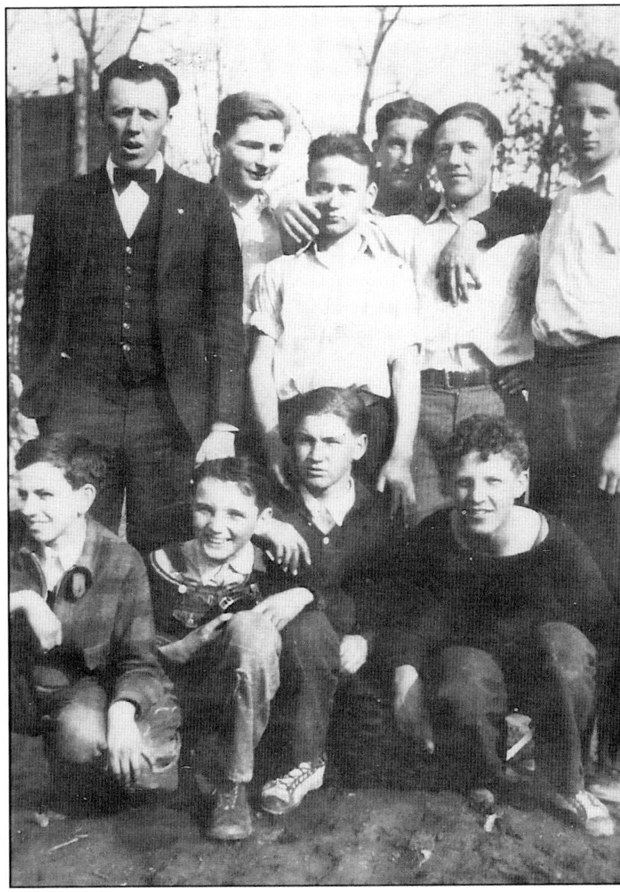

The White Plains school destroyed by fire had 205 students. The school was rebuilt for $25,000. Classes were held at the White Plains Methodist Church, the jailhouse, the White Plains Missionary Baptist Church, and other areas until the building project was completed. The White Plains school building that now stands has been converted into a great youth center for teens called the Damascus Road House. (WPM.)

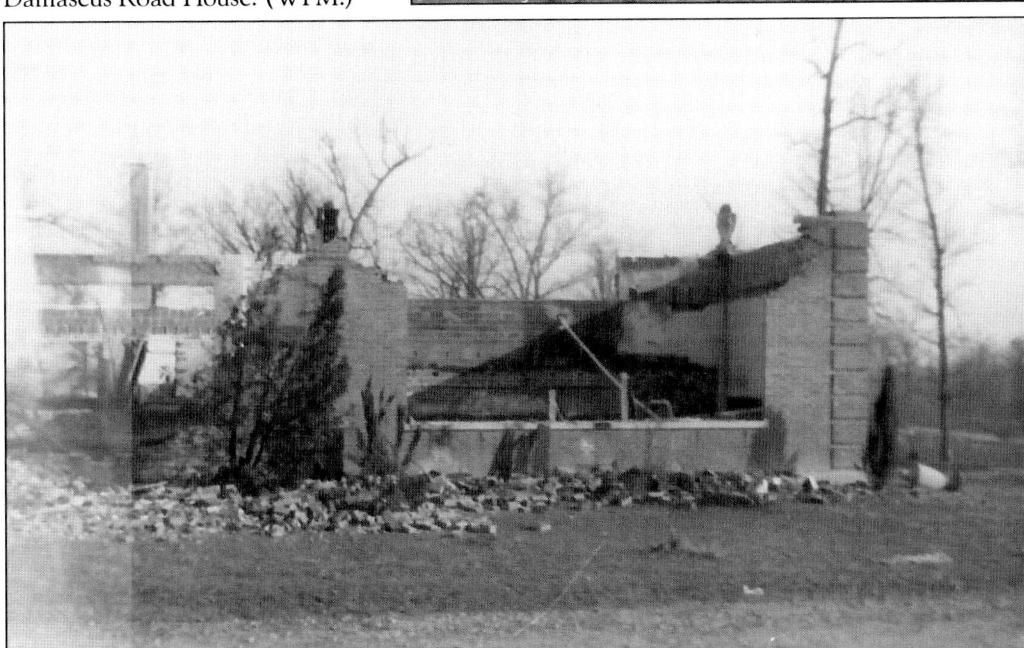

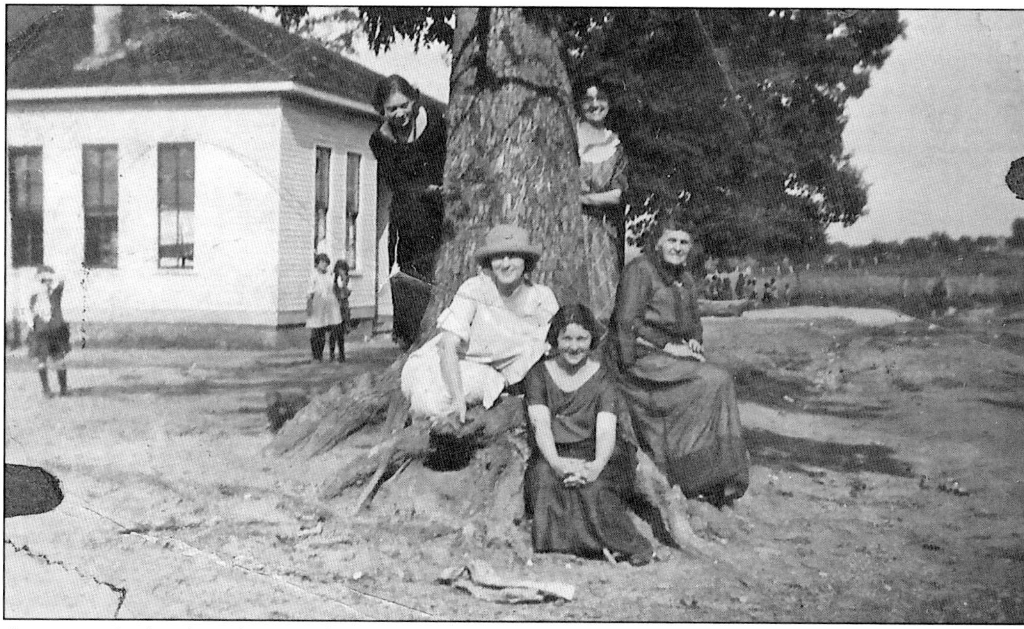

A group of schoolteachers at the old Mortons Gap School poses by a tree in front of the school. The teachers identified are Minnie Kington, Grace Ezell, Ophelia Davis, and ? Winsett. In 1934, Minnie Kington married the Reverend Claude D. Cole, who pastored the First Baptist Church in Mortons Gap. (Gail Warren.)

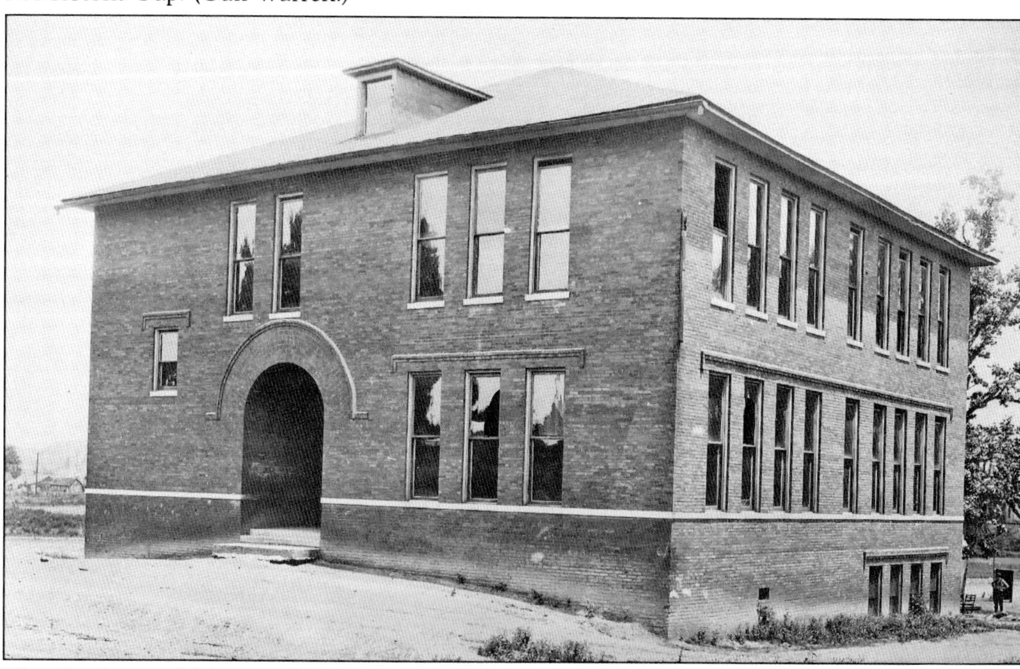

The St. Bernard Mining Company built the J. W. Million School for African Americans in Earlington in 1912. The school was one of the finest schools in its day. It replaced a wood-frame building located near the lake where the AME Zion Church now stands. The building was demolished in 1964. The Reverend J. W. Million was the pastor of the Mount Zion Missionary Baptist Church. (HSHC.)

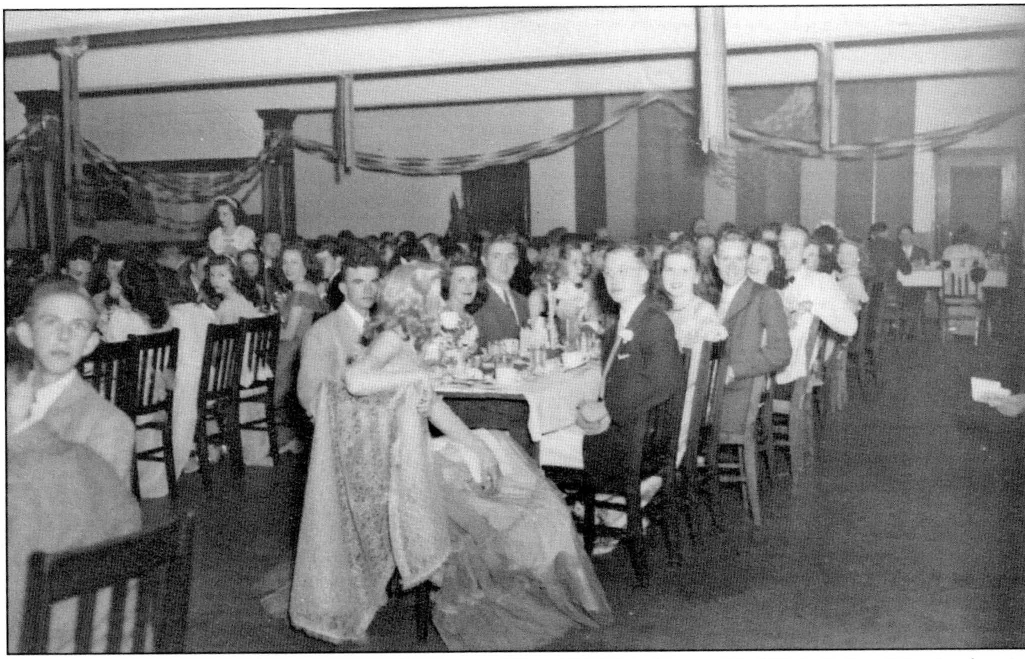

The look of prom has changed over the years. The 1946 Madisonville High School junior/senior prom was captured in this photograph. Identified at the far left looking toward the camera is Jess McGary. Jess now lives in Nortonville. He is a descendant of one of the McGarys who donated land for the founding of Madisonville. (Anita Pate Cartwright.)

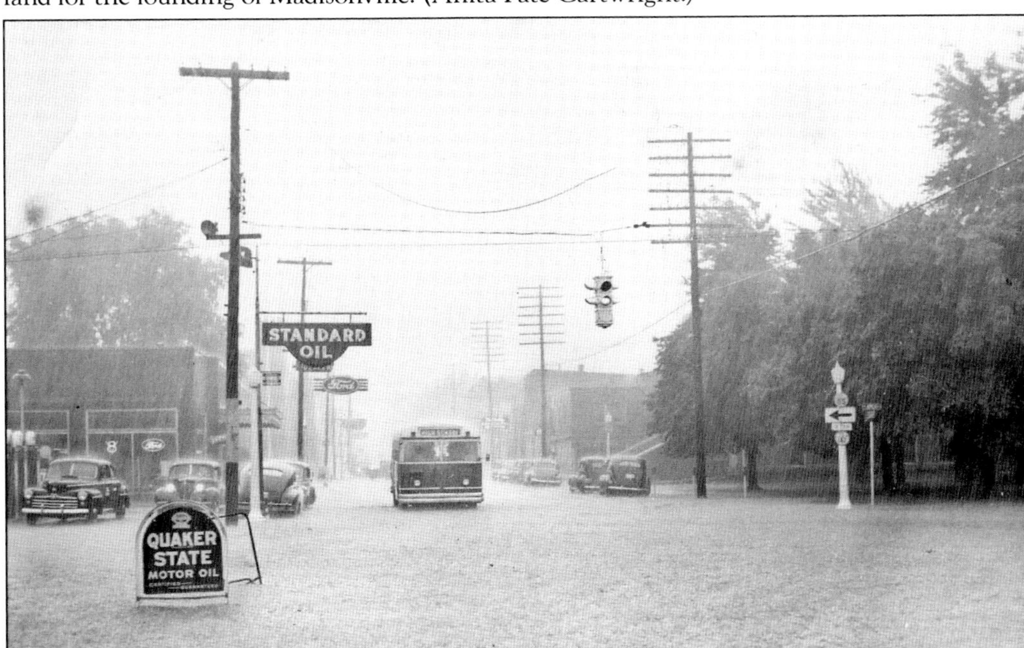

During a heavy rain in the summer of 1947, the intersection of North Main and Arch Streets was flooded. W. W. Williams started the city bus line on March 29, 1947, and this is the bus that ran to the high schools through the flooded streets. The city school system did not have buses in 1947, so the city buses transported the students. (HSHC.)

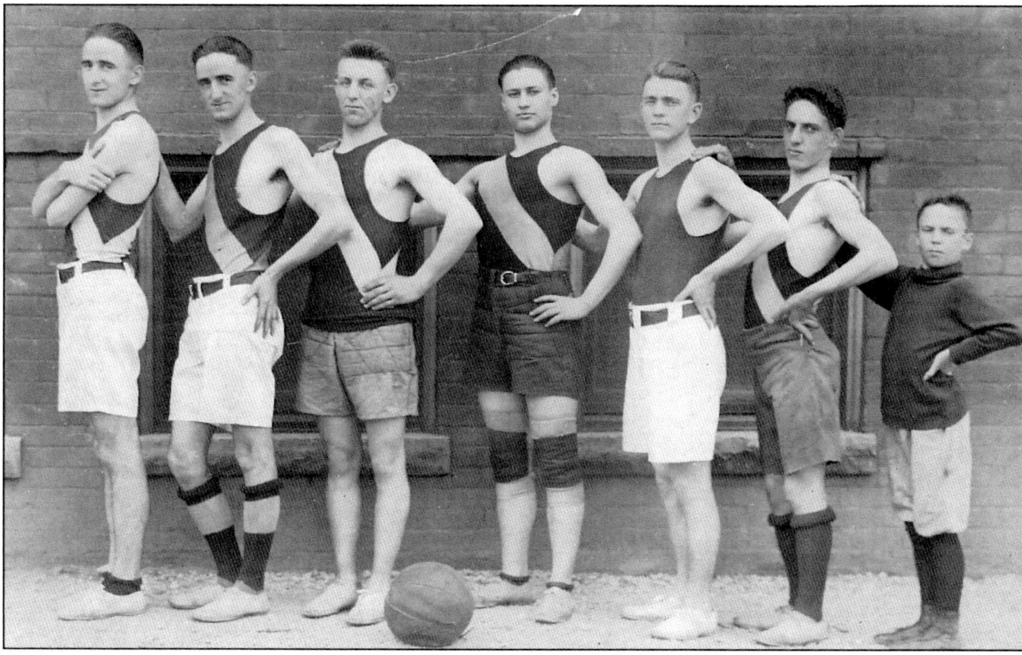

A proud team of ballplayers from Mortons Gap School poses in this photograph for the photographer in the 1920s or 1930s. The only two team members identified are twins. E. W. Jones stands on the left with his arms crossed, and his brother Paul M. Jones stands behind him. (HSHC.)

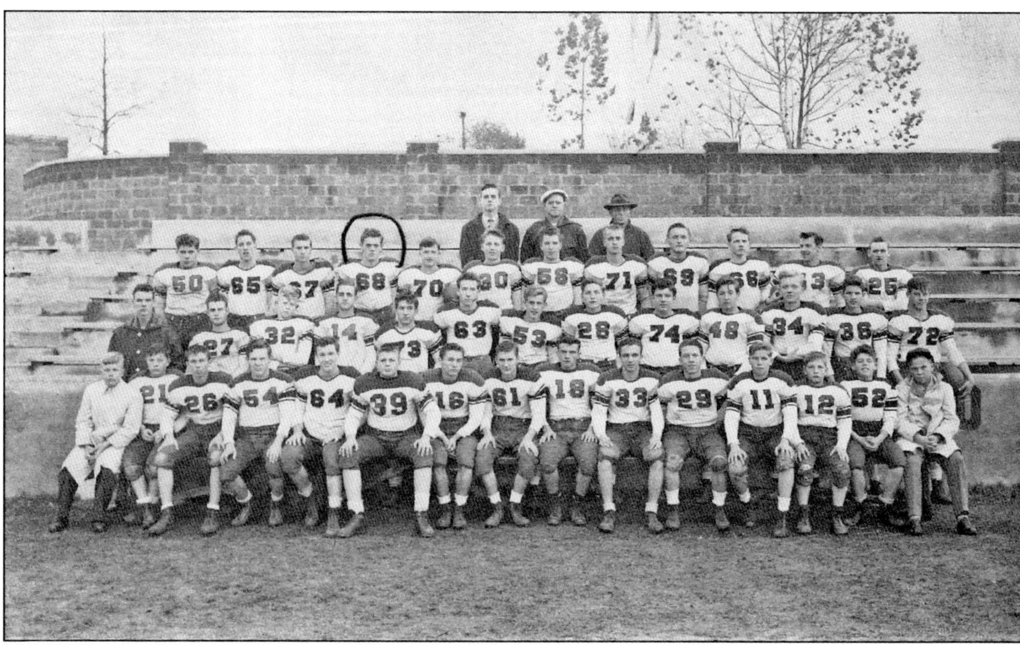

The Madisonville High School football team sits together in this photograph in front of their coaches. The student identified with the mark around his head is Henry Cartwright, who worked at Parish Friendly Shoes. The boy on the right in the center row is holding an old football. The photograph is not dated. (Anita Pate Cartwright.)

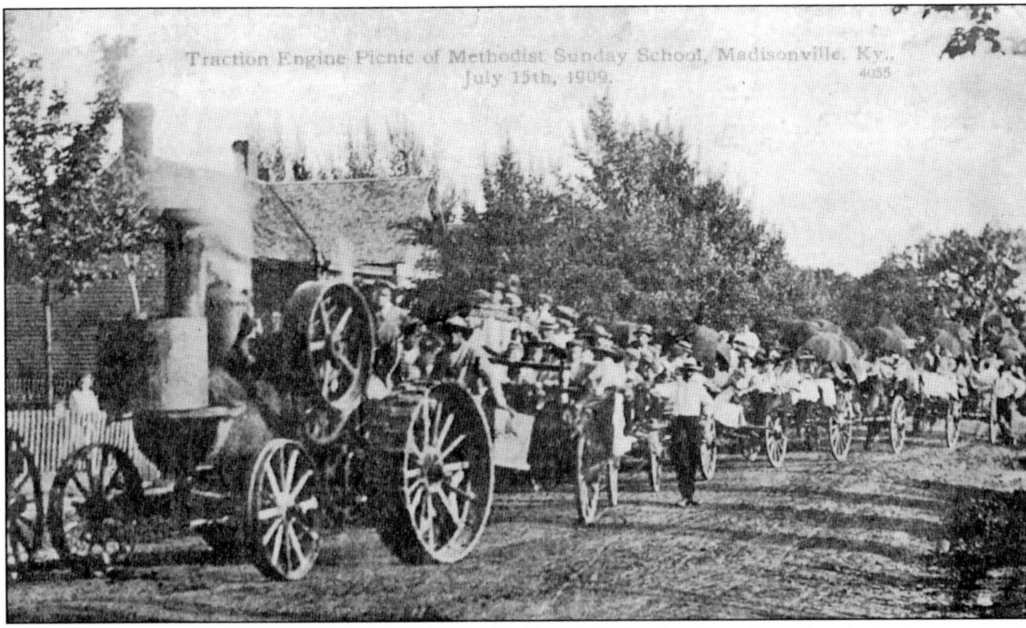

A Wheeler traction engine is shown pulling the First Methodist Sunday school picnic wagons in Madisonville on July 15, 1909. This steam engine was rented out to local farmers to harvest their crops. On this day, at least five farm wagons were attached to it for the kids to ride. This was the first steam engine in the county. (HSHC.)

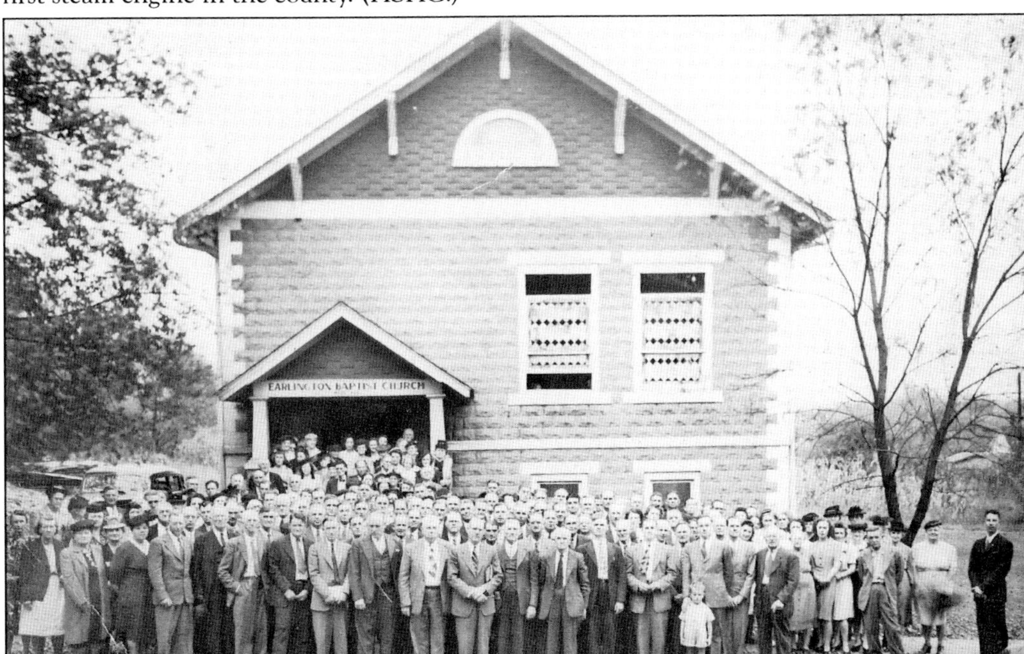

This undated photograph shows the Earlington Baptist Church members standing in front of the building that the church moved into on June 4, 1916, on East Moss Avenue. This building was torn down in 1959, and a new sanctuary was built. The new building became the First Baptist Church. Prior to 1916, the congregation met in a church on South Robinson Street. (HSHC.)

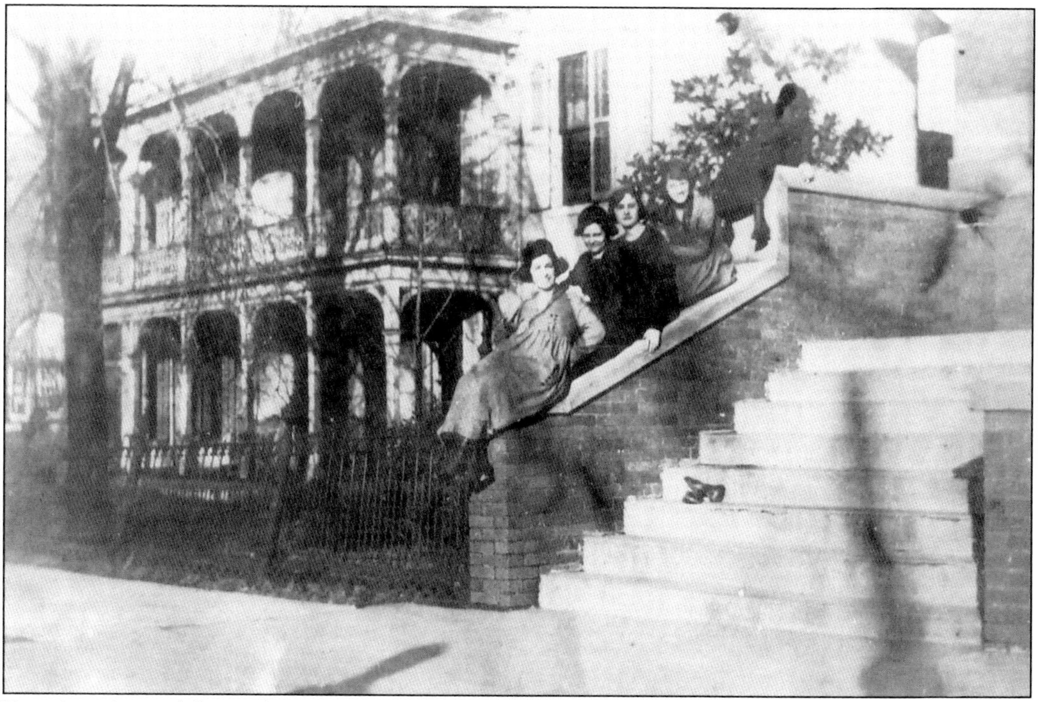

Five friends model on a banister of the First Christian Church on South Main Street between 1915 and 1920. The Morton House is the building on the left. Cassie Shadrick (later Mrs. Herbert Barton) is seated in the front. Helen Morton Hall is the fourth girl from the front. Notice that someone left her shoes on the steps of the church. (HSHC.)

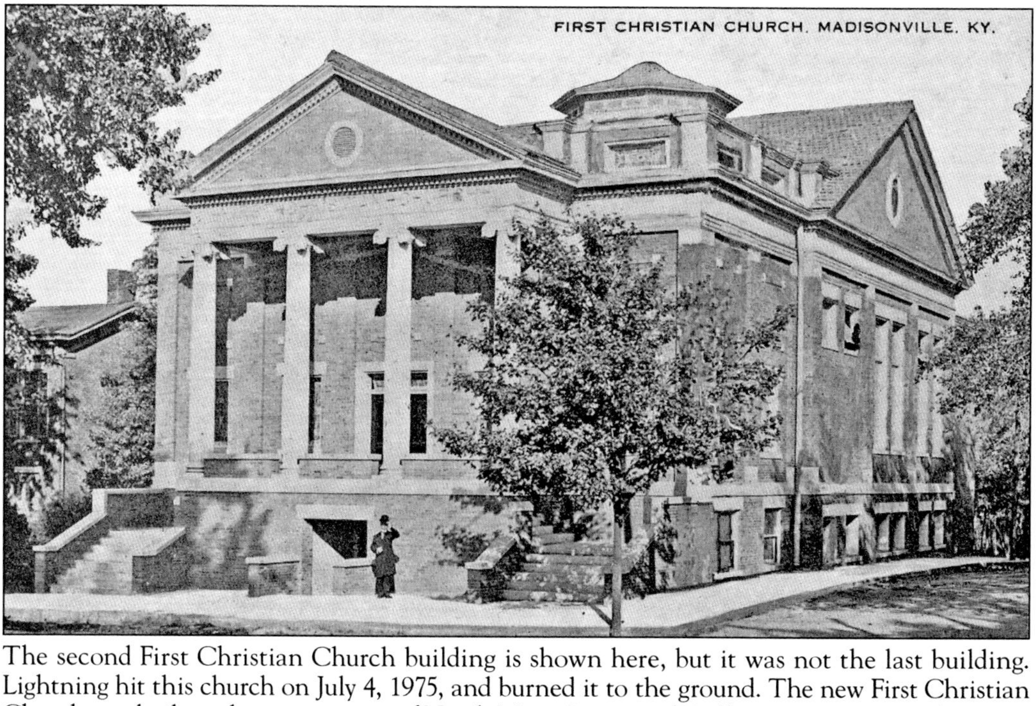

The second First Christian Church building is shown here, but it was not the last building. Lightning hit this church on July 4, 1975, and burned it to the ground. The new First Christian Church was built at the intersection of North Main Street and College Drive. (HSHC.)

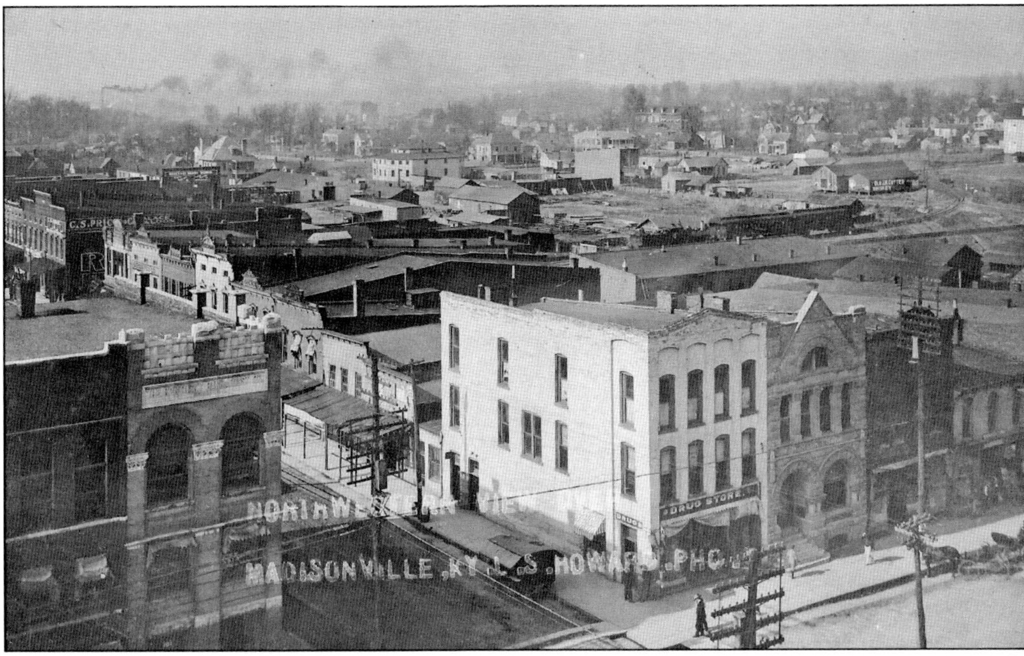

This northwest view of Madisonville was captured from the roof of the courthouse in 1909. The photograph shows the now-demolished building called the Tabernacle in the background. The smokestack in the upper left is from the Eureka Mine Reinecke Coal Company. The Tabernacle was built through a community interdenominational effort. (J. Harold Utley.)

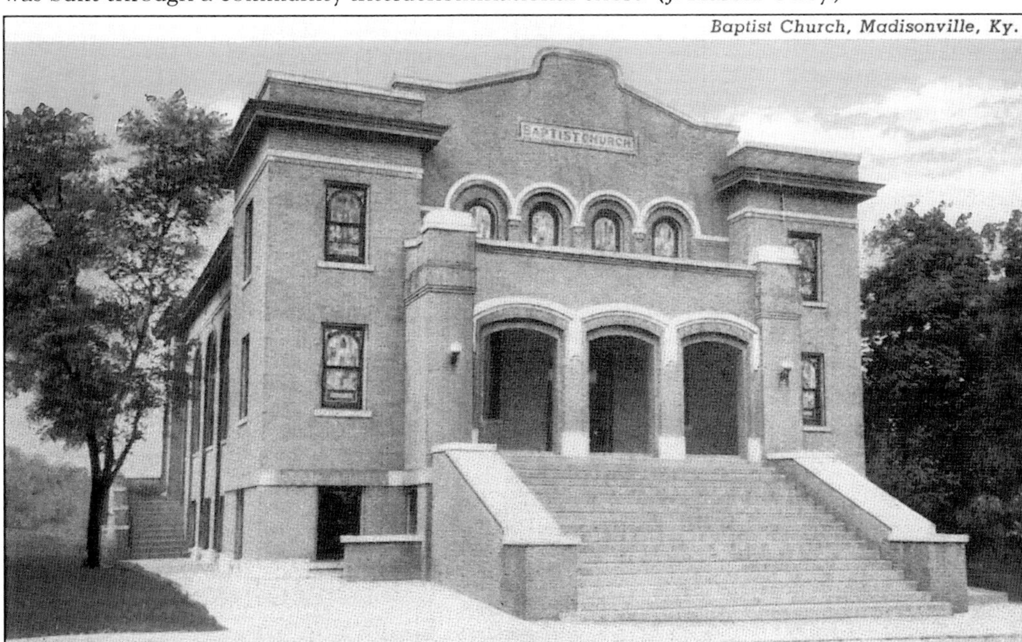

The second building of the First Baptist Church is shown here. While the new building was constructed, the congregation met at the Tabernacle. The church building was erected in 1912 but was torn down in 1954. This property is now the parking lot of the Old National Bank. The First Baptist Church is now located farther north on Main Street in Madisonville. (HSHC.)

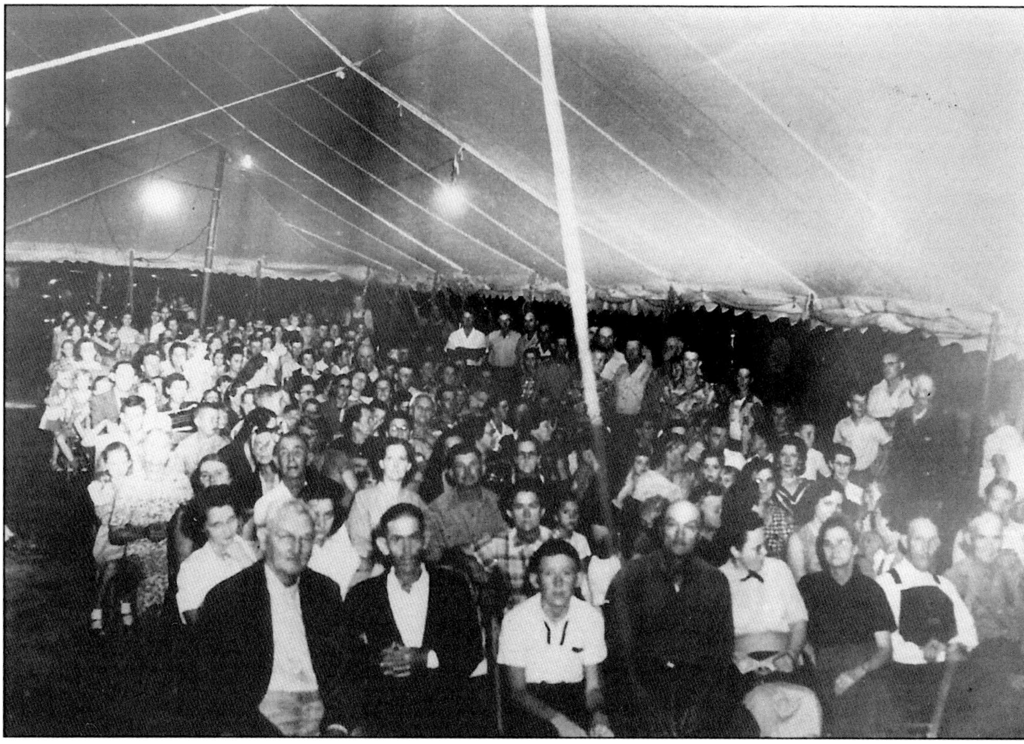

Many tent revivals were held in Nortonville, and several area churches were birthed out of the efforts of those revivalists. The tents were packed full, as shown in these photographs. There were no empty seats, and the tents were surrounded with people standing to hear the Gospel message and listen to music. Many were seated inside vehicles that surrounded the tent. This particular tent was owned by Harold Lam and was erected for the revival shown in the 1950s. Gail Warren is sitting in the first chair in the fifth row in the above photograph. Identified in the crowd of the photograph below are Charlie and Pearlie Carlton, Ray and Evelyn Miller, Betty Carlton, Martha Helen Smith, Mae Hartline, and Zadie Knowles. (Both, Gail Warren.)

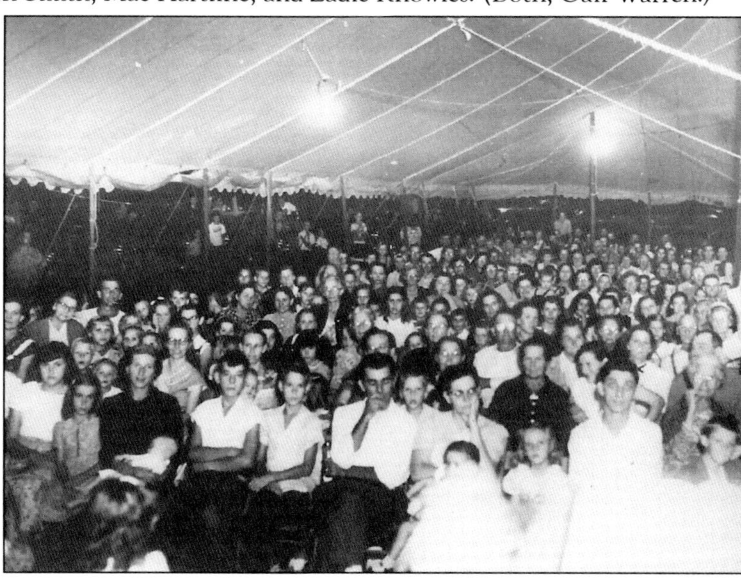

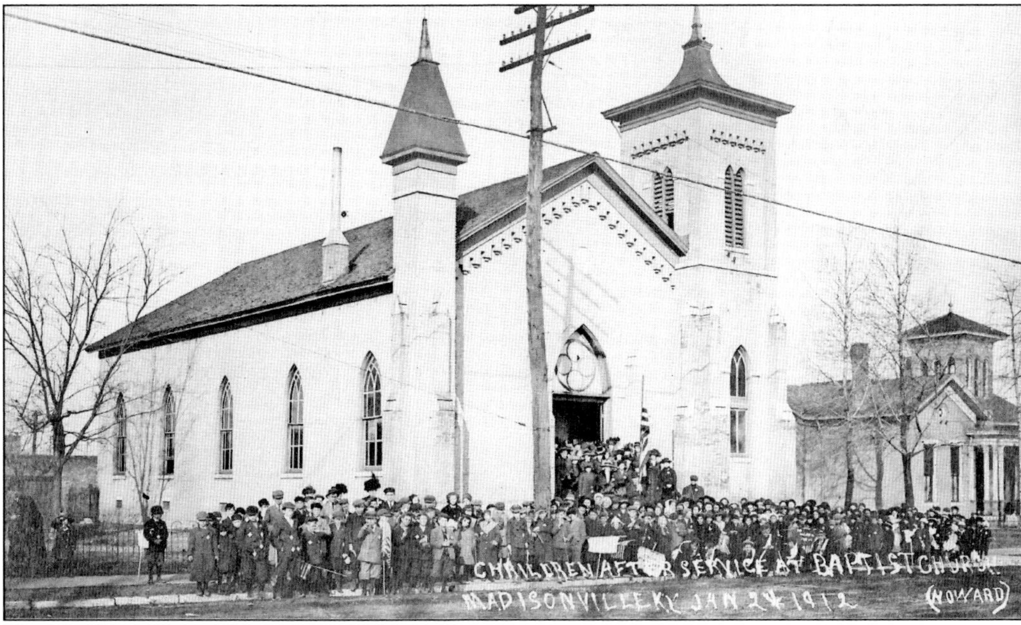

Children and adults spill out of the First Baptist Church in this photograph after a service in Madisonville to celebrate the success of the efforts for Prohibition. The postcard is dated January 24, 1912. Well over 150 men, women, and children can be counted in this photograph. This is an incredible number considering that it would have been a cold day and most would have traveled by foot, horse, or wagon. (HSHC.)

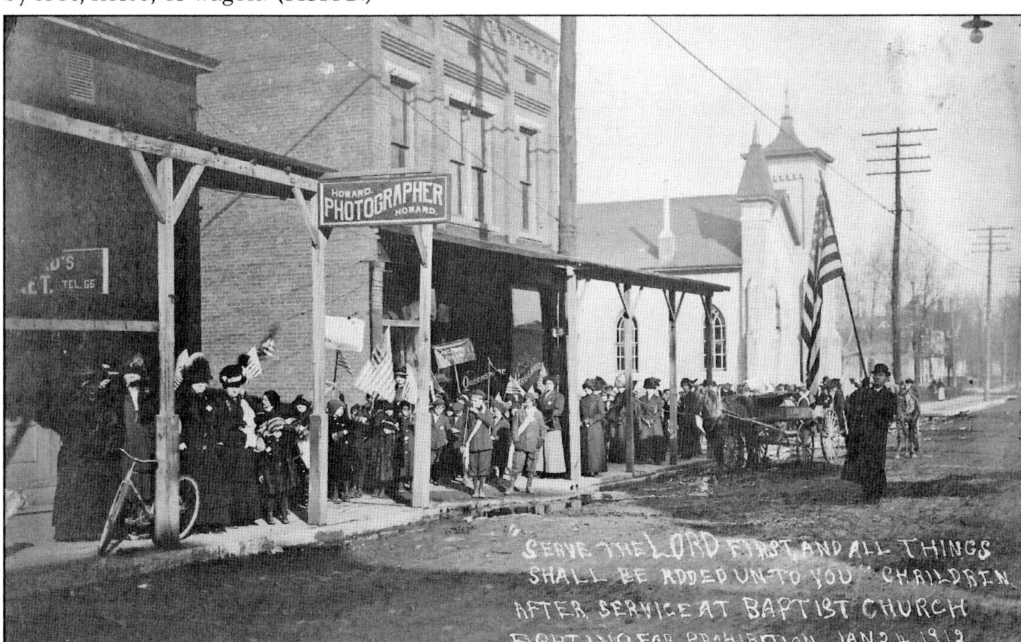

The congregation of the First Baptist Church in Madisonville is shown fighting for Prohibition on January 24, 1912. The postcard reads, "Serve the Lord first, and all things shall be added unto you." A sign held in the background says "No Saloon for Us!" The door in the background advertises "Queensware Groceries." (HSHC.)

Consistent with our mission to preserve history on a local level, this book was printed in South Carolina on American-made paper and manufactured entirely in the United States. Products carrying the accredited Forest Stewardship Council (FSC) label are printed on 100 percent FSC-certified paper.

MADE IN THE USA